Bleeding Hearts, Corydalis, and Their Relatives

Bleeding Hearts, Corydalis,

AND THEIR RELATIVES

Mark Tebbitt,
Magnus Lidén, and
Henrik Zetterlund

with illustrations by
Adèle Rossetti Morosini and
Paul Harwood

BROOKLYN
BOTANIC
GARDEN

Timber Press
Portland • London

Title page illustration: Bleeding heart, *Lamprocapnos spectabilis*.
Drawing by Paul Harwood.

Published in 2008 by
Timber Press, Inc.
The Haseltine Building
133 S.W. Second Avenue, Suite 450
Portland, Oregon 97204-3527, U.S.A.
www.timberpress.com
For contact information regarding editorial, marketing, sales,
and distribution in the United Kingdom, see www.timberpress.co.uk.

Printed in China

Library of Congress Cataloging-in-Publication Data

Tebbitt, Mark C.
  Bleeding hearts, Corydalis, and their relatives / Mark Tebbitt, Magnus Lidén,
and Henrik Zetterlund ; with illustrations by Adèle Rossetti Morosini and Paul Harwood.
      p. cm.
  "Published in association with Brooklyn Botanic Garden."
  Includes bibliographical references and index.
  ISBN-13: 978-0-88192-882-2
 1. Papaveraceae. 2. Corydalis. 3. Papaveraceae—Identification. 4. Corydalis—
Identification. I. Lidén, Magnus. II. Zetterlund, Henrik, 1953– III. Title.
  QK495.P22T43 2008
  635.9'3335—dc22
                                                                    2007038226
A catalog record for this book is also available from the British Library.

Contents

Color plates follow page 80

Preface

THE FERNY LEAVES and curious flowers of the bleeding heart family have long held a fascination for me. While growing up in England I grew several of the species in a rock garden and shaded woodland site. Since moving to the States to join the Brooklyn Botanic Garden as Horticultural Taxonomist I have also had the chance to become acquainted with, and study, the many members of the bleeding heart family that grow wild in North America—*Adlumia fungosa*, *Capnoides sempervirens*, nine species of *Corydalis*, and seven species of *Dicentra*—all of which can be found in European as well as North American gardens. Many of these plants now grace my current garden in Pennsylvania.

This book owes its genesis to Neal Maillet at Timber Press, who suggested that I write an authoritative book for gardeners covering all the cultivated members of the bleeding heart family. While I have a background in botany and experience growing some members of the family, this idea was at first daunting, especially since I knew that, as far as the genus *Corydalis* was concerned, I was a novice. Luckily two experts soon agreed to co-author the book with me: Magnus Lidén and Henrik Zetterlund. They are also the authors of *Corydalis: A Gardener's Guide and a Monograph of the Tuberous Species*, published in 1997 by the Alpine Garden Society.

Magnus Lidén has spent much of his career (first at Gothenburg Botanic Garden and currently at Uppsala Botanic Garden) studying the taxonomy of the bleeding heart family (Fumariaceae). He is particularly knowledgeable about *Corydalis*, the largest genus in the family, having studied these plants and their closest relatives for his doctoral thesis. Henrik Zetterlund brings to the book knowledge of a different and complimentary kind, practical gardening experience. He is a gifted plantsman and grower of rare and challenging alpine and woodland plants at Gothenburg Botanic Garden. Part of the incredible collection of rare plants that Henrik has helped amass at that garden is what must be the most comprehensive collection of *Corydalis* and related genera to be found anywhere in the world. This collection has been built up not only through the generosity of other growers and enthusiasts but also through collecting trips conducted by both Henrik and Magnus. Jointly or separately they have visited almost all the places where *Corydalis* and its relatives abound—Mediterranean Europe, western North America, the Himalaya, China, Iran, Turkey and Mongolia. In the process they have collected many new and interesting species, and have introduced them into cultivation. Just as importantly, this field-collecting experience has given them useful insights into the conditions required to successfully grow these sometimes challenging plants.

With cool summers and mild winters, Gothenburg Botanic Garden is blessed with a particularly favorable climate for growing a wide range of species from the bleeding heart family. Even the usually difficult-to-grow *Dicentra peregrina* flourishes there in the open garden. Gardeners from regions that experience higher summer temperatures are likely to find that this species offers a severe test of their growing skills. However, the family does include several members much more amenable to warmer climates. In fact, readers will find species adapted to nearly every climatic zone of the temperate regions. Likewise, gardeners of every level of experience will discover in this book plants to interest them. As chapter one states, there are species suited not only to the alpine house but also to the formal border, to outdoor containers, and to woodland and naturalistic gardens. Indeed one of the things that first attracted me to these plants was their versatility in the garden.

Surprisingly, no previous books have been written for gardeners that cover the bleeding heart family in its entirety. This is particularly unexpected since members of the family have been cultivated in Europe for as long as detailed records go back. John Gerard, whose herbal of 1596 provides the earliest comprehensive record of British garden plants, reported several cultivated species, including the ever-popular *Pseudofumaria lutea* (syn. *Corydalis lutea*). Furthermore, by the early to mid 1900s all the genera found in cultivation today had been introduced to gardens in both Europe and North America. The lack of any previous books is most likely due to successful introduction of the bulk of the currently cultivated species only since the mid 1970s. For this flood of new introductions we can largely thank the advent of cheap airline travel. Intercontinental flights allowed plant material, for the first time, to be transported rapidly around the globe. Prior to this the success rate of new introductions was low because many members of the family have ephemeral seeds that must be sown as soon as they are mature. Now, almost every year, our gardens are enriched with new species, especially those from the *Corydalis*-rich Himalaya and western China. The introduction discusses this intriguing history and introduces a few garden-worthy plants yet to be brought into general cultivation. This chapter also relates how these plants have been and continue to be used in gardens.

In chapter one general cultivation techniques are presented. Specific cultural needs are also given later in the book, alongside the plant descriptions in chapters four, five, and six.

In writing this book, I and my co-authors also saw a need to update gardeners (and botanists) with some recent (and not so recent) name changes in the family. This is presented in chapter two. We expect that few gardeners will be pleased to hear that the beloved *Dicentra spectabilis* is now correctly named *Lamprocapnos spectabilis*. We hope, however, that by explaining in non-technical terms the scientific reasons for this and a few other name changes, the necessity for these changes will become readily apparent, and the new names accepted in gardens. Chapter two, along with the glossary, also provides background information on the morphological features important in identification. Additionally, chapter two covers the fascinating natural history of these plants including their intriguing interactions with animal pollinators and seed dispersers.

Chapter three provides an identification key to all the genera in the bleeding heart family. This key may be used in conjunction with the more detailed species keys in chapters four, five, and six.

The remaining three chapters each focus on a particular group of related species. Chapter four describes *Dicentra* and five other genera with heart-shaped flowers, including the climbing dicentras (*Dactylicapnos*) and bleeding heart (*Lamprocapnos spectabilis*). Chapter five discusses *Corydalis*. And lastly, chapter six presents five genera, which, like *Corydalis*, have zygomorphic flowers but in other respects are distinct from that genus. These include *Pseudofumaria* and two fascinating cliff-dwelling genera grown by rock gardeners, *Rupicapnos* and *Sarcocapnos*. Together, these chapters provide readers with descriptions and practical information covering almost all the species, hybrids, and cultivars of the bleeding heart family found in cultivation. In the case of *Corydalis*, which has well over 150 cultivated species and is the largest genus in the family, the book focuses on only the best and/or most popular cultivated species. That way the text has been kept within bounds and gardeners are not forced to wade through numerous obscure species of interest only to the botanist.

As a comprehensive guide to the bleeding heart family, this book offers something for all enthusiasts of this intriguing and beautiful group of plants, and will, I hope, even produce some new adherents. But newcomers should be warned; if Gothenburg Botanic Garden is anything to judge by, collecting these plants is likely to become addictive.

MARK TEBBITT

Acknowledgments

WE WISH TO THANK the many people who helped with this book. We are particularly grateful to Neal Maillet for suggesting a book on cultivated Fumariaceae to fill a gap in gardener's libraries.

Brooklyn Botanic Garden (BBG) is very gratefully acknowledged for its financial support. We thank BBG's past and current presidents, Judy Zuk and Scot Medbury, and the Garden's Vice President for Science, Steve Clements, all of whom showed good taste in thinking this book a worthwhile project.

We are also very grateful for the beautiful artwork provided by Adèle Rossetti Morosini and Paul Harwood.

Several people provided helpful information, editorial time, and/or plants. For these we thank Laura Tebbitt; the library staff at BBG: Atiba Alexander, Kathy Crosby, and Patricia Jonas; Marie Long, of the New York Botanical Garden's LuEsther T. Mertz Library; Alison Kelly of the Library of Congress (Science, Technology, and Business Division); Adrian Bennett (BBG), Kerry Barringer (BBG), Louis Cesario (BBG), Carol Fyler, Dan Heims (Terra Nova Nurseries), Roy Herold, Linda Marschner (BBG), Gerry Moore (BBG), Darrell Probst, Meghan Ray; and F. MacRoni. We also wish to thank Aaron Schusteff for providing the photograph of *Dicentra nevadensis*, Mats Hagberg for providing the photograph of *Sarcocapnos pulcherrima*, and Dan Heims for providing photographs of various *Corydalis* cultivars.

Richard Sanford (Royal Horticultural Society) is gratefully acknowledged for his assistance in producing the list of awarded plants that appears in Appendix C.

Our Latvian friends, Jānis Rukšāns and Arnis Seisums, have earned our deep gratitude by carrying *Corydalis* knowledge further.

We also wish to acknowledge the following institutions for the use of their resources: Brooklyn Botanic Garden; California University of Pennsylvania; Gothenburg Botanic Garden; Linnaeus's Hammarby Estate; New York Botanical Garden; Royal Botanic Garden Edinburgh; Royal Botanic Gardens Kew; and Botanic Garden Uppsala University.

Introduction
Old Friends and New Acquaintances

HARDLY A GARDEN must exist in Europe or North America that does not contain at least one member of the bleeding heart family. This family, known to botanists as the Fumariaceae, includes a multitude of good garden plants, although not all of them are grown as widely as they deserve. Bleeding heart (*Lamprocapnos spectabilis*) and rock fumewort (*Pseudofumaria lutea*) will be especially familiar to gardeners, though perhaps, in both these cases, they will be known under their older names: *Dicentra spectabilis* and *Corydalis lutea*, respectively. The numerous cultivars of *D. formosa* are also garden mainstays as is the blue-flowered *C. flexuosa*, at least in regions with mild summers.

Other members of the family, while just as attractive and hardly more difficult to grow, are much less frequently seen in cultivation. Examples include the climbing dicentras (*Dactylicapnos* species), the Californian eardrops (*Ehrendorferia* species), and the large-flowered dicentra (*Ichtyoselmis macrantha*), all of which merit wider recognition. Likewise, only rock gardeners and alpine enthusiasts are likely to grow still other members of the family, including the species of *Rupicapnos* and *Sarcocapnos,* as well as certain *Corydalis* and *Dicentra* species. However, in the case of these plants, their more exacting growing requirements will continue to exclude most gardeners, especially those lacking an alpine house or bulb frame.

Since the late 1990s the bleeding heart family as a whole has become increasingly popular. Some of its members are being grown for the first time, while others are

Bleeding heart, *Lamprocapnos spectabilis*.
Reproduced from *Curtis's Botanical Magazine* (1848, plate 4458).

11

experiencing a renaissance. The genus *Corydalis* has particularly grown in popularity. Newer introductions of blue-flowered *Corydalis* are especially prominent in several current nursery catalogs and no doubt are helping to inspire a wider appreciation of this genus. A few of the blue-flowered newcomers, but chiefly *C. omeiana*, have proven suitable for growing in areas with warm summers, further expanding the possibilities offered by this large genus.

Even though the bleeding heart family has never been as popular in gardens as it is now, some of its members have been cultivated for centuries in both Europe and China. In Europe the native species of *Corydalis*, *Fumaria*, and *Pseudofumaria* were the first to be grown for their medicinal properties. Like their close relatives in the poppy family, many bleeding heart species contain medicinally important alkaloids. *Corydalis cava*, for example, was once commonly grown in monastic herb gardens and used to ease tension, lower blood pressure, and prevent muscle contractions. This species can even now sometimes be found surviving among the ruins of abandoned monasteries. In many parts of the world, *Corydalis* species are still used as herbal medicines. The boiled and dried tubers of *C. yanhusuo* are a particularly famous example, being one of the best known Chinese herbal drugs. This drug, known as yanhusuo, yuan hu, or yanfusuo, is used to treat a variety of ills, including coronary heart disease and menstrual pain.

Corydalis cava. Reproduced from John Gerard's *The Herball, or, General Historie of Plantes* (1633, p. 1090).

Many European species of *Corydalis* and *Pseudofumaria* that were grown in monastic apothecary gardens have very attractive flowers and for this reason were among the first members of the family to be grown as ornamentals. *Corydalis cava*, *C. solida*, and *Pseudofumaria lutea*, all of which have medicinal properties, were grown in European flower gardens as early as the mid 1500s. Even after ornamental flower gardens became fashionable, apothecary gardens continued to play an important role in facilitating early plant introductions. The first North American species to be introduced to European gardens, rock harlequin (*Capnoides sempervirens*), arrived in 1683 at a garden that later became the Edinburgh Physic Garden. Another North America native, Dutchman's breeches (*Dicentra cucullaria*) was introduced in 1759 via the Chelsea

Physic Garden. No doubt in both cases these plants were grown for their ornamental value at least as much as for their medicinal properties. Interestingly, these same plants, *Corydalis cava*, *C. solida*, *Pseudofumaria lutea*, and *Capnoides sempervirens* (but surprisingly not *Dicentra cucullaria*), were the first members of the family to be sold by American nurseries in the late eighteenth century.

Like the monks of medieval Europe, the ancient Chinese were also accomplished gardeners and were responsible for many early introductions. Bleeding heart (*Lamprocapnos spectabilis*) is a particularly notable example since it has been grown in Chinese flower gardens for hundreds of years. Today it is one of the most popular garden plants in the West.

Prior to the introduction of bleeding heart into European gardens, the great taxonomist Carl Linnaeus saw a drawing of the plant in one of his student's theses. Linnaeus was very much taken by it and longed to see a live plant. When in 1765 he was sent seeds of "*Fumaria spectabilis*" from Siberia, he was delighted, thinking that at last he had received the plant he desired. The seeds, though, turned out to be those of a different species—that which we now grow as *Corydalis nobilis*. While Linnaeus had hoped for bleeding heart, he must not have been too disappointed, for *C. nobilis* is a particularly beautiful member of the family. From Linnaeus's garden at Hammarby, north of Stockholm, plants of *C. nobilis* were distributed to other gardens in Europe, eventually reaching Britain in 1783. This *Corydalis* has not, however, seen widespread acceptance in European gardens, as Linnaeus once predicted it would.

The late 1700s and early 1800s also saw the introduction to England of three North American species, the vine *Adlumia fungosa* (in 1778) and two dicentras, *D. eximia* (just prior to 1815), and *D. canadensis* (just prior to 1830). Through the exploits of early American plant collectors, like John Bartram and his cousin Humphry Marshall, a steady stream of North American plants entered British gardens at the turn of the nineteenth century. Particularly notable British gardeners, with pockets deep enough to finance these collectors, included such luminaries as Peter Collinson and John Fothergill. Despite the avid interest of British gardeners in American plants, the first North American *Corydalis* species was not introduced to Britain

Corydalis nobilis. Reproduced from *The Gardener's Chronicle* (9 June 1883, p. 725, fig. 119).

until *C. caseana* entered the scene in 1886. The more garden-worthy *C. scouleri* arrived even later, around 1895, although, in this case the species was brought to Britain from continental Europe, where it had been introduced earlier.

Surprisingly little is known about when these and other North American species were first grown in North American gardens. It appears likely though that in several cases they initially became established in European gardens and then returned to North America as nursery-grown stock. However, in a few cases these attractive wild flowers were no doubt collected locally and brought into cultivation by North American gardeners. This certainly appears to have been true of Dutchman's breeches (*Dicentra cucullaria*), since this species is mentioned in the early American horticultural literature but does not appear to have been available from American nurseries until much more recently.

The early to mid 1800s saw the first introductions from Asia. The earliest species to grace European gardens was the beautiful yellow-flowered climbing *Dactylicapnos scandens* (syn. *Dicentra scandens*), which arrived in 1831 from the Himalaya. Other Asian species soon followed, especially as China tentatively began to open its doors to European trade. In 1846 Robert Fortune successfully introduced bleeding heart (*Lamprocapnos spectabilis*) as part of a collecting trip to China sponsored by the Royal Horticultural Society. At that time foreign access was restricted to the treaty ports. However, since *L. spectabilis* had long been established in Chinese gardens, Fortune was able to send the species back as part of the first major shipment of Chinese plants to reach European shores. From 1830 to 1890, several Central Asian *Corydalis* species also entered the horticultural stage. Most of these introductions were made by Albert von Regel, who traveled widely throughout Central Asia bringing back plants, which he distributed from St. Petersburg to prominent gardens and bulb dealers in mainland Europe, as well as in the British Isles.

The late 1800 to early 1900s, that "golden age of plant collecting," resulted in surprisingly few new introductions. This was largely due to almost all members of the bleeding heart family having seed intolerant of dry storage. Famous collectors of this period like George Forrest, Frank Kingdon-Ward, Ernest Wilson, and Reginald Farrer encountered and sent home seeds of many Chinese *Corydalis* species. However, few of their introductions, other than the low-altitude crevice species, like *C. wilsonii* and *C. saxicola*, and a few woodland species, like *C. cheilanthifolia*, were successfully germinated and raised in gardens. Today collection is much easier and, with the advent of intercontinental flights, transport is considerably faster. As a result, more and more new species are now entering our gardens.

While relatively few new members of the family entered gardens around the turn of the twentieth century, the early 1900s did witness some historically significant introductions. In 1900 the first *Sarcocapnos* species entered British gardens. This plant, the Spanish cliff-dwelling *S. enneaphylla*, has been grown by rock gardeners ever since. Shortly afterward in 1905, Maurice de Vilmorin's Paris nursery introduced from the Himalaya the climbing annual *Dactylicapnos torulosa*. Also from Asia came the large-flowered dicentra, *Ichtyoselmis macrantha*, collected in 1904 by Ernest Wilson while working for Veitch and Sons Nursery. With beautiful serrated leaves and remarkably large, pale yellow, fiddle-shaped flowers, this is a wonderful plant for the woodland garden. Sadly, it has never been common in cultivation.

After World War I, the Veitch nursery was also responsible for introducing a spectacular border species, golden eardrops (*Ehrendorferia chrysantha*). It arrived in England in 1932 from a collection made in California by William Lobb. Again, it has never been as common in cultivation as it deserves. In 1933 the first *Rupicapnos* species entered gardens, seed of *R. africana* having been collected that year by a British rock gardener, while visiting the Rif mountains of Morocco. A year later the first of the blue-flowered *Corydalis* species, *C. cashmeriana*, made a well-publicized debut at the Alpine Garden Society spring show. The Royal Horticultural Society afterward gave the species its prestigious Award of Merit, as it did several other members of the family (see Appendix C).

World War II quieted the horticultural stage, and indeed few introductions of note entered European gardens before the late 1970s though a second blue-flowered *Corydalis*, the Japanese *C. fumariifolia*, was introduced to England a little before 1970.

From the late 1970s to early 1980s horticultural interest in *Corydalis* increased dramatically. Many new adherents were created in 1981 when Kew Gardens bulb expert Brian Mathew gave a lecture on the genus at the fifth international rock garden plant conference in Nottingham, England. Further interest also resulted from an influx of new plants. Gardeners in particular began to reap the fruits of botanical expeditions to Turkey, Iraq, Iran, and Afghanistan, which had taken place in the sixties and early seventies.

Plant enthusiasts from Eastern Europe had also in the 1960s and early 1970s traveled widely within the Soviet empire, introducing some fantastic plants into cultivation. For years these plants had been trapped behind the Iron Curtain, only reaching the West in the 1980s. From the Caucasus these Eastern European gardeners brought back such gems as *Corydalis kusnetzovii*, *C. nariniana*, and *C. seisumsiana*. From Central Asia came *C. glaucescens*, *C. macrocentra*, *C. maracandica*, *C. nudicaulis*, *C. ruksansii*, and *C. schanginii*. From easternmost Siberia were introduced *C. buschii*, *C. ornata*, and *C. turtschaninovii*.

Likewise, in the 1970s, when tourism increased in Turkey and the Caucasus, many bulb enthusiasts traveled there, revealing additional species like *Corydalis hausmknechtii*, *C. henrikii*, *C. lydica*, *C. paschei*, *C. triternata*, and *C. wendelboi*. In the 1980s better forms of blue-flowered *C. fumariifolia* were introduced from Japan, along with four more blue-flowered gems: *C. fukuharae*, *C. lineariloba*, *C. orthoceras*, and *C. papilligera*. Interest in the genus continued into the 1990s as new forms of already well-known *Corydalis* species were selected in Europe, and additional species and subspecies of the North American *Corydalis* species were introduced into cultivation.

Since 1981 a series of expeditions have brought back numerous plants from China, including additional species of climbing dicentra (*Dactylicapnos* species) and *Adlumia asiatica*, although the latter species is still so rare in cultivation that it has not yet reached the general public. China is especially rich in *Corydalis*, with more than two-thirds of all the species in the genus. To date, more than 50 Chinese species have been introduced. The first to thrill us was the *C. cashmeriana*-like *C. pachycentra*, introduced from Cangshan, in Yunnan by the SBEC (Sino-British Expedition to Cangshan). Later expeditions brought back other exciting blue-flowered species, including *C. curviflora*, *C. flexuosa*, *C. hemidicentra*, *C. omeiana*, and *C. pseudoadoxa*. Some, like *C. flexuosa* and *C. omeiana*, have performed extremely well in gardens. Others, like *C. hemidicentra*, are proving difficult to grow and may well be lost from cultivation, a particular shame in the case of *C. hemidicentra* since its succulent hepatica-like leaves make it one of the most striking members of the genus. Other notable Chinese *Corydalis* introductions of recent years include purple-flowered *C. calcicola*, *C. smithiana*, and *C. taliensis*. Many more *Corydalis* species are now entering gardens through the activities of commercial Chinese Internet-based companies. Despite this continuous high level of collecting within China, a surprisingly large number of desirable *Corydalis* species still await introduction.

Horticultural hybridization and selection have also been ongoing since 1953, at which time the first artificial dicentra hybrid was created—*Dicentra* 'Bountiful'. Many more such hybrids have since followed. In the 1980s, work also began on hybridizing and selecting the red and pink forms of *Corydalis solida* and a few other *Corydalis* species. Even a couple of named clones of the climbing dicentra, *Dactylicapnos scandens*, have now been selected. There remains, however, a great deal of room for future development of improved hybrid cultivars and selections throughout the family.

At present about 180 species and 65 cultivars of the bleeding heart family are in cultivation in Europe and North America. Approximately 150 of these species belong to the genus *Corydalis*. With more and more plants entering cultivation each year, no wonder the group's popularity continues to rise.

1

Cultivation

THIS CHAPTER EXAMINES cultivation techniques as they relate to the bleeding heart family—how and where to use plants in the landscape, how best to propagate them, how to create new hybrids, and how to keep plants free of pests and diseases or treat them if necessary. The principles presented here are very general. Any specific cultural requirements are noted in the plant descriptions, in chapters four through six.

Their Use as Garden Plants

Coming from a wide variety of natural habitats, members of the Fumariaceae require a wide range of garden situations if they are to prosper in cultivation. For example, some members of the family are suitable for naturalizing in the woodland garden, while at the opposite end of the spectrum other members require the protection of an alpine house or bulb frame. A few suggestions as to garden location and plant associations are given here, along with more specific cultivation techniques.

Woodland Garden

The bleeding heart family includes many species that naturally grow in woodlands. In the garden these perform well and look their best in a shaded position, especially under trees and shrubs.

Dense Deciduous Woodland

Dense deciduous woodland is a particularly suitable environ for the spring ephemerals that are able to conclude their annual life cycle just as the canopy closes. An area like this with dense summer shade under trees and shrubs is among the most difficult to adorn in the garden. However, it is perfect for *Corydalis solida* and its relatives (section *Corydalis*), *C. cava*, *C. nobilis*, and the North American *Dicentra cucullaria* and *D. canadensis*. Furthermore, all these plants mix beautifully with other suitable spring bulbs such as *Anemone blanda*, *Crocus*, *Scilla*, snowdrops, spring snowflakes, and winter aconites. Few summer-active plants will thrive in such a position, but *Helleborus, Podophyllum, Polygonatum,* and *Trillium* as well as some shade-tolerant ferns will provide good company. The spring ephemerals need a good supply of nutrients during their short active period. In nature they prefer neutral to slightly alkaline mineral soils with a high content of humus thoroughly worked in by earthworms. In the garden this typically corresponds to a good fertile loam.

During planting the soil should be improved by mixing in a generous supply of phosphate in the form of bonemeal and/or wood ashes. The latter should be derived from deciduous broadleaved trees and will also assist in raising the pH. Well-rotted manure or compost should also be added since this will improve the soil structure.

Planting depth depends upon the species. *Dicentra canadensis* will commonly be found with its nose at soil surface. However, if the tubers to be planted look dry, bury them to at least 10 cm so that the soil moisture rehydrates them; eventually they will reach the surface. Species of *Corydalis* section *Corydalis* (*solida* group) should be planted with their top about 10 cm below the surface, the tap-rooted *C. nobilis* with the top of the tap-root about 3 cm below soil surface, and the forms of *C. cava* at a depth of approximately 20 cm.

After planting, the ground should be watered if it is dry. Future care will include an annual feeding (preferably of manure) in October, accompanied by a medium dose of bonemeal.

Open Mixed Woodland and Shady Border

These garden situations provide the perfect sites for many species that appear later in the year than those just mentioned. Here water and some degree of light should be present during the summer. The soil should be enriched by a mixture of leaf mold, well-rotted manure, and peat to give it an open structure and a good content of nutrients and other beneficial properties. The combination of dappled shade and summer moisture is perfect for *Adlumia fungosa, A. asiatica, Dicentra eximia, D. formosa, Ichtyoselmis macrantha,* and *Lamprocapnos spectabilis,* as well as many *Corydalis* species, such as *C. caseana, C. chaerophylla, C. flexuosa, C. omeiana,* and *C. scouleri,* along with several other of the recently introduced Chinese species. The spring ephemerals mentioned previously will likewise be equally at home here as in the dense, deciduous woodland.

In the wild, shade-loving Fumariaceae are found growing alongside other desirable woodland plants. For gardeners who enjoy imitating nature, we suggest growing these plants with species of *Arisaema, Epimedium, Erythronium, Jeffersonia, Lilium, Nomocharis, Podophyllum, Polygonatum, Tiarella, Trillium, Vancouveria,* anemones of the nemorosa clan and various ferns. Several of the species that are suitable for a shady border combine well with large-leaved plants, such as hostas and certain arums, since the bold leaves of these plants provide contrast to the ferny leaves of the Fumariaceae. Members of the family will, however, associate equally well with their close relatives the poppies, especially *Eomecon*, *Hylomecon*, and *Stylophorum*, as well as with ferns, all of which have leaves similar to those of the bleeding hearts. A glaucous-leaved *Dicentra* hybrid like *D.* 'Luxuriant' next to a green-leaved fern is a particularly pleasing combination. Larger ferns and *Lamprocapnos spectabilis* also combine well since the latter plant has a tendency to die down in mid summer, particularly when planted in dry soils. The blue-flowered corydalis look especially attractive next to other herbaceous plants with yellow flowers or foliage. Alternatively, they may be used as an underplanting to the pale yellow-flowered *Corylopsis pauciflora* for a stunning effect.

To provide shade a variety of slow-growing trees and shrubs such as *Abies*, *Acer*, *Halesia*, *Magnolia*, *Quercus*, *Tsuga*, and azaleas can be used. Many Fumariaceae will not only thrive in the open woodland but also will naturalize. *Adlumia fungosa*, *Dicentra eximia*, and *D. formosa* are particularly suitable for naturalizing in woodland gardens. White-flowered dicentras, such as *D. eximia* 'Alba', naturalized among a group of white-stemmed birches, such as *Betula papyrifera* or *B. utilis*, make for an especially pleasing effect.

Perennial or Mixed Borders

Some members of the family can be used in more formal garden situations. Many of the woodland species mentioned previously will, for example, be equally at home here. The most important candidates are *Dicentra eximia*, *D. formosa*, the hybrid dicentras, and *Lamprocapnos spectabilis*. All of these are already familiar border plants that enjoy a fertile garden loam and continuous summer moisture. Less well known are the two species of eardrop, *Ehrendorferia chrysantha* and *E. ochroleuca*, both of which are suitable for a well-drained, hot, sunny border. The white-flowered *E. ochroleuca* can reach a height of 3 meters, and would make a real conversation piece at the back of a border. Sadly, it is rarely if ever cultivated outside of its native California. The yellow-flowered *E. chrysantha* is shorter at about 1 meter tall and is occasionally grown in perennial borders in England, and to a lesser extent the United States. But, again, this is a species that deserves wider recognition. Some of the *Corydalis* from section *Corydalis* that we later recommend for the rock garden, such as *C. glaucescens*, *C. malkensis*, and *C. solida* in its best forms, can also be grown in a sunny border.

Herb Gardens, Containers, and Walls

Since many members of the family have medicinal properties, they make obvious additions to the ornamental herb garden. Examples include *Corydalis cava*, *Dicentra cucullaria*, *Fumaria officinalis*, and *Pseudofumaria lutea*—all of which were traditional mainstays of the apothecary garden.

Dicentra formosa, *D. eximia*, the hybrid dicentras, and the two species of *Pseudofumaria* can all be grown to great effect in a container as long as they are divided and given fresh soil every few years.

Forcing of bleeding heart (*Lamprocapnos spectabilis*) was once common, though it is rarely practiced these days, as we discuss in chapter four.

Pseudofumaria alba and *P. lutea* grow naturally on cliffs and rock outcrops and have long been grown upon old garden walls to great effect. In gardens of a more Mediterranean climate, *Rupicapnos*, *Sarcocapnos*, and chasmophytic *Corydalis* like *C. rupestris*, *C. tomentella*, and *C. wilsonii* can be tried. Perpetuation by means of self-sown seedlings will be important in such situations since all these species are rather short-lived.

Climbers

Climbing members of the family with their often subtle flowers and restful ferny leaves look attractive when allowed to scramble over low-growing shrubs, rocks, or old logs in a woodland garden. *Adlumia fungosa* and *A. asiatica* are particularly suited to this approach. The already strikingly pale green stems and leaves of these species can be even further accentuated by growing them over shrubs with dark green foliage.

The showier yellow-flowered climbing dicentras, *Dactylicapnos macrocapnos*, and *D. scandens*, are sometimes grown against the wall of a house, as can be seen at the Old Vicarage Garden in North Norfolk, England, where the former species intermingles with a purple-flowered clematis to great effect (Plate 14). Tony Lord's useful book, *The Encyclopedia of Planting Combinations* (2002), suggested a more unusual combination—*D. scandens* intertwined with the purple-flowered climbing monkshood (*Aconitum hemsleyanum*). Again the yellow and purple flowers complement each other beautifully.

Rock Garden and Alpine Trough

A well-drained rock garden provides the ideal site for many species. Here the soil should be rich, open, and water-retentive. A mix of equal parts good loam, peat, sand, and grit that is neutralized with lime and enriched with bonemeal, and an annual sprinkle of a complete fertilizer gives the plants a good environment. Some species will prefer a hot, southerly exposure. These include the non-tuberous *Corydalis adunca*; the tuberous *C. glaucescens*, *C. henrikii*, *C. nudicaulis*, *C. schanginii*, and *C. wendelboi*; *Dicentra formosa* subsp. *oregana*; and the two species of *Pseudofumaria*. The two remarkable ehrendorferias are probably also best in a hot site.

A cooler north exposure will suit an increasing variety of species including *Corydalis cava*, *C. cheilanthifolia*, *C. malkensis*, *C. pakistanica*, *C. pseudobarbisepala*, *C. solida*, *Dicentra formosa*, and *D. eximia* as well as the short-lived *C. incisa*, and *C. linstowiana*, *C. smithiana*, and *C. speciosa*. The cooler north exposure approaches the peat wall in its horticultural qualities so many species can be grown in either structure.

A cool and easily attended area is the obvious spot to try *Corydalis alpestris*, *C. emanuelii*, and the choice *Dicentra peregrina*, as well as the blue species of *Corydalis* section *Corydalis* from the Far East.

An "alpine trough" gives gardeners the ultimate control and is really the best outdoor area for tiny jewels like *Corydalis emanuelii* and its closest relatives, *Dicentra pauciflora*, *D. peregrina*, and *D. uniflora*. Major benefits of a trough are the excellent drainage it provides and the relatively deep root-run which buffers plants against sudden changes in moisture and temperature. The trough should be situated in a lightly shaded and readily accessible part of the garden.

Peat Beds

With their fertile, humus-rich, cool, and slightly acid soil, peat beds and peat walls are the most important garden structures for growing Fumariaceae. In a peat garden the building material as well as the compost and the plants evaporate water to give a high degree of atmospheric humidity. This is especially appreciated by the majority of the *Corydalis* species hailing from the monsoon areas of the Sino-Himalaya. The site should be an open north slope and the peat terraces should be filled with a good mix of well-rotted manure, peat, sand, and loam. The area must, naturally, be under scrutiny regarding weeds, water, and nutrients and be given a little more care than the average backyard. A structural backbone can be created by planting smaller rhododendrons and other ericaceous shrubs in the peat blocks, along with a few deciduous shrubs such as *Hamamelis*, hydrangeas, smaller magnolias, *Sorbus reducta*, and *S. rosea*. All will provide summer shade, as well as support for *Dactylicapnos* species.

Here among Asiatic primulas, dwarf lilies, *Meconopsis*, and *Nomocharis* we can imagine planning an advanced connoisseur garden of Fumariaceae. In it the early spring would see the golden *Corydalis bracteata* surrounded by the dwarf, lacey, azure *C. lineariloba* and the ivory-white *C. malkensis*. Other blue easterners like *C. turtschaninovii* and *C. fumariifolia* would follow, with icy-white and celestial-blue *C. ornata*, golden *C. gorinensis*, and greeny pinkish-white *C. magadanica* later succeeding in a gentle order. The shadier parts would be the perfect place for *Ichtyoselmis macrantha* to present its translucent, red-green foliage and large sulfur "gold-fish" flowers. In early summer the clear-blue flowers of *Corydalis flexuosa*, *C. omeiana*, and their hybrid *C.* 'Craigton Blue' would look wonderful in the dappled shade under pink and white azaleas. In fact, most of the more recently introduced Chinese species would be at home in an area like this, including *C. davidii*, *C. elata*, *C. flaccida*, *C. leucanthema*, *C. temulifolia*, *C. tenerrima*, and *C. yunnanensis*, to mention just a few.

To grow the rarest and most choice members of the family, sharpen the drainage with sand and grit, elevate the area to a comfortable height, and create a raised peat bed with extra drainage. The fairest of alpine corydalis will then stand a chance in this select spot. Besides the alpine house, this is the ultimate corner for the true alpine species. Even *Corydalis benecincta*, *C. emanuelii*, and *C. hemidicentra* from the high screes above 4000 m (13,000 ft) can sometimes survive here for a few years. The same can be said about the tiny dicentras—*Dicentra pauciflora*, *D. peregrina*, and *D. uniflora*. Really durable in a site like this though are *C. cashmeriana* and *C. pachycentra*; both will flower in late spring and make wonderful company with the sweetly fragrant, ivory-white *Primula reidii* var. *williamsii*. Other jewels such as *C. calcicola*, *C. hamata*, and *C. kokiana* are also safest in the raised peat bed.

Alpine House

Some members of the family are not ideally suited to the open garden and require the protection of an alpine house or bulb frame, especially if grown in wetter or colder climates. Others are simply too frail or too scarce to risk in the open garden. Such plants include *Dicentra nevadensis*, *D. pauciflora*, *D. peregrina*, *D. uniflora*, *Rupicapnos africana*, *Sarcocapnos enneaphylla*, and many *Corydalis* species. Most of these plants are typically grown in pots, but all species of *Rupicapnos* and *Sarcocapnos* and certain cliff-dwelling corydalis, like *C. rupestris*, *C. tomentella*, and *C. wilsonii*, are best displayed on a tufa wall where the occasional self-sown seedlings will perpetuate the species. Other plants, including *D. canadensis* and *D. cucullaria*, and any *Corydalis* shorter than 30 cm, while readily grown outdoors, also take well to a pot in an alpine house. Cultivating them this way not only allows them to be grown to perfection but also enables them to be positioned at a convenient height for viewing their intriguing flowers. It is also a good way of safeguarding any rare or new plants for future propagation.

All tuberous and most dwarf to medium-sized species of *Corydalis* are lovely subjects for pot cultivation in an alpine house. Together with *Crocus* and vernal *Colchicum*, *Eranthis*, and *Galanthus* they are the first plants to greet spring, which makes them particularly precious.

Since the cultural needs of plants suitable for an alpine house differ, they are discussed here under two distinct categories reflecting their different watering needs.

Summer-Dormant Species

The tuberous summer-dormant species should have a dry summer—dust-dry in the case of members of *Corydalis* section *Leonticoides* such as *C. popovii* and *C. macrocentra* and "just a trifle moist" for the species of sections *Corydalis* (*solida* group) and *Radix-cava*.

The compost should be open, air- and water-retentive, and have a decent supply of nutrients. We have had good results with a mix of equal parts of loam, peat, sand, and grit. During the active season (August to May) the pots receive a light dose (about 1 part per thousand) of liquid fertilizer (the same kind as used for house plants) with each watering.

Deep pots (long toms) best suit *Corydalis* sections *Leonticoides* and *Radix-cava* since their tubers are naturally deeply seated. The species from section *Corydalis* should be more shallowly planted like most pot-grown bulbs, including *Fritillaria* and *Crocus*. Annual repotting is best done from August to September for sections *Corydalis* and *Radix-cava*, which should be watered and kept slightly moist from then on. Plunging the pots in sand is beneficial. It allows more accurate regulation of the moisture level around the plants since the plunge material, rather than the potting medium itself, can be watered. The species of section *Leonticoides* should be repotted and started much later (November to early December) to prevent winter growth. It is of vital importance that the pots don't dry out after they have received their first sip of water because this will have initiated rooting. Also, be alert when the thaw comes, since the pots may freeze-dry in the winter and may need to be thoroughly soaked. The plants discussed here will be among the first to appear in spring, present their lovely flowers, and set seed before quickly withering in May. From then on water should be withheld. If clay-pots are being used, the just-a-trifle-moist state can be achieved by watering the plunge material every week or fortnight.

Summer-Active Species

These plants demand a cooler part of the alpine house. Generally, they require a slightly more acidic compost and some shade during the summer. Some species might go partly dormant in the hottest summer but must not be kept too dry. Fertilizer should be provided as mentioned previously. Such a regime suits the four tuberous species of *Dicentra* and is the safest way to make *D. uniflora* and *D. pauciflora* long-lived and regularly flowering. Species of *Corydalis* section *Dactylotuber*, such as *C. benecincta*, *C. emanuelii*, and *C. hemidicentra*, also appreciate this treatment. *Dicentra peregrina* and *Corydalis cashmeriana* are outstanding pot subjects that can be grown together with dwarf Asiatic primulas, androsaces, dwarf gentians, and other alpines. *Corydalis flexuosa* and several of the recently introduced Chinese species of this genus can be grown into excellent show plants in the alpine house.

Bulb Frame

The bulb frame—a well-drained bed filled with compost and covered by glass—is the perfect place to grow the beautiful and bizarre *Corydalis* section *Leonticoides*. The ability to plant the tubers at an ample depth (30–50 cm), to have total control of watering, and the protection provided by the glass in late winter all help keep these challenging plants in character and long-lived (25 years or more). Some members of section *Corydalis* are also at their best here. *Corydalis glaucescens*, *C. henrikii*, *C. integra*, *C. nudicaulis*, *C. paschei*, *C. ruksansii*, *C. schanginii*, *C. tauricola*, *C. triternata*, and *C. wendelboi* are all suitable for the bulb frame. While a bulb frame is, in many ways, similar to an alpine house, the former has the advantage of providing plants with a free root-run and allows moisture to be more evenly available during the watering season. A bulb frame is also often easier to ventilate.

In the bulb frame, use compost made by mixing equal parts loam, peat, sand, and grit, as previously recommended for pot-grown plants. The compost should be kept moist from October to May and dry during the remaining months. The bulb frame should be placed in a sunny site away from trees and provided artificial shading as needed.

Propagation

For purposes of propagating the Fumariaceae, the plants are divided into two groups by their underground parts: tuberous species and non-tuberous, or fibrous, species. Both have different requirements.

The Tuberous Species

The tuberous species include *Dicentra canadensis*, *D. cucullaria*, *D. pauciflora*, *D. uniflora*, and *Corydalis* sections *Corydalis* (*solida* group), *Radix-cava*, *Duplotuber*, and *Leonticoides*.

Seed

The spring ephemerals produce seed that is best sown fresh because the embryo in it is not fully developed by the time the seed is dispersed and does not really start to enlarge until cool autumn days arrive. If the seed is sown as soon as it is harvested, or no later than September, one can expect excellent germination the following spring. Old seed might occasionally produce a few seedlings, so don't feel deterred to order older seed if it is the only source available to you.

Sow the seeds thinly on a compost composed of equal parts loam, peat, sand, and grit; cover them with a layer of sharp sand; and top with a layer of grit. Keep the seed-pot slightly moist and expose it to the winter weather. In early spring the cotyledon will appear but expect no more top-growth that season. This single leaf produces "power" for the little tuber that forms underground, so try to nurse it and keep it green as long as possible. Do not disturb the young plant by pricking out during the first season. When the cotyledon turns yellow, it is time to let the pot dry out. Since the corms are so minute (2–5 mm in diameter), they should be kept slightly moister during the summer than the adult versions. As long as the pots are watered with liquid fertilizer, they may stay untouched for three seasons. After three or four years the first plants will have reached flowering size.

Division

The dicentras and *Corydalis* sections *Corydalis* (*solida* group) and *Duplotuber* proliferate underground and can easily be divided in early autumn (September) before new roots are formed. Exceptions are *C. caucasica*, *C. malkensis*, and *C. pumila*; because their tubers rarely split, these species are best propagated by seed.

The species from *Corydalis* sections *Leonticoides* (*C. popovii* and its allies) and *Radix-cava* have tubers that don't increase in numbers but can grow to a large size and eventually, through partial deterioration, increase that way. Accordingly, larger tubers have several adventitious buds and can be propagated by simply breaking or cutting them into smaller parts. This operation should be carried out in early autumn. The divided tubers of *C. blanda* and *C. cava* must go directly into compost and be kept moist, while those of *C. popovii* and its allies must be allowed to heal their wounds in the open air of the potting shed and should not be planted before November. After that they should be nursed like an adult plant.

The Non-tuberous Species

The non-tuberous species include *Dicentra eximia, D. formosa, D. nevadensis, D. peregrina*, all the *Corydalis* species not mentioned in the previous category, *Adlumia, Capnoides, Dactylicapnos, Ehrendorferia, Ichtyoselmis, Lamprocapnos, Pseudofumaria, Rupicapnos*, and *Sarcocapnos*.

Seed

The summer-active species have seeds that store better than those of the spring ephemerals. There is a lot of variation in their longevity, however, so it is always safest to sow as soon as possible. The seeds of woodland, streamside, and alpine species store less well, whereas the seeds of species from drier ground and the cliff-dwellers have longer viability. Some of the annual species can survive storage for several years.

The seeds should be treated as recommended for the tuberous species. They will require at least one long cold period before they are ready to germinate. Sometimes they may take two to three years before they show, so save your seed-pots.

Ehrendorferia seed is triggered to germinate by smoke. The easiest method is to use "liquid smoke" that can be purchased from the Seed Room at Kirstenbosch National Botanical Garden (see appendix A for the address).

After germination all these plants will produce true leaves the same season. Prick out the seedlings when their size allows and grow on like ordinary herbaceous plants. The type of compost and exposure depends on the needs of the individual species and is discussed elsewhere in this book.

Division

This is a particularly useful method for species with well-developed rhizomes like *Dicentra formosa, Lamprocapnos, Ichtyoselmis, Corydalis scouleri*, and many of the Chinese woodland species, such as *C. flexuosa, C. omeiana*, and *C. yunnanensis*. *Corydalis cashmeriana* and the other species from section *Fasciculatae* can (and should) be propagated by carefully separating their crowded root bundles.

Division is best carried out in the autumn. Root growth will be promoted by the cooler weather and high humidity. Even plants that have gone partly dormant by that time, such as *Dicentra formosa* and *Corydalis scouleri*, should be lifted in autumn. Division in spring is not advisable for any Fumariaceae, though it may work with strong-growing species.

Cuttings

For species that are difficult to divide, spring cuttings by means of compact rosettes may provide another possibility for propagation. This method works well with *Dicentra eximia* and those *Corydalis* with winter-green leaf rosettes, such as *C. davidii*, *C. pseudobarbisepala*, and *C. sheareri*. With these species simply detach the individual rosettes and insert them in a good cutting compost. Keep the cuttings in a transparent enclosed container and check them once a week. After roots have formed, transplant them to compost suitable for mature plants. At this time keep them in the enclosed container for a few more days and then gradually open the lid up until the cuttings are fully exposed to the air.

Cuttings are also a good method to propagate the frail, juicy species of *Sarcocapnos* and *Rupicapnos*, as well as the cliff-dwelling *Corydalis* species, like *C. rupestris*, *C. tomentella*, and *C. wilsonii*. These, however, are trickier and require a drier rooting medium, such as pumice.

In Vitro Propagation

The rooting of micro-cuttings in flasks appears to be readily achieved as far as most summer-growing species are concerned. The spring ephemerals should, in theory, be more difficult to root, with problems associated with temperature and dormancy breaking.

Creating Hybrids

Hybrids within the different sections of *Corydalis* frequently occur spontaneously in cultivation and can be repeated if desired. The safest way to control the offspring is to chose a self-sterile seed parent and pollinate it with the desired pollen parent. Many hybrids have been created within the tuberous species. Several have appeared within the summer-growing species with *C.* 'Craigton Blue' (*C. omeiana* × *C. flexuosa*) being an outstanding example. The startling *C.* 'Kingfisher' even breaks the section barriers, being a hybrid between members of sections *Elatae* and *Fasciculatae*. Clearly there is much scope for new, fantastic hybrids in the future.

Many superb *Dicentra* hybrids are also on the market. For those wishing to produce their own hybrids it should be noted that dicentras regularly self-pollinate if the style is rubbed too severely. For this reason, artificial pollination is best carried out by first cutting off the inner petals, carefully removing the stamens on the flower to be pollinated, and then artificially pollinating it repeatedly over the course of a few days. Interestingly, *D. cucullaria* and *D. canadensis* do not form hybrids, nor have these species been crossed with other dicentras. Attempts to cross *Lamprocapnos* or *Ichtyoselmis* with other species have also, so far, failed, which is not surprising considering their isolated positions within the family.

Pests and Diseases

Generally, the bleeding heart family is a healthy plant group and its members are usually trouble-free in the garden. However, when any collection of related plants is amassed, the higher density of species—all with similar pest and disease susceptibilities—may generate problems. This is particularly true when plants are being commercially mass-produced.

In nature, species of *Dicentra* and *Corydalis* often have their own highly specialized parasites. While few of these pests have yet been inadvertently introduced into our gardens, we can count on an enemy with a taste for a particular species being equally happy to feed upon most cultivated members of the family. For this reason, prevention of pests and diseases starts with avoiding the accidental introduction of problems into a garden via diseased plants. Appropriate cultural practices, the use of sterilized potting soils, and the regular removal of dead and dying plant parts are also good preventative measures. If frequent monitoring is maintained, few pests or diseases should be encountered, and those that are can be easily controlled before they become a serious problem.

Mammals

In early spring when food is short in supply, deer, rabbits and hares may sometimes acquire a taste for the bitter foliage of *Corydalis* and *Dicentra*. This rarely happens though later in the season.

Mice, voles and other rodents can also acquire a taste, especially for the particularly bitter tubers of the ephemeral *Corydalis* species. Once they have developed such a hankering they can often completely strip an area of tubers in a very short time. In-

Mouse. Drawing by Paul Harwood.

deed, their eagerness makes one suspect that they find the opium affect as pleasant as the nourishment properties. Be especially alert in the autumn when rodents move in from the fields. A resident cat can be effective, but only as long as it is trained not to scratch in the gravel around choice plants. Otherwise, use traps and take other precautions to keep the rodent populations down. If poison is used it works best when applied among the rodent colonies. It must, of course, be protected from rain, as well as from other mammals and birds.

Insects and Mites

Several species of apollo butterfly (genus *Parnassius*) are wholly dependent on particular species of *Dicentra* and *Corydalis*. Should any of these lovely butterflies, such as the western North American *Parnassius clodius*, or the European *P. mnemosyne*, choose your garden as a hatchery, we suggest that you should be proud and neglect the damage caused.

Wasps of the genus *Aylax* may also use corydalis fruits as nurseries for their larvae, with infested fruits becoming swollen, spongy, and sterile. This parasite has been recorded for *Corydalis* species from different sections, but not on the spring ephemerals, and never on cultivated plants.

The vine weevil, *Otiorhynchus sulcatus*, is not usually a great threat to plants but on rare occasions the white maggotlike grubs can attack the thick-rooted species. One method of controlling these pests is to routinely walk around the garden or alpine house at night when the adults are active and remove them by hand. Most chemical treatments focus on the larvae, as chemical control of the adult weevils is difficult. The grubs can be controlled by nematodes like *Steinernema* (formerly *Neoaplectana*) and *Heterorhabditis* that are commercially available. These are extremely efficient and eliminate the need for chemicals. To prevent unexpected infestations, always examine the roots of severely wilted plants for larvae and routinely tidy the alpine house to reduce the number of potential hiding places for the adults.

Greenfly, also known as aphids, can sometimes be a problem on the summer-active species but is easy to control by insecticidal soaps and horticultural oils. Red spider mite, *Tetranychus urticae*, may also occasionally become a problem in summer if plants are grown too hot and dry, but once present may be similarly controlled. Be aware that the chemicals used to treat such insects often tend to scorch the fragile foliage of this family. The best thing is to improve the cultural conditions for your plants.

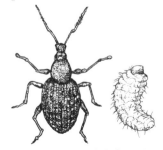

Adult vine weevil (left) and larval vine weevil (right).
Drawing by Paul Harwood.

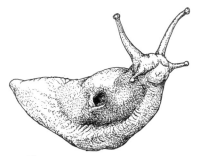

Slug. Drawing by Paul Harwood.

Other Creatures

Snails and slugs will not choose members of the bleeding heart family as a main course, but sometimes as their dessert. These pests are usually only a problem in the open garden, and there they can be controlled by a variety of methods. For example, a sprinkling of soot or diatomaceous earth around the base of the susceptible plants will help deter slugs. For a more permanent solution, set beer traps or routinely walk around the garden with a flashlight on a damp night, when these pests are active, and remove them. Removal of dead and dying plant material and other debris will also make your garden a less hospitable place for slugs and snails. Most slug pellets are not recommended because they can be harmful to pets and wild birds.

Fungal Diseases

A wide range of fungi has the potential to parasitize plants, but only a few species present a serious problem. By optimizing light, air movement, watering, nutrients, and hygiene, it should not be necessary to resort to chemical treatments. For the ordinary garden we particularly recommend the collect-and-destroy tactic as the safest, most efficient method of control.

A particularly serious fungal plague has recently occurred on the ephemeral *Corydalis* species. This as-yet-unidentified fungal pathogen has provisionally been called the black corydalis disease. The first sign is spots of wilt on the foliage that rapidly spread over the lamina and stalk, giving the impression of heat damage. Underground parts look blackish and distorted. On the tubers, black spots signal the forthcoming rot and eventual death. We have seen the same fungus attack *Helleborus thibetanus*, as well as anemones of the nemorosa clan. The infection spreads rapidly when plants are grown in full sun. Possibly it is caused by *Rhizoctonia tulipanorum*, and if so it can be controlled with a fungicide containing tolclofos-methyl, such as Rizolex. A fungicide of mono- and di-potassium salts of phosphorus acid such as Fosphite also seems to control the disease, if used when the foliage is developing. However, it must be combined with hygiene; in particular, exchange the soil around affected plants and destroy any infected plant parts.

Young seedlings are susceptible to most of the widespread fungal "propagation diseases." *Alternaria, Botrytis, Fusaria, Phytium, Phytophthora*, and *Rhizoctonia* will all show their presence if conditions are right, or rather, wrong. However, if you improve conditions slightly by increasing light levels and air circulation, you can avoid most problems.

Stem and crown rot, *Sclerotium rolfsii*, also known as southern blight, causes a wilt. Leaves will become juicy at the base and collapse, after which a cobwebby, white mycelium covers the infected area. Later, the small, reddish brown to blackish, seedlike sclerotia will form and perpetuate the fungus. This disease is particularly bad for *Hosta* but is noted here since it can also attack *Dicentra* and *Lamprocapnos*. Stem and root rot can also be caused by *Rhizoctonia solani*. Maintenance of hygienic conditions and good cultural practice should prevent both these diseases. Appropriate fungicide sprays are also available.

In eastern Asia wild *Asarum* species share a rust fungus, *Cerotelium asari*, with *Corydalis lineariloba*. In eastern North America, a related species of rust, *Cerotelium dicentrae*, shares its life between *Laportea canadensis* (wood nettle) and *Dicentra cucullaria* (but interestingly not with *D. canadensis*). Other rusts said to grow on members of the family are *Puccinia aristidae* and *P. brandegei*. None of these, however, are widespread or problematic in gardens.

On cultivated *Corydalis flexuosa*, leaf spots have been reportedly caused by *Colletotrichum gloeosporioides*, a common disease in horticulture. The best control is to not accidentally introduce this fungus into your garden, especially since once noticed it will likely have already damaged your plants.

Powdery mildew, probably an *Erysiphe* species, can also attack plants in summer, rarely in the open garden but more frequently in the greenhouse. It seems to be the same species that also infests many plants in the family Ranunculaceae. These minute fungi produce unsightly white-powdery patches on leaves, stems, and buds. Powdery mildews prefer cool temperatures, high humidity, and wet leaves, and may be problematic when plants are stressed. In a greenhouse, good air circulation and ventilation are effective preventative measures. Severe cases may be treated with a fungicide.

Yellow to brown spots on the leaf combined with, in humid conditions, a white "fur" on the lower surface of the leaf are the symptoms of downy mildew, *Peronospora corydalis*. In mass-produced crop plants like *Corydalis yanhusuo*, it can be lethal. The fungus is systemic in *C. yanhusuo*, *Dicentra cucullaria*, and *D. canadensis* and can occur in the tubers. It is also known to infest *Capnoides sempervirens*, so it can occur on the summer-active species as well. It is, however, rarely a problem in cultivation and can be prevented in a greenhouse, where it is usually most prevalent, by providing good air circulation and ventilation.

2

Natural History

THIS CHAPTER EXAMINES the natural environment of the Fumariaceae and particularly the natural distribution of the plants in the wild, their habits and habitats, and their interactions with pollinators and seed dispersers. It also provides background information on the morphological features important in plant identification. But first we begin with a brief survey of taxonomic relationships in the family—what the species and genera have in common and what features distinguish them from each other.

The Bleeding Heart Family

At first glance, the distinctive, somewhat heart-shaped flowers of dicentras, which have two planes of symmetry (see Plate 1) look very different from the two-lipped, long-spurred flowers of a typical corydalis, which have a single plane of symmetry (see Plate 2). However, even a brief study of their foliage and flowers will reveal a number of common features that reflect the shared ancestry of these plants. Both, for example, have deeply dissected, somewhat fernlike leaves, and flowers with four petals arranged in two pairs. Even more striking is that in both flowers the two inner petals are fused together at their tips into a distinct hoodlike structure that blocks the flower's entrance and hides the anthers and stigma. In fact, as you examine a corydalis flower you will find that it is constructed using exactly the same basic plan as found in *Dicentra*, but instead of having two planes of symmetry it has only one. *Capnoides sempervirens*, a species that was once classified in *Corydalis*, further illuminates this link, as its flowers are even more similar to those of *Dicentra*, except that they are oblique (Plate 105).

Since the early 1800s botanists have recognized that *Corydalis*, *Dicentra*, and a number of other genera compose a distinct evolutionary lineage that is most closely related to the poppies. The bleeding hearts and the poppies share numerous similarities in vegetative, floral, and DNA characters, as well as a suite of distinct chemicals, including some of the potent alkaloids for which the poppies are so well known. The two groups, while similar, nonetheless have obvious structural differ-

32

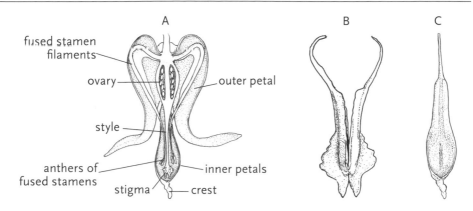

Dicentra eximia: A: A cross section of flower showing anthers and stigma inside hoodlike structure formed by the two fused inner petals. B: A pair of inner petals showing fused tips, side view. C: A single inner petal, inner surface viewed face on. Drawing by Paul Harwood.

ences and can be readily distinguished. The *Corydalis-Dicentra* group, as we have already seen, has a distinct petal arrangement. Its members, unlike the poppies, also have, on one or both of their outer petals, a spur or sac that collects nectar. Furthermore, their stamens are very unusual and few in number, and their sap is colorless and watery. The poppies, in contrast, have petals that are never fused at their tips and are spread wide, and since their flowers don't produce nectar they never have nectar-collecting spurs or sacs. The poppies also differ in having numerous stamens and a sap that is milky or colored.

Some botanists have chosen to highlight the differences between the bleeding hearts and poppies by classifying them in two families: Fumariaceae, the bleeding heart or fumitory family, and Papaveraceae, the poppy family. Other scientists have stressed their similarities by classifying them in the same family—the Papaveraceae. Neither system is incorrect, as each in its own way reflects evolutionary history.

In this book we recognize the Fumariaceae as a distinct family, which in addition to its traditional members also contains *Hypecoum* (Plate 3), a rarely cultivated genus that is intermediate in certain floral characters between the bleeding hearts and the poppies. For instance, *Hypecoum*, in common with the bleeding hearts, has two dissimilar pairs of petals; however, the outer petals are not spurred and the inner petals are not fused at their tips, and in this way they resemble the poppies. Nevertheless, the 20 species of *Hypecoum* share many more features with the Fumariaceae than they do with the poppies and are classified in the former family, albeit in a separate subfamily. The following list summarizes the classification of the Fumariaceae:

Family: Fumariaceae
  Subfamily: Fumarioideae   Tribe: Corydaleae
    Tribe: Fumarieae   *Adlumia*
      Ceratocapnos   *Capnoides*
      Cryptocapnos   *Corydalis*
      Cysticapnos   *Dactylicapnos*
      Discocapnos   *Dicentra*
      Fumaria   *Ehrendorferia*
      Fumariola   *Ichtyoselmis*
      Platycapnos   *Lamprocapnos*
      Pseudofumaria   Subfamily: Hypecoideae
      Rupicapnos   *Hypecoum*
      Sarcocapnos
      Trigonocapnos

Excluding the genus *Hypecoum*, Linnaeus, in the mid-eighteenth century, knew only 13 species in the family Fumariaceae, and included them all in the genus *Fumaria*. Today we count about 550 species divided into 20 genera. The vast

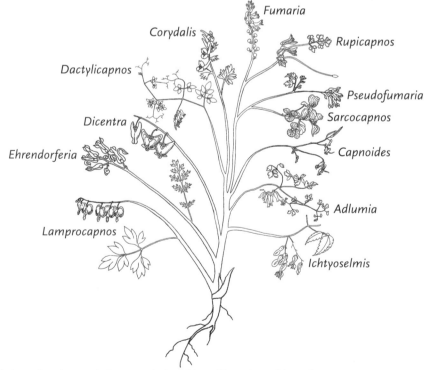

Family tree showing evolutionary relationships of just the cultivated genera. Drawing by Adèle Rossetti Morosini.

majority of these species are classified in *Corydalis*, with most of the other genera consisting of a single or less than 10 species. After *Corydalis*, the next largest genera are *Fumaria* with 50 species, *Hypecoum* with 16 species, and *Dactylicapnos* with 10 species. The genus *Dicentra*, as we will see shortly, has recently been split up, and as currently circumscribed includes eight species.

Evolutionary relationships among the genera of Fumariaceae, which have been determined using molecular sequence data (see family tree on page 34), are also confirmed by morphological features. For example, all genera except *Lamprocapnos* share a unique type of seed coat, an evolutionary novelty arising after the split between *Lamprocapnos* and the others.

Recent Taxonomic Changes

It is often said that botanists change the names of plants just to see their own names in print. While name changes can be a disquieting experience for gardeners, for whom a plant's name has become common usage, botanists usually have good reasons for renaming a plant. Discovering that a species has been misidentified in cultivation requires correction. Sometimes new information requires dividing a variable genus or species, or, in other cases, merging two or more genera or species. Recent research in the bleeding heart family has led to some taxonomic reshuffling, which has in turn necessitated some name changes among the commonly cultivated members. To alleviate confusion over the naming of these plants, we summarize here the reasons for these changes.

The biggest taxonomic change, and the one that has resulted in the most new names, is the division of the genus *Dicentra* into five smaller genera. This change followed a molecular study (Lidén et al. 1997), which found that the 21 species previously recognized as comprising *Dicentra* do not constitute a distinct evolutionary lineage. Instead these species had been lumped together solely because they lacked certain evolutionary novelties found in other lineages of the bleeding heart family. The principal character that had been used to construct the previous classification was the bisymmetry of *Dicentra* flowers. However, as bisymmetric flowers are also found in *Hypecoum* and *Adlumia* (as well as in the poppy family!), this characteristic is not suitable for recognizing *Dicentra*. In fact, the DNA study showed that some species of *Dicentra* are more closely related to *Fumaria* and *Corydalis* than they are to other species of *Dicentra* in the classical sense. Since modern-day classifications aim to reflect evolutionary relationships, the 21 species of *Dicentra* have been split into five smaller genera, each of which represents a natural evolutionary lineage. This may at first seem rather drastic, but the groups are all readily identifiable. Unique, and often prominent, morphological features that correlate with the DNA traits characterize each genus.

Thus today, all 10 species of climbing Himalayan dicentra are classified in the genus *Dactylicapnos*. The most commonly cultivated bleeding heart, *Dicentra spectabilis*, is correctly known as *Lamprocapnos spectabilis*. The two species of Californian eardrops, which have upright flowers, are classified in the genus *Ehrendorferia*. The large-flowered Chinese *Dicentra macrantha*, which has pendant fiddle-shaped flowers and toothed leaf margins, is correctly known as *Ichtyoselmis macrantha*. Only eight species of stemless herbs remain in the genus *Dicentra*, seven of which are North American and one of which is native to northeastern Asia. So distinct are each of these new genera that they had previously been recognized as subgenera of *Dicentra*, or in the case of *Dactylicapnos*, commonly as a genus.

The genus *Corydalis* has also had three commonly cultivated species removed from it and placed in two distinct genera. Thus *C. lutea* and *C. ochroleuca* are now respectively named *Pseudofumaria lutea* and *P. alba*, while *Corydalis sempervirens* is named *Capnoides sempervirens*. Again, these changes reflect a better understanding of evolutionary relationships. The three species were removed from *Corydalis* because morphological characteristics indicate that these plants are not directly related to the remaining species of *Corydalis*, a conclusion later confirmed by DNA sequences. In the case of *Capnoides sempervirens*, this outcome should not be too surprising, since its flowers are rather different from *Corydalis* and resemble somewhat oblique flowers of *Dicentra eximia*. In contrast, the floral differences between the two species of *Pseudofumaria* and *Corydalis* are, at first glance, harder to see but no less important. Most notable is the difference in the styles. In *Corydalis* they persist in fruit, while in *Pseudofumaria* they quickly fall off. This trait, the small bracts, and the short rounded spur show that *Pseudofumaria* is instead closely related to *Fumaria*.

The renaming of *Corydalis ochroleuca* to *Pseudofumaria alba* requires further explanation, since the name of the species as well as the genus has changed. In this case, the name *alba* was validly published for the species earlier than the name *ochroleuca*, and for this reason has priority under the rules of botanical nomenclature. The following list summarizes the name changes affecting commonly cultivated Fumariaceae:

Previous name	Current accepted name
Corydalis lutea	*Pseudofumaria lutea*
Corydalis ochroleuca	*Pseudofumaria alba*

Previous name	Current accepted name
Corydalis sempervirens	*Capnoides sempervirens*
Dicentra chrysantha	*Ehrendorferia chrysantha*
Dicentra macrantha	*Ichtyoselmis macrantha*
Dicentra scandens	*Dactylicapnos scandens*
Dicentra spectabilis	*Lamprocapnos spectabilis*

Morphology

Members of the bleeding heart family typically have hairless, juicy, brittle stems. The leaves of most species are alternate and spirally arranged along the stem, but in a few *Corydalis* species they are opposite (see Plate 65 for an example), while in *Dicentra* and *Hypecoum* all leaves are basal. All members of the family lack stipules (save for a few *Corydalis* species). Likewise, the leaves are usually either pinnately or ternately divided, except in one Tibetan *Corydalis* species, which has simple leaves.

Certain species of *Corydalis* and *Dicentra* have evolved an unusual characteristic involving the number of seed leaves, or cotyledons, that their seedlings produce. Flowering plants are traditionally divided into those whose seedlings have two cotyledons—the dicots—and those with only one—the monocots. However, a few dicots have in the course of their evolution lost one of their seed leaves. This is the case with all tuberous species of *Corydalis*, some of the non-tuberous Himalayan *Corydalis* species, and some species of *Dicentra*. The loss of one seed leaf has occurred independently in the monocots and different groups of dicots, and is an example of convergent evolution (Plate 4).

Sepals and Petals

All members of the bleeding heart family have two sepals (see Plate 26 for an example). In many species these are small and easily overlooked, but in some *Corydalis*, such as *C. macrantha* and *C. peltata*, they are conspicuous. In certain species the sepals soon fall off, while in others they remain attached to the pedicel almost until fruit maturity.

All Fumariaceae flowers have four petals arranged in two dissimilar whorls. In *Hypecoum* the four petals are separate from each other, while in *Adlumia* they are fused for most of their length. In the remaining genera the outer petals are separate, but the inner petals are fused at their tips.

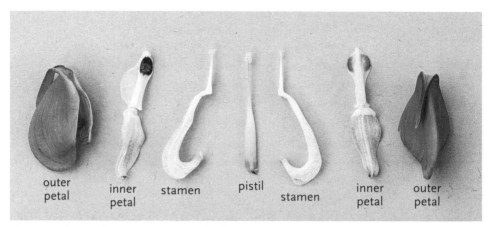

Dissected flower of *Lamprocapnos spectabilis*. Photo by Mark C. Tebbitt.

In most species either one (for example, *Corydalis*) or both (for example, *Dicentra*) of the outer petals are swollen at the base to form a sac or spur that collects nectar (see Plates 18 and 69 for examples). In *Corydalis* the outer petals often have a crest that runs along the center of each petal on its outer surface.

The inner petals of almost all species have a constriction at their middle, which acts as a flexible joint. Both of the inner petals have a well-developed wing, or crest, that runs along the center of the outer surface, as well as—on each side of the central crest—low ridges that run from the apex to the joint. *Pseudofumaria* and *Platycapnos* (Plate 5), however, differ by having inner petals that are only unilaterally indented, rather than fully jointed. The lower margin of their inner petals is instead continuous and rather firm. This feature makes possible their distinct method of pollination.

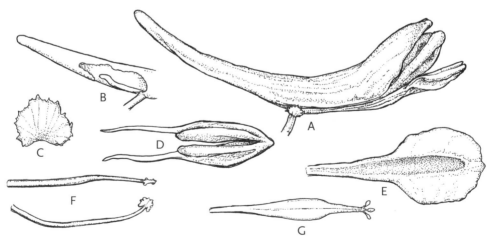

Dissected corydalis flower. A: Flower. B: Spur, with a section removed to show nectary. C: Sepal. D: Pair of fused inner petals. E: Lowermost outer petal. F: Pistil. G: Fused stamens. Drawing by Paul Harwood.

In most members of the family the inner petals are internally (and often also externally) blotched with blackish purple at the apex. This blotch is absent, however, in *Pseudofumaria* and a few species of *Corydalis* and *Fumaria*. The function of the blotch is still open to conjecture.

Inner petal of *Pseudofumaria lutea* showing unilateral indentation. Drawing by Paul Harwood.

Stamens and Nectaries

Flowers of *Hypecoum* have four stamens, each with two pollen sacs. Flowers of most other genera have two bundles of stamens. Each bundle consists of one central stamen that has two pollen sacs and two lateral stamens, each with a single pollen sac. In most genera, the filaments of the stamens are usually firmly fused throughout their length, but in *Ehrendorferia, Ichtyoselmis, Lamprocapnos*, and most *Dicentra* species, they are less firmly stuck together, or only cohere just below the anthers.

The flowers of all genera except *Adlumia* have nectar-producing tissue at the base of the stamens. In *Ehrendorferia, Hypecoum, Ichtyoselmis, Lamprocapnos*, and most *Dicentra* species, the nectaries are no more than small swellings. In *Capnoides* and *D. cucullaria*, the nectaries are simple peglike structures, and in *Corydalis, Dactylicapnos*, and the *Fumaria* group (*Fumaria, Pseudofumaria, Rupicapnos*, and *Sarcocapnos*), the nectary is a prolonged structure that reaches into the spur and is partly fused to it.

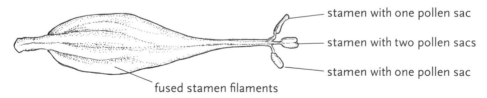

stamen with one pollen sac

stamen with two pollen sacs

stamen with one pollen sac

fused stamen filaments

Typical stamens of Fumariaceae showing fused structure unique to that family. Drawing by Paul Harwood.

Ovary and Style

All members of the Fumariaceae have a 1-locular ovary and parietal placentation, but the styles and stigmas vary greatly and are consequently of great taxonomic value. In the subfamily Fumarioideae the style ends in a single stigma. However, it differs significantly between different genera. In the *Fumaria* group the style soon falls off, and is white and semitranslucent, while in the rest of the genera it persists

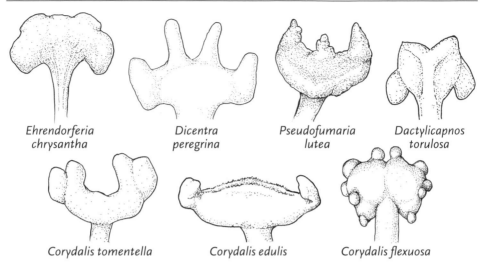

| Ehrendorferia chrysantha | Dicentra peregrina | Pseudofumaria lutea | Dactylicapnos torulosa |

| Corydalis tomentella | Corydalis edulis | Corydalis flexuosa |

Variation in stigma morphology (not to scale). Drawing by Paul Harwood.

in fruit and is usually green. In *Hypecoum*, which is classified in its own subfamily (Hypecoideae), the style has two long branches.

Differences in stigma shape are found between different genera in the same tribe, and often between different species within a particular genus. For example, in *Dicentra* the stigmas have four papillae, while in *Corydalis* few to several papillae may be arranged around the margin of each stigma, depending upon the species. Comparable differences are also found in the tribe Fumarieae, with *Sarcocapnos enneaphylla* and the genus *Pseudofumaria*, for example, having a large stigmatic crest while *Fumaria* lacks such a crest.

Natural Distribution

The first members of the Fumariaceae are believed to have originated in Asia. Certain genera, like the bleeding heart (*Lamprocapnos spectabilis*), large-flowered dicentra (*Ichtyoselmis macrantha*), and all 10 climbing dicentras (*Dactylicapnos* species), still have distributions restricted to this continent, while other groups long ago migrated either westward into Europe or eastward into North America, or, in the case of *Corydalis*, in both directions. Some westward-migrating species colonized Africa from western Asia via the Middle East, while others entered that continent from southern Spain via the Strait of Gibraltar.

If you look at a world map you can imagine how the ancestors of the modern-day Fumariaceae may have spread across the Asian continent into adjoining Europe or even nearby Africa, but it is less apparent how North America was colonized, since a great expanse of ocean separates the two continents. Nevertheless, genera like *Adlumia*, *Corydalis*, and *Dicentra*, which have representatives in both Asia and North America, are by no means alone among the flowering plants. Many scientists have commented upon the striking similarity between the plant life of eastern Asia and North America, which is such that botanists from one region will often experience déjà vu when botanizing in parts of the other. Even though the continents of Asia and North America are today separated by thousands of kilometers of ocean, we now know that during past ice ages sea levels were considerably lower. This was because much of the world's water was locked up in huge glaciers. At these times a land bridge extended between the two continents allowing the gradual migration of both plants and animals.

Today the Fumariaceae are found throughout the temperate zone of the Northern Hemisphere—in Asia, North America, Europe, and both North and East Africa. Nevertheless, they are most abundant in the Mediterranean and the Sino-Himalaya. In addition, three small genera, *Cysticapnos*, *Discocapnos*, and *Trigonocapnos*, have distributions far removed from the rest of the family and are found in the South African cape. Most likely they reached this region by migrating in leaps along the temperate mountains of otherwise tropical East Africa. As weeds of gardens and agriculture, some *Fumaria* species occur outside the family's natural range. Their current distributions owe more to the impact of humans than to natural seed dispersal. A prominent example is *F. officinalis*, which is now found as a weed throughout much of the world. Aside from such weeds, the bleeding heart family is notably absent from Central and South America, Tropical Africa (with the exception of the East African mountains), and Australasia.

Habits and Habitats

A wide range of life-forms is found in the Fumariaceae, including both annual and perennial herbs and climbers, and tuberous geophytes. As would be expected from such a diverse group of plants, the various species make their home in an equally diverse range of natural habitats. Most members of the family, including most species of *Corydalis* and *Dicentra*, are rhizomatous perennials and are found in woodland, scrubland, meadows, or alpine scree. They typically occur either on gravelly or rich alluvial soils, but usually where there are plenty of outcropping rocks.

Other members of the family favor more extreme habitats, which are often largely devoid of competing plants. The two species of *Ehrendorferia* are noteworthy

examples. These Californian natives are usually found in scrubland that recently
has been consumed by fire (see Plate 32). In fact, their seeds germinate most readily after they have been exposed to smoke, enabling these plants to colonize the
largely lifeless but nutrient-enriched soils left by the fire. Other species, including
many of the numerous Chinese corydalis and a few dicentras, favor life on alpine
scree or talus slopes (see Plate 6) and have long rhizomes and a perennial life cycle.

The genera *Cryptocapnos*, *Fumariola*, *Rupicapnos*, and *Sarcocapnos* and some
Corydalis species occupy what is perhaps the most extreme habitat of any member
of the family (see Plate 7). These plants typically grow on vertical or, more often,
overhanging dry limestone cliffs. Such plants are much-branched and form cushions dotted along the cliffs. The commonly cultivated *Pseudofumaria lutea* (syn.
Corydalis lutea) inhabits both cliffs and screes and will on occasion escape from
gardens and grow on walls and other artificial structures.

Some species of *Corydalis* have evolved a different strategy and avoid competition and other unfavorable conditions by being spring ephemerals. They have perennial tubers that enable them to become dormant beneath the ground during
much of the year. Other species, particularly those in *Fumaria*, *Hypecoum*, and
Platycapnos, have condensed their life cycle and are annuals of open or disturbed
areas. Again these habitats are largely devoid of competition. For example, most
agricultural land is artificially kept free of large trees and other tall vegetation. Two
weedy fumitories, *F. occidentalis* and *F. purpurea*, are of particular note. They inhabit arable land and waste places in the British Isles but occur nowhere else on
earth. Roughly one percent of the British flora is unique to these islands, and of this
tiny fraction the two fumitories are the only endemic arable weeds.

Pollination

The unusual flower structure of the bleeding heart family underlies a fascinating
pollination mechanism. The flower's nectar-containing spurs or sacs, the jointed,
partially fused inner petals, and the curiously flattened stigma all play a prominent
role in promoting cross-pollination.

The process by which pollination occurs is readily observed in *Dicentra cucullaria*, a common spring ephemeral of North American woodlands. When the flowers are still in bud, protuberances at the edges of the stigma interlock with the
nearby anthers so that as a flower matures its stamens are pulled downward, causing the sticky pollen to be deposited on the stigma. The stigma is hidden between

the apically fused inner petals. Energy-rich nectar accumulates in the hollow spurs at the base of the two outer petals and is very attractive to bees.

When a bee visits the flower in search of nectar, it pushes the hooded inner petals and stamens aside and thrusts its head into the flower so that its long tongue can reach the nectar in a spur. In doing this, the bee rubs its head and body against the rigidly held stigma and gets dabbed with pollen. When the bee flies off in search of more nectar, the hinged inner petals spring back into their original position, ready for the next visitor. Upon reaching a new flower the bee repeats the process. This time though, in addition to getting dusted with new pollen it will, in all likelihood, also rub off some of the pollen already on its body onto the stigma of the new flower. Thus cross-pollination occurs.

This process works because pollen will only germinate and bring about fertilization when it comes in contact with the stigma of a flower on a different plant. Pollen deposited on the stigma of its own flower does not receive a chemical signal to germinate and hence self-pollination is prevented. Such a complex mechanism has evolved because it encourages the mixing of genetic material, which increases genetic diversity favoring the survival chances of at least some of the offspring in a variable environment. Some normally cross-pollinated species can, however, be self-pollinated after disturbance of the stigmatic surface, for example, *Dicentra peregrina* and *Corydalis caseana*.

Some bees have learned to steal the nectar by biting through the spur. These holes may then be used over and over again, and can be also used by bees that are not strong enough to bite through the petals themselves. This damage does little to affect seed set, however, since longer-tongued bees or pollen-collecting bees will still visit and pollinate such flowers.

While the pollination mechanism described for *Dicentra cucullaria* also holds true for many other members of the Fumariaceae, slight modifications have evolved in certain species in response to different pollinators and ecological situations. The zygomorphic flowers of most corydalis, for example, have a broad lower petal providing guidance and support to the visitor.

The flowers of *Pseudofumaria* also differ in their pollination mechanism. In these plants the inner petals and the

Short-tongued honeybee stealing nectar from *Corydalis solida*. Photo by Magnus Lidén.

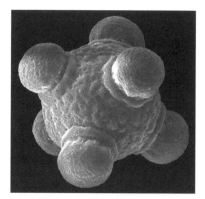

Magnified pollen of *Rupicapnos africana*. Photo by Magnus Lidén.

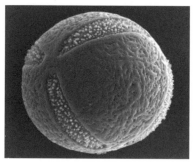

Magnified pollen of *Corydalis edulis*. Photo by Magnus Lidén.

style-stamen apparatus are held under tension so that they strive to move in opposite directions, but are prevented from doing so by flaps on the inner petals that embrace the style and stamens. When an insect visits, the style with its pollen is suddenly and irreversibly released from the inner petals, forcefully dabbing the bee with pollen. Consequently each flower can be visited only once. In spite of this elaborate mechanism, both species are fully self-compatible.

Ehrendorferia ochroleuca, a native of California's Santa Ynes and Santa Monica Mountains, is unique within the family in being pollinated by hummingbirds. Several features of the plant adapt it to its pollinators. Its flowers are relatively large, produce copious nectar, and are tough enough to withstand a hummingbird's bill. The species is also (except for the climbers) the tallest member of the family, reaching a height of up to 3 meters. The bright cream- to yellowish-white flowers are produced at the top of the plant in a large mass, where they are clearly visible from a distance. Most striking is the flowers' orientation skyward, making them accessible to hummingbirds.

An evolutionary switch to regular self-fertilization requires no structural modification, since the sticky pollen in all species is already deposited onto the stigma as the flower unfolds. Self-compatibility has evolved in several lineages in the family, and is mostly coupled to short generation times. All annuals and biennials in the family, except one, are self-compatible and usually self fertilized. Among the perennials we find self-compatible species mainly (but not exclusively) occupying dry cliffs, where the presence of a seed reserve is extremely important for survival. Self-fertilization also occurs in a few tuberous species, like *Corydalis caucasica*, *C. pumila*, and *C. uniflora*. However, the possibility for self-fertilization does not mean that cross-pollination never occurs in these species.

The structure of the pollen grains is also worth a brief mention since *Fumaria* and *Rupicapnos* have very unusual pollen. In these plants the inner layer of the two-layered surface coating bulges out through pores in the outer layer.

Seed Dispersal

Myrmecochory, or seed dispersal by ants (Plate 8), is common in the bleeding heart family. For example, it is found in all species of *Dicentra* and *Pseudofumaria*, and in all *Corydalis* species except two. These plants have fleshy, whitish, fat-rich appendages attached to their seeds. The appendages, or elaiosomes, are very nutritious and highly attractive to ants. Ants are immensely strong and can carry or drag the seeds to their homes, where they remove the elaiosomes and feed them to the colony's young. The seeds themselves are discarded and left to develop into the next generation of plants. Many species give their seeds an extra helping hand by explosively releasing them from the pods.

A different, but equally ingenious, dispersal mechanism is found in the cliff-dwelling species of *Rupicapnos* and *Sarcocapnos*, where the fruit stalks curve toward the substrate and bury the seeds at the base of the plant. This is an adaptation for life on a cliff, because if these seeds were released in the normal manner they would fall to the ground where they would be very unlikely to prosper. The fruits are sometimes further dispersed along the cliff by ants that are attracted by a fatty collar at the base of the fruit.

Bleeding Hearts and Butterflies

While few herbivores relish eating the toxic leaves of members of the bleeding heart family, most species in the butterfly genus *Parnassius* are wholly dependent upon *Corydalis*, *Dicentra*, and the unrelated, but for most animals equally poisonous, *Aristolochia* and *Telephium*. This butterfly group is distributed throughout much of Europe, Asia, and western North America, with each species usually having a limited distribution that largely mirrors that of a particular *Corydalis*, *Dicentra*, *Aristolochia*, or *Telephium* species. The clodius parnassian (*Parnassius clodius*), for example, is found in western North America and its caterpillars rely largely upon the similarly distributed *D. formosa* for their food source. Likewise, caterpillars of the arctic parnassian (*P. ammosovi*) feed only upon *C. gorodkovii*, and as a result this butterfly, like the corydalis, has a distribution restricted to East Siberia. The clouded apollo (*P. mnemosyne*) is also wholly dependent on *Corydalis*, but its larvae feed upon several tuberous European species, including *C. cava*, *C. intermedia*, and *C. solida*. The sensory system of this butterfly is truly miraculous. Despite there being hardly any trace of these plants above ground, by midsummer when the adult lays her eggs, she can, amazingly, pick out the right spots. The butterfly selects dead, withered leaves or grass above the dormant plants, apparently guided by the smell of the underground tubers. The following spring when the new leaves begin to emerge the eggs will hatch and the caterpillars can then begin to feed on the leaves.

Such specificity to a particular food plant is not unusual among butterflies. Many famous examples exist, including the passionflower butterflies (*Heliconius* species) and the monarch butterfly (*Danaus plexippus*), whose caterpillars exclusively eat milkweeds (*Asclepias* species). In each of these cases the host plants are extremely toxic to most creatures, but the caterpillars have evolved to be able to eat the poisonous leaves without harm. Furthermore, they retain the plant poisons in their adult butterfly bodies, where the chemicals protect them from predators, such as birds and mammals.

A pair of *Clodius parnassius* on Pacific bleeding heart. Drawing by Adèle Rossetti Morosini.

3

Identification Key to Genera

A DICHOTOMOUS IDENTIFICATION KEY is provided as a means to identify the genus to which an unknown plant belongs. The key consists of a series of paired, contrasting statements. To use the key, start at the first pair of statements and determine which one best describes the characteristics of your unknown plant. The number after that statement will lead you to the next pair of statements to be compared with your plant. This process is continued until you arrive at a name for your unknown plant.

Once you have arrived at a genus name, check that your plant matches the relevant description of that genus in chapter four, five, or six, as well as the associated artwork and photograph(s). If your plant does not match the description and illustrations, then you must start again and recheck the decisions you made previously. Technical terms used in the keys are explained in both chapter two and the glossary.

After you have identified the genus to which your plant belongs, the species name can then be determined. Again this may be achieved by comparing your plant with the relevant descriptions in chapters four, five, or six, and with the photograph(s). Identification keys to the species in three of the genera best represented in cultivation, *Dactylicapnos* (chapter four), *Dicentra* (chapter four), and *Sarcocapnos* (chapter six), are also provided for this purpose. We decided not to present a dichotomous key to all the cultivated species of the very large genus *Corydalis* for two reasons. Firstly, the list of cultivated species is forever changing, and secondly, if such a key were to be restricted to just those species currently in cultivation—during this snapshot in time—it would be very long and unwieldy. Instead, we recommend that readers match up unknown *Corydalis* species with the descriptions in chapter five and with the associated photographs. Readers are also referred to the identification keys for cultivated tuberous corydalis published in Lidén and Zetterlund (1997).

Key to the Genera of Fumariaceae

1a. Flowers bisymmetric (with two planes of symmetry), either both or none of the outer petals spurred 2

1b. Flowers zygomorphic (with one plane of symmetry), one of the outer petals spurred or saccate. 8

2a. Petals free, more or less flat; stamens 4 (rosulate annuals) . . . . *Hypecoum*

2b. Inner petals united at tip; stamens 2 or 6 in 2 bundles. 3

3a. Leaves all basal, flowering stems leafless . . . . *Dicentra*

3b. Leaves borne along the stem and sometimes also at base of plant. 4

4a. Flowers yellow or cream 5

4b. Flowers pink or white 7

5a. Plant climbing; leaves with tendrils . . . . *Dactylicapnos*

5b. Plant not climbing; leaves lacking tendrils. 6

6a. Flowers erect, ca. 2 cm long. . . . . *Ehrendorferia*

6b. Flowers pendent, ca. 5 cm long . . . . *Ichtyoselmis*

7a. Plant climbing and often sprawling; outer petals fused for most of their length, persisting in fruit. . . . . *Adlumia*

7b. Plant not climbing, more or less erect; outer petals fused only at base, falling off before fruit matures . . . . *Lamprocapnos*

8a. Plant not climbing; perennial, annual, or biennial. 9

8b. Plant climbing; annual 18

9a. Style persistent on the fruit 10

9b. Style soon falling, not persisting on the fruit. 11

10a. Flowers pink or white, with a yellow apex, inflorescence cymose; upper petal with a short blunt spur to 3–4 mm long. . . . . *Capnoides*

10b. Flowers variously colored but very rarely pink or white with a yellow apex, inflorescence racemose; upper petal with a prominent spur . . . . *Corydalis*

11a. Fruit 1-seeded 12

11b. Fruit 2- to many-seeded 17

12a. Plant very dense or cushionlike on vertical rock surfaces; flowers in a corymb; fruiting stalks recurved and elongating to 20–50 mm 13

12b. Plant not cushionlike, rarely growing on vertical rock surfaces; flowers in a spikelike raceme with stalks 2–7 mm long. 16

13a. Leaf lobes rounded to cordate . . . . *Sarcocapnos*

13b. Leaf lobes obovate to linear 14

14a. Flowers yellow; nut cylindric. . . . . *Fumariola*

14b. Flowers white or pink; nut rounded to ovoid. 15

15a. Nut with a conspicuous projecting beak with concave sides . . . . *Cryptocapnos*

15b. Nut with a short acute beak, or without a beak. . . . . *Rupicapnos*

16a. Flowers in a dense head; leaf lobes threadlike, 0.5–1 mm wide. . . . . . . *Platycapnos*

16b. Flowers in an elongate spike; leaf lobes linear to obovate 1–7 mm wide. . . *Fumaria*

17a. Leaf lobes obovate, not fleshy; fruit many-seeded; seeds with elaiosomes
    . . . . *Pseudofumaria*

17b. Leaf lobes rounded to cordate, fleshy; fruit 2-seeded with longitudinal ribs; seeds
    lacking elaiosomes . . . . *Sarcocapnos*

18a. Fruit many-seeded. . . . .*Cysticapnos*

18b. Fruit 1- to 5-seeded 19

19a. Fruit discoid with a persistent style, 1-seeded. . . . . *Discocapnos*

19b. Fruit not round and flat; style soon falling, 1- to 5-seeded 20

20a. Fruit 3-angled, 1-seeded; pedicels ca. 10 mm long, very thin . . . .*Trigonocapnos*

20b. Fruit not 3-angled, 1- to 5-seeded; pedicels thick, 2–4 mm long . . . . . *Ceratocapnos*

4

The Bleeding Hearts

THIS CHAPTER COVERS genera with bisymmetric flowers (with two planes of symmetry), of which most were until recently classified in the genus *Dicentra*. Included are many good garden plants, ranging from the ever-popular bleeding heart, *Lamprocapnos spectabilis* (syn. *Dicentra spectabilis*) to the climbing species of *Adlumia* and *Dactylicapnos* and the desirable woodland and subalpine species of *Dicentra*. Two less well-known genera are also treated: *Ehrendorferia*, with two pyrophilous species from California and, in one case, northern Baja California, and *Ichtyoselmis macrantha*, a woodland plant from China and Myanmar (Burma) with very large, pale yellow flowers.

Adlumia   PLATES 9–11
Allegheny vine

> Biennial or rarely summer annual climbing vines; if biennial forming a basal rosette the first year and developing a leafy stem 1–5 m (occasionally to 8 m) long the second year. *Leaves* (2–)3–4 times pinnately divided, lowermost leaves stalked, upper leaves sessile; *leaflets* cut into 2–4 ovate lobes, leaflet stalks tendril-like. *Inflorescences* axillary, short, few- to 30-flowered cymes. *Flowers* with two planes of symmetry, drooping, urn-shaped, 10–17 × 3–7 mm, white, or pale pink to purplish; *petals* persistent, eventually enclosing the ripe capsule and becoming increasingly spongy, all petals and stamens fused for most of their length, base of outer petals pouchlike; *nectary* absent. *Fruit* many-seeded, dehiscent. *Seeds* without elaiosomes.

Adlumia includes two species, *A. fungosa* Greene ex Britton, Sterns & Poggenburg (Plate 9) from eastern North America and *A. asiatica* Ohwi (Plate 10) from eastern Asia. It has long been recognized as a genus distinct from *Dicentra* and is easily identified by its vinelike habit, biennial (or rarely annual) life cycle, twining leaflet stalks, and spongy, urn-shaped petals that are almost completely fused together. The genus is unique in the family in that all inflorescences are axillary. Naturalist Constantine Rafinesque first coined the name *Adlumia* in 1807. It honors John

Adlum (1759–1836), an American horti-
culturalist, expert on viticulture, and frequent correspondent with Thomas Jef-
ferson on the subject of winemaking.

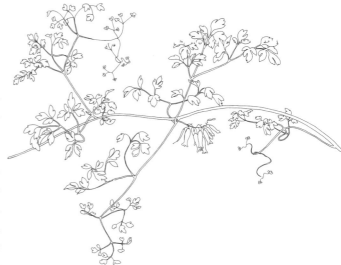

The only obvious morphological
difference between the two *Adlumia*
species is that the flower of *A. asiatica* is
sharply rectangular in cross section,
while the flower of *A. fungosa* is rounded. The species also differ in the shape
of their stigmatic lobes and the length
of their style branches. However, such
subtle characteristics are less likely to be
noticed by the casual observer. The species occupy similar natural habitats.

Adlumia fungosa. Drawing by Adèle Rossetti Morosini.

They grow in moist rocky woodlands (Plate 11) and thickets and use their leaflet
stalks to grasp onto and scramble over surrounding vegetation.

That *Adlumia* consists of two very similar species with widely separated distributions in eastern Asia and eastern North America is not as unusual as it may at
first appear. Sixty-five other genera of flowering plants share this pattern, including
Liriodendron (tulip-trees), *Sassafras*, and the *Corydalis pallida-aurea* group. Furthermore, numerous genera of fungi, insects, and freshwater fishes have a similar distribution. This pattern is thought to have resulted from a process that can be divided into three stages: dispersal, local extinction, and speciation.

At some time between 23 and 3.5 million years ago a species of *Adlumia* must
have dispersed either from eastern Asia into western North America or vice versa.
During this period various ice ages led to the lowering of global sea levels, which in
turn caused a broad strip of land to periodically emerge from the ocean between
eastern Asia and western North America. Once *Adlumia* had migrated across one
of these temporary land bridges, its populations in western North America died out
due to the climate of that region becoming increasingly dry, a trend that started
about 3.5 million years ago and continues to the present day. With its remaining
populations isolated in the climatically stable mountains of eastern Asia and eastern North America, the original species of *Adlumia* has slowly diverged to become
two distinct, yet similar species.

Today, *Adlumia fungosa*, the horticulturally most important of the two species,
is distributed from southeastern and south-central Canada southward to eastern
Tennessee, primarily along the Appalachian Mountain range. Its relative abun-

dance in the Allegheny Mountains, which compose part of the Appalachian range, is reflected in the species's common name, Allegheny vine. The plant's scientific name *fungosa* is derived from the Latin for spongy, a reference to the texture of the plant's petals. *Adlumia fungosa* grows from near sea level to an altitude of 1500 m (4920 ft) and is typically found in moist wooded coves, rocky woods, alluvial slopes and thickets, often on lime-rich soils. *Adlumia asiatica*, in contrast, is very rarely encountered both in cultivation and in the wild. It is native to Russia's Far East and neighboring parts of northeastern China and Korea, where it grows in similar habitats to its North American counterpart.

Adlumia fungosa was first grown in England around 1778 in the garden of plantsman John Fothergill. Fothergill was an avid collector of North American plants and had most likely received seed of this plant from American botanist William Bartram. Bartram being a keen gardener may have even cultivated this plant himself in Philadelphia. Frederick Law Olmsted was also fond of this species and apparently used it in his naturalistic-style plantings at the 1893 Chicago World Fair. In contrast, *A. asiatica* appears to be a 21st-century introduction and is currently not grown outside of botanic gardens.

Both *Adlumia* species require a cool, shady site and protection from strong winds. They perform best in light humusy, moist but well-drained soils. Propagation is from seed, and once plants become established they will often self-sow. Both species are cold-hardy to –20°C (–4°F) and flower from late June to September. They will add interest to the garden, especially when allowed to twine up a showier-flowered climber, such as a clematis; in this setting the relatively pale green foliage of the *Adlumia* contrasts to great effect against the darker leaves of its support. Variants with white or pink flowers are cultivated and are available from specialist seed lists and a few nurseries.

Dactylicapnos   PLATES 12–14
Climbing dicentras

> Perennial or annual climbing vines. *Stems* 1–10 m long. *Leaves* ternately divided (perennial species) or pinnate (mainly annual species); *lateral leaflets* entire, rarely 1 or 2 times ternately divided; *terminal leaflet* transformed into a branched tendril. *Inflorescences* terminal, leaf-opposed, umbellate, 14-flowered. *Flowers* with two planes of symmetry, heart-shaped to oblong, pendent, 10–24 × 4–15 mm; *petals* pale yellow to orange, apex of outer petals hardly reflexed, base pouchlike; *nectary* conspicuous.

A large vine of climbing dicentra covered with bright yellow, heart-shaped, pendent flowers is an unforgettable sight, especially when seen in the warm glow of late summer, a time when relatively few other ornamentals are at their best. Why then are none of the species of *Dactylicapnos* common in gardens? Certainly it is not because these plants are newcomers to cultivation; *D. scandens* (D. Don) Hutchinson has been grown since at least 1838, at which date it is mentioned in Sweet's *British Flower Garden* (1838). The rarity of the climbing dicentras is likely due to a combination of their intolerance for freezing temperatures and their fragile form which makes them more or less impossible to handle in the nursery trade. Perhaps for this reason the main commercial source of these plants tends to be mail-order nurseries whose plant savvy customers are more likely to see the potential in a flowerless twig. That said, the nursery that currently offers the widest selection of *Dactylicapnos* species offers both a mail-order service and welcomes in-person visits. This is Crûg Farm Plants, of North Wales. The nursery's owners, Bleddyn and Sue Wynn-Jones, sell four species, three of which they collected in the wild themselves in the mountains of western China and northern India.

Gardeners outside of the United Kingdom have to content themselves with a smaller selection of species. In the United States *Dactylicapnos scandens* is the only species available commercially, though *D. torulosa* (J. D. Hooker & T. Thompson) Hutchinson has been offered since 2004 in the North American Rock Garden Society's annual seed lists. Also in the United Kingdom, it is *D. scandens* with which most gardeners are familiar. At least this is the name most commonly appearing in trade—although in our experience most British plants labeled as *D. scandens* have turned out to be the very similar *D. macrocapnos* (Prain) Hutchinson. The true *D. scandens* is nevertheless available commercially both in the United Kingdom and North America, having been reintroduced in 1995 from seed collected on a joint Heronswood Nursery–Crûg Farm Plants expedition to Nepal. Anyway, the two species offer the gardener much the same. Both are tall climbing, frost-tender herbaceous perennials with attractive, bright yellow heart-shaped flowers. *Dactylicapnos macrocapnos* (Plates 13, 14) has the advantage of poten-

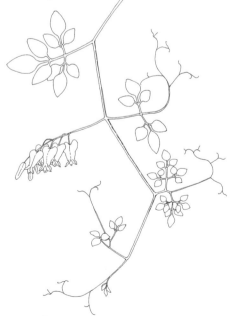

Dactylicapnos macrocapnos. Drawing by Adèle Rossetti Morosini.

tially climbing to far greater heights, with annual stem growth of 10 meters or more not being unheard of (versus 4 meters in *D. scandens*). Its fruits, however, are much less interesting than the purple, bullet-shaped ones that appear each autumn on *D. scandens*. In very northerly districts, the growing season may be too short for these perennial species to flower, as they seem to be short day plants. A third perennial species has recently been introduced to cultivation in the United Kingdom. It is *D. ventii* and may be distinguished by its opposite leaflets. This plant grows to a height of about 3 meters.

The other two cultivated species, *Dactylicapnos torulosa* (Plate 12) and *D. roylei* Hutchinson, are slender annuals, which rarely climb to a height above 4 meters and have paler, smaller, less-showy flowers than either of the two cultivated perennial species. *Dactylicapnos torulosa* was first introduced into French gardens in 1905 from seed sent by a French missionary in Tibet to Paris nurseryman Maurice de Vilmorin. This annual appears, however, to have been subsequently lost from cultivation and is now represented in gardens by a collection made on a Crûg Farm Plants expedition to Yunnan. *Dactylicapnos roylei*, an introduction from Kangding in Central Sichuan, has much broader and more conspicuous lemon-yellow flowers, but is as yet rare in cultivation. A third annual species, *D. lichiangensis*, may also be in cultivated but we cannot confirm this since the only material we have seen labeled as this species was a misidentified individual of *D. macrocapnos*.

All 10 species of climbing dicentra are native to Asia. Collectively, they are distributed from northwestern India, through Nepal and Bhutan to Northern Myanmar (Burma), western China, and northern Vietnam. Many of the species individually occur throughout large parts of the generic range. *Dactylicapnos scandens* is distributed from Nepal eastward to China's Yunnan Province and southward to central Myanmar (Burma) and northern Vietnam. *Dactylicapnos torulosa*, *D. roylei*, and *D. lichiangensis* range from Sikkim eastward through northeastern India to southwestern China. *Dactylicapnos macrocapnos* is distributed from northeastern India to Nepal. All four species naturally grow on the margins of moist forests, on shrubby rocky slopes, open hillsides, and occasionally on roadside banks. They are typically found at altitudes of 750 to 3000 m (2460 to 9840 ft), with *D. lichiangensis* reaching the higher altitudes. *Dactylicapnos scandens* is almost unique within the family (save for a couple of Sichuanese *Corydalis* species) in that the valves of the short red or purple capsule are very fleshy, suggesting bird dispersal. It should be noted, however, that the seeds still carry elaiosomes, so ants most likely also play a part in their dispersal. The annual *Dactylicapnos* species, however, have long linear capsules, and their abundantly produced seed is dispersed locally once the capsule walls split apart.

The name *Dactylicapnos* is derived from the Greek words *dactylos*, finger, and *capnos*, smoke. The first part of the name is a reference to the resemblance of the individual fruits of the type species, *D. scandens*, to a grape or fig. The second part of the name is common to other genera in the family, and most likely refers to the smokelike effect created by the often finely dissected leaves.

Like many other plants from the Himalaya, northern Myanmar (Burma), and western China, the perennial climbing dicentras prefer climates with mild winters and cool, moist summers (though *Dactylicapnos scandens* 'Athens Yellow' is said to perform well in the hot-humid southeastern United States). The climbing dicentras also need a sheltered site that gives them protection from strong winds and late frosts. While they tolerate light frosts, they will succumb to temperatures below −5°C (23°F). The annual life cycle of *D. roylei*, *D. torulosa* and *D. lichiangensis*, however, allows them to be grown in areas with much colder winter temperatures. Only three *Dactylicapnos* cultivars are available commercially: *D. scandens* 'Athens Yellow', a plant with particularly deep yellow flowers, which was selected by Allan Armitage, of the University of Georgia in Athens, from a batch of seed he collected in the Dublin garden of Helen Dillon, *D.* 'Golden Tears' from Summer Hill Seed nursery, said to have flowers 2.5 cm long, and *D. scandens* 'Shirley Clemo', a cultivar with almost silver leaves that has been commercially available since 2000 from Shirley Clemo's nursery at the beautiful Pine Lodge Gardens near St. Austell in South West England. To remain true to type the cultivars should be propagated vegetatively.

Key to Cultivated Species of *Dactylicapnos*

1a. Annuals; sepal margins fringed with hairs; capsules more than 40 mm long; upper leaves pinnately divided; inflorescence 2- to 6-flowered; flowers 10–20 mm long. . 2

1b. Perennials; sepal margins entire; capsules less than 30 mm long; upper leaves usually ternately divided; inflorescence usually 7- to 16-flowered; flowers 13–22 mm long 4

2a. Flowers rounded in profile, more than half as broad as long . . . . *D. roylei*

2b. Flowers narrow, much less than half as broad as long 3

3a. Capsule wall constricted between each seed. . . . . *D. torulosa*

3b. Capsule wall smooth, not following contours of each seed . . . . *D. lichiangensis*

4a. Leaves once ternately compound. . . . . *D. ventii*

4b. Leaves bi- or tri-ternately compound 5

5a. Capsule fleshy, 12–25 mm long, with a rounded base; leaflets usually 7- to 8-veined . . . . *D. scandens*

5b. Capsule membranous, 22–29 mm long, with a tapering base; leaflets usually 9- to 13-veined . . . . *D. macrocapnos*

Dicentra
Dutchman's breeches, bleeding hearts

Perennial herbs with leafless flowering stems. *Leaves* triangular, 1–3 times pinnately divided. *Inflorescences* 1- to 30-flowered, cymose. *Flowers* with two planes
of symmetry, more or less heart-shaped, 11–30 × 3–20 mm, occasionally pleas-
antly fragrant; *petals* pink to rose-purple or white, or sometimes cream or pale-
yellow; *outer petals* with a strongly reflexed apex, base pouchlike or shortly
spurred; *inner petals* with or without a crest; *nectary* present.

Following the removal of several species with leafy stems, the genus *Dicentra* now
only contains species with bisymmetric flowers and a stemless, scapose habit. Eight
species are recognized in the genus, seven from North America, and one from eastern Asia. All are desirable garden plants but they differ widely in their ease of culture. *Dicentra eximia, D. formosa,* and almost all the hybrid dicentras are very amenable in most garden situations and are long blooming. The two spring ephemerals,
D. canadensis and *D. cucullaria,* are likewise readily cultivated but are best grown in
a woodland setting. *Dicentra nevadensis, D. pauciflora, D. peregrina* and *D. uniflora*
are the most demanding and typically require alpine house cultivation.

In the wild, *Dicentra* species occupy
a wide variety of habitats and geographical regions, which explains the differences in their ease of cultivation. *Dicentra canadensis* and *D. cucullaria* grow in
rich, moist alluvial soils in deciduous
forest, from sea level to 1500 m (4920 ft)
in altitude. These two species occur
throughout much of eastern North America and in the case of *D. cucullaria* also in
the Columbia River Basin in Washington, Oregon, and western Idaho. A third
eastern species, *D. eximia,* is restricted to
the Appalachian Mountains. It tends to
inhabit woodland sites at elevations of
100 to 1700 m (330 to 5575 ft) that are
rockier than the sites occupied by the
other two eastern species. All the other
North American species are restricted to

Dicentra canadensis. Drawing by Paul Harwood.

the western portion of the continent. Almost all of them favor gravelly soils derived from limestone, serpentine, or granite and occur at intermediate to high elevations (Plate 15). *Dicentra nevadensis*, *D. pauciflora*, and *D. uniflora* occur at the highest elevations and are found up to 3350 m (11,000 ft) in elevation. Nevertheless, these and other western species are not true alpines since they typically occur in open sites in, or at the margins of, sub-alpine forests. *Dicentra peregrina*, the sole Asian species, also favors gravelly soil but is an arctic-alpine. It grows in open habitats on the summits and sides of extinct volcanoes, at altitudes ranging from 600 to 2100 m (1970 to 6890 ft).

The name *Dicentra* is derived from the Greek words, *dis*, two, and *kentron*, spur, a reference to the two-spurred flowers of *D. cucullaria*, the first species described in this genus. *Dicentra* is not, however, the oldest name for these plants but is predated 70 years by the name *Bikukulla*. While *Bikukulla* would normally be given priority over any later name, the name *Dicentra* is recognized today because it was conserved under the rules of the International Code of Botanical Nomenclature and given priority.

A key to the species of *Dicentra* is provided below. Precise cultivation requirements and other pertinent information are presented under each species.

Key to the Species of *Dicentra*

1a. Bulblets and tubers never present; leaves usually numerous 2
1b. Bulblets or tubers or a mixture of both always present; leaves usually few 5
2a. Leaves very glaucous, finely divided, lobes ca. 1 mm wide; plant ca. 10 cm tall
. . . . *D. peregrina*
2b. Leaves green to glaucous, twice pinnately divided, lobes coarsely toothed or themselves shortly lobed, 2–5 mm wide; plant at least 20 cm tall 3
3a. Reflexed apical portion of outer petals 4–8 mm long . . . . *D. eximia*
3b. Reflexed apical portion of outer petals 2–5 mm long 4
4a. Petals purple-pink, pink, cream, or pale yellow, rarely white; central filament of stamen bundle almost straight; leaflets usually not sharply pointed . . . . *D. formosa*
4b. Petals white to pale yellow or rose-tinted; central filament of stamen bundle forming an angular loop between its center and base; leaflets sharply pointed at their apex . . . . *D. nevadensis*
5a. Apical portion of outer petals weakly reflexed for 2–5 mm long; inner petals with a prominent crest 6
5b. Apical portion of outer petals strongly reflexed for 4–11 mm long; inner petals lacking a crest 7

6a. Rootstock a cluster of pink to white bulblets; flowers odorless; outer petals with diverging pointed spurs 3–13 mm long . . . . *D. cucullaria*

6b. Rootstock a cluster of yellow bulblets; flowers fragrant; outer petals with rounded pouchlike sacs 2–6 mm long . . . . *D. canadensis*

7a. Non-reflexed basal portion of outer petals 4–8 mm long; apical part of inner petals triangular to lanceolate or spoon-shaped; leaflets obovate . . . . *D. uniflora*

7b. Non-reflexed basal portion of outer petals 10–15 mm long; apical part of inner petals narrowly spoon-shaped, never triangular to lanceolate; leaflets elliptic
. . . .*D. pauciflora*

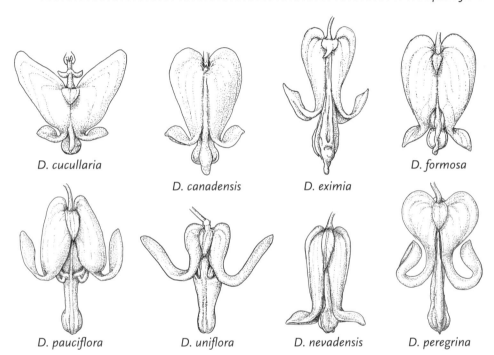

D. cucullaria

D. canadensis   *D. eximia*

D. formosa

D. pauciflora   *D. uniflora*   *D. nevadensis*   *D. peregrina*

Dicentra flowers. Drawing by Paul Harwood.

Dicentra canadensis (Goldie) Walpers   PLATE 16
Squirrel-corn

Rootstock a cluster of yellow (or reddish if sun exposed) globose bulblets. *Leaves* few to several, green on upper surface, glaucous on lower surface, broadly triangular, 4–11 × 6–15 cm, 2 or usually 3 times pinnately divided; *leaflets* deeply dissected into linear to linear-elliptic or linear-obovate lobes; *petioles* 6–18 cm long. *Inflorescences* 3- to 12-flowered, usually exceeding length of leaves. *Flowers* pendent, very fragrant; *petals* white; *outer petals* 10–20 mm long, apex reflexed for 3–5 mm long, base pouchlike; *inner petals* 10–18 mm long, crest conspicuous. *2n* = 64.

Despite its scientific name of "canadensis," this species is found in the wild throughout the northeastern United States and the adjoining mountains of the Southeast and is only marginally distributed in Canada in the far south of the provinces of Ontario, Quebec, and New Brunswick. Nevertheless, the species was first described from herbarium material collected by Scottish naturalist John Goldie near Montreal. The vernacular name, squirrel-corn, refers to the yellow corn-on-the-cob-shaped bulblets of this species, which resemble a squirrel's hoard of shallowly buried seed.

Dicentra canadensis is a spring ephemeral and in its native lands is one of the first woodland wildflowers to reemerge from the ground, in some areas as early as mid February, although, at the highest elevations and most northerly latitudes, plants will not produce flowers until May. After flowering, plants persist vegetatively until the trees form a dense leafy canopy and then die back to subsurface bulblets. The bulblets are not completely dormant though during this time, but in the autumn, with a burst of underground activity, form the next spring's leaf and flower buds. The species is usually found in rocky, deciduous woodlands in rich, loamy soils at elevations from sea level up to 1500 m (4920 ft).

Dicentra canadensis was first cultivated in Great Britain shortly before 1830, at which time plants that a Mr. Cleghorn had been sent from Canada flowered at Glasgow Botanic Garden. It is likely (but difficult to prove) that this species was brought into cultivation in North America around the same time. At least it is easy to envision early North American gardeners collecting local plants of this beautiful wildflower for their own gardens. The species does not, however, appear in North American horticultural literature until the early 1900s and even then does not appear to have been available commercially. Today it is still rare in cultivation, being much less often grown than the other eastern North American spring ephemeral, *D. cucullaria*. Nor is it as common in the wild as that species, having a much smaller and patchier distribution. For some reason, these two plants are often confused, even though they are not difficult to distinguish. The flowers of *D. canadensis* are fragrant and have pouchlike bases, while those of *D. cucullaria* are odorless and have diverging spurs at their bases. *Dicentra canadensis* usually also flowers about a week later than *D. cucullaria* and has few relatively large yellow bulblets that are only partially buried and turn red when exposed to the sun, whereas *D. cucullaria* has numerous small pink to white bulblets that are completely buried, often as deep as 5 cm, and are arranged in a way that makes them look like a lily bulb (Plate 17). The difference in the rootstock is an especially useful means of distinguishing the two species once they have finished flowering, a time when gardeners may want to divide or relocate plants.

Dicentra canadensis is best grown in a shady site in a rich, humusy soil and is especially suited to the woodland garden. The species is commercially available from several sources and is readily cultivated. Propagation is by seed or detached bulblets. Plant breeders have ignored D. canadensis and no named cultivars are available commercially.

Dicentra cucullaria (Linnaeus) Bernhardi   PLATES 18, 19
Dutchman's breeches

> Rootstock a cluster of pink to white teardrop-shaped bulblets. Leaves few to several, green on upper surface, glaucous on lower surface, broadly triangular, 10–36 × 4–18 cm, 2 or 3 times pinnately divided; leaflets deeply cut into linear to linear-elliptic or linear-obovate lobes; petioles 6–18 cm long. Inflorescences 3- to 14-flowered, usually exceeding length of leaves. Flowers pendent; petals white, sometimes suffused pink, apex yellow to orange-yellow; outer petals 10–20 mm long, apex reflexed for 2–5 mm long, base with pointed usually diverging spurs; inner petals 7.5–14 mm long, crest conspicuous. 2n = 32.

This charming woodland spring ephemeral is commonly called Dutchman's breeches because its flowers, with their diverging basal spurs, resemble the baggy pantaloons worn by 18th-century Dutchmen. An alternative name, staggerweed, alludes to the toxicity of this plant to livestock. Cases of poisoning in cattle, horses, and sheep are rare, but sometimes the plant is eaten when more palatable forage is unavailable and can lead to the animals developing breathing difficulties and convulsions. Interestingly, Native Americans in the past used this plant as a love charm. Young men would reportedly chew the rootstock and circle their intended while breathing out the fragrance from the bulblets. The historical records do not, however, say how effective this seductive dance was. The species was also used in the treatment of syphilis and as a blood purifier. All parts of this species and the closely related Dicentra canadensis contain high levels of toxic alkaloids.

In the wild, Dicentra cucullaria is distributed throughout the northeastern United States, in the adjoining parts of Canada up into Nova Scotia and Prince Edward Island, and in the mountains of the southeastern United States. In addition the species has a disjunct distribution in the Columbia River Basin in Washington, Oregon, and western Idaho. At one time after the last ice age these eastern and western populations must have been in contact, but the intermediate populations have since died out because the intermediate region has become increasingly arid In the past, the western populations were recognized as the variety *occidentalis* (Rydberg) M. Peck, since they are frequently coarser in their features than are most of the eastern plants. Nevertheless, plants from the Blue Ridge Mountains of Virginia and elsewhere are indistinguishable from those from the Columbia River Basin, and accordingly the variety is no longer accepted. The fact that no definitive morphological differences exist between the western and eastern populations suggests that they have only been separated a few thousand years, a flicker in geological time.

On the East Coast, where *Dicentra cucullaria* is most abundant, it is occasionally found growing alongside its close relative *D. canadensis*. Nevertheless, the two species differ in chromosome number and do not hybridize.

Both species usually have white flowers, but those of *Dicentra cucullaria* can very occasionally be suffused with a pink tinge. Two such clones have been named: 'Pittsburg' turns light pink in favorable conditions, whereas 'Pink Punk' (Plate 19), collected by H. Zetterlund on Saddle Mountain in Oregon, is always deep pink.

Dicentra cucullaria has been grown in England since at least 1759, when Philip Miller cultivated it at the Chelsea Physic Garden. Miller most likely received the species from John Bartram, the botanist who established the first American botanic garden at his home in Philadelphia. Bartram may even have grown the plant in Philadelphia before sending it to Miller, though no records of this exist. In fact the species is not mentioned in American horticultural literature until the turn of the 19th century, although it is hard to believe that such a pretty plant as this was not collected from the woods and brought into colonial gardens at a much earlier date.

Dicentra cucullaria is best grown in a shady location in a rich, humusy soil and is especially suited to the woodland garden. When happily situated plants may form large patches and produce a delightful display of flowers each spring. Particularly notable patches, several meters across, may be seen both in Brooklyn Botanic Garden's native flora garden and in the woodland garden at the Royal Botanic Gardens Kew. The species is available from several commercial sources.

Dicentra eximia (Ker-Gawler) Torrey   PLATES 20, 21
Turkey-corn

> *Rootstock* a slender, fleshy, horizontal rhizome, producing rosettes of leaves from which arise few to several leafless flowering stems 25–70 cm tall. *Leaves* numerous, green on upper surface, glaucous on lower surface, triangular, 10–55 × 5–30 cm, 2 or 3 times pinnately divided; *leaflets* coarsely toothed or themselves shortly

lobed into acute lobules; *petioles* 5–40 cm long. *Inflorescences* 5- to many-flowered, usually exceeding length of leaves. *Flowers* pendent, broadest near the base and here 9–14 mm wide; *petals* rose-purple to pink, occasionally white; *outer petals* with apex reflexed for 4–8 mm long, base pouchlike; *inner petals* 17–25 mm long, crest conspicuous. *2n* = 16.

This eastern North American species is in many respects similar to its western counterpart *Dicentra formosa*. In fact, so alike are these plants that they are often confused in gardens. The most obvious distinguishing feature is the length of the reflexed apical portion of the outer petals. In *D. eximia* this measures 4–8 mm long, while in *D. formosa* it is only 2–4 mm long. The flowers of *D. eximia* are also more narrowly heart-shaped than are those of *D. formosa*. This difference is best seen when flowers of both species are available for comparison (Plate 21). Furthermore, the flowers of *D. eximia* have a distinct jasminelike fragrance, cherished by some, by others considered repulsive. Both species vary in their tendency to spread by underground rhizomes; some strains of *D. eximia* are more clump-forming, short-lived, and more prone to self-seed.

Dicentra eximia is found in the Appalachian Mountains from southwestern Pennsylvania southward to Tennessee and North Carolina. The species typically grows in rock crevices at the base of large outcrops in woodland at an altitude of 100 to 1700 m (330 to 5575 ft). It is the latest of the three dicentras from the eastern United States to flower and has a much longer flowering season than either *D. canadensis* or *D. cucullaria*. In nature, the flowering season lasts from mid spring to early fall, but garden plants will often bloom until the first hard frosts cut them down. In this respect the species is similar to *D. formosa*. Nevertheless, in most regions of the world, *D. eximia* is much less commonly cultivated than that species or the numerous garden hybrids between *D. eximia* and *D. formosa*. However, in recent years *D. eximia* has become more common in gardens and is now the most commonly grown of these plants in the eastern United States. This is in part because it is a native of that region and is thus more tolerant of the hot-humid summers. Growers in the eastern United States also report that *D. eximia* is not often eaten by deer, a great advantage in a region where these creatures are a major garden pest.

Dicentra eximia has been grown in English gardens since three to four years prior to 1815, at which time it was illustrated in volume one of *The Botanical Register* (Edwards 1815) under the synonymous name *Fumaria eximia*. A Mr. Lyon had introduced it from the United States, where it was most likely already being grown in a few gardens.

Dicentra eximia is readily cultivated in most gardens in a shady to semi-shady position in a moist, but well-drained soil. Because *D. eximia* (like *D. formosa*) has a creeping rhizome, it needs a relatively large patch of garden in which to roam. For this reason *D. eximia* is best suited to the woodland or wildflower garden, though it is possible to grow this species in more confined spaces. To prolong bloom time inflorescences may be removed as the flowers begin to fade; that way the plant will bloom in flushes until the first frosts.

In addition to the typical pink-flowered species at least two white-flowered selections are grown: 'Alba' and 'Snowdrift', the latter of which has larger flowers making for a better garden plant. The pale pink-flowered selection 'Dolly Sods' was introduced by Plant Delights Nursery of North Carolina from a collection made at Dolly Sods Wilderness area in West Virginia. It has blue-green foliage and is particularly tolerant of heat and humidity.

Dicentra 'Ivory Hearts' also has pure white flowers and is a Japanese hybrid between *D. peregrina* and *D. eximia* 'Alba'. The cultivar's *D. peregrina* parentage makes for a particularly beautiful plant, but one that is resentful of hot-humid climates and sun. It is a close kin to the equally outstanding rose-pink 'Candy Hearts' with the same species in its ancestry. Both have the same gray, rather finely cut leaves. Hybrid cultivars between *D. eximia* and *D. formosa* are discussed further under *D. formosa*.

Dicentra formosa (Haworth) Walpers   PLATES 21–23
Pacific bleeding heart

Rootstock a slender, horizontal rhizome, producing rosettes of leaves from which arise one to several leafless flowering stems 25–60 cm tall. *Leaves* numerous, green to glaucous on upper surface, glaucous on lower surface, triangular, 15–55 × 8–35 cm, 2 or usually 3 times pinnately divided; *leaflets* coarsely toothed or themselves shortly lobed; *petioles* 5–40 cm long. *Inflorescences* 2- to 30-flowered, usually exceeding length of leaves. *Flowers* pendent; *petals* rose-purple, pink, cream, or pale yellow, rarely white; *outer petals* 12–24 mm long, apex reflexed for 2–5 mm long, base pouchlike; *inner petals* 12–22 mm long, crest conspicuous. $2n = 16, 32$.

The Pacific bleeding heart is a wonderful garden plant, which if periodically deadheaded and given sufficient soil moisture will bloom in waves from April right up until the first hard frosts, with a peak flowering in late spring. The species is the most variable of all the dicentras and many of the natural variants are now cultivated. These, along with the numerous garden hybrids between this species and *D.*

eximia, *D. nevadensis*, and *D. peregrina*, offer the gardener a wide choice in terms of color, shape, and size of flowers and foliage.

Dicentra formosa is native to western North America, where two subspecies are generally recognized, subsp. *formosa* (Plates 21, 22) and subsp. *oregana* (Plate 23). (Some authors recognize a third subspecies, subsp. *nevadensis*, but this is treated here as a distinct but closely related species). The two subspecies differ in the color of their flowers and leaves. Subspecies *formosa* usually has pink to pinkish-purple flowers and green leaves, while subsp. *oregana* has cream or pale yellow flowers and blue-green leaves and is also often shorter in stature. Both are widely cultivated. In several places in Europe subsp. *formosa* has escaped from cultivation into nature, and once established is very long-lived, due both to efficient vegetative spread through rhizome growth, and the occasional seedlings.

Dicentra formosa subsp. *formosa* grows naturally in the region stretching from Vancouver Island and southern British Columbia, south along the Cascade Range, Coast Range, and Sierra Nevada to central California. It is a plant of loam or gravel soils, and grows in moist woods and along stream banks at elevations from sea level to 2250 m (7380 ft). Two natural chromosome races occur that do not interbreed, a diploid race with a more inland distribution growing in drier areas in pine woodlands, and a tetraploid race with a more coastal distribution. They are difficult to distinguish morphologically, although the diploid possibly has more grayish leaves and a deeper flower color. Apparently, only the diploid race will form hybrids with the diploid *D. eximia* from the eastern United States. The second subspecies, subsp. *oregana*, is found only in a small area straddling southern Oregon and northern California, in the Siskiyou Mountains. This region is rich in local endemics, including *Vancouveria chrysantha* and the carnivorous cobra-lily *Darlingtonia*. Like these other endemics the dicentra is adapted to grow on serpentine soils, which are toxic to most plants.

Dicentra formosa subsp. *formosa* was first discovered by Scottish surgeon and naturalist Archibald Menzies, while serving with Captain Vancouver on the *Discovery*'s voyage around the world. Menzies appears to have collected seed at Nootka Sound in 1792, which upon returning to England in 1795 he gave to the Royal Botanic Gardens Kew. From Kew the species entered nearby nurseries and that way soon became more widely cultivated. The plant was most likely not grown in North American gardens until several years later, apparently first being offered for sale in 1835 by the Boston nursery of William Kenrick. This nursery presumably acquired the species from England. The more locally distributed subsp. *oregana* is a 20th-century addition to our gardens, apparently entering cultivation in both the United States and Great Britain around 1932, when it was first offered for sale by the Oregon nursery firm of Borsch and Sons. It is still relatively uncommon today. It has been important in hybridization, but is trickier to grow and requires a more well-drained soil than does subsp. *formosa*.

Dicentra formosa has now been brought into gardens on several occasions and is represented by numerous clones, which range in flower color from white through pink to dark red, and in foliage color from green to bluish- or even grayish-blue-green. One commonly cultivated clone with white flowers and bluish-green leaves is grown under the name *D. formosa* f. *alba*. Another good wild-collected plant is *D. formosa* 'Cox's Dark Red', with particularly dark red flowers and green foliage.

More important than these wild selections of *Dicentra formosa* are the numerous hybrids involving *D. formosa* and other dicentras. Richard Manske patented the first commercially available hybrid in 1953, *D.* 'Bountiful', a pink-flowered cross between *D. formosa* subsp. *oregana* and *D. eximia*. It was soon followed by other hybrids of the same parentage, including the first white-flowered cultivar, *D.* 'Silversmith'. Since then well over 30 hybrids between these and other bleeding hearts have entered our gardens. The finely cut blue-green leaves of *D. formosa* subsp. *oregana* have been inherited by many of these crosses, including *D.* 'Bountiful', but several also show their subsp. *formosa* parentage in having green leaves. *Dicentra peregrina* and to a lesser extent *D. nevadensis* have also occasionally been used as parents in these hybrids. *Dicentra* 'King of Hearts' (Plate 24), a complex hybrid between *D. peregrina* × (*D. formosa* subsp. *oregana* × *D. eximia*), is a particularly fine example.

Most of the *Dicentra formosa* hybrids are easy to grow and have long bloom times. However, those with *D. peregrina* and *D. nevadensis* parentage tend to sulk during hot weather and are best suited to regions with cooler summers, like Great Britain. Nevertheless, even in warmer climates they can be grown if given a shady position and soil that is never allowed to dry out. While these hybrids are certainly more amenable in gardens than are either *D. peregrina* or *D. nevadensis*, better adapted still to regions with hot humid summers are hybrids with *D. formosa* subsp. *formosa* and especially *D. eximia* parentage. A list of the most widely available *D. formosa* hybrids follows:

White-flowered Cultivars

'Langtrees' (syn. 'Pearl Drops')—flowers white, leaves bluish green.

'Margaret Fish'—flowers pure white, leaves bluish-gray-green.

'Quicksilver'—flowers pure white, leaves bluish-gray-green; resentful of hot-humid climates and sun.

Snowflakes = 'Fusd'—flowers pure white, leaves green; a Blooms of Bressingham introduction.

'Sweetheart'—flowers pure white, leaves green.

Pink-flowered Cultivars

'Bacchanal'—flowers particularly deep red, leaves bluish-green.

'Coldham'—flowers deep burgundy, leaves bluish-green, finely cut.

'Zestful'—flowers deep rose-pink, leaves bluish-green.

Hybrid Cultivars Involving *D. formosa*

'Adrian Bloom'—flowers dark pink, leaves bluish-green, particularly finely cut, said to be relatively sun tolerant; a Blooms of Bressingham introduction, from a chance seedling of *D.* 'Bountiful'.

'Aurora'—flowers pure white, leaves gray-green; particularly tolerant of hot-humid climates; a German hybrid with *D. eximia* parentage bred by Ernst Pagels.

'Bountiful'—flowers rosy red, leaves bluish-green; a Canadian hybrid of *D. formosa* subsp. *oregana* × *D. eximia* bred by Richard Manske.

'Gothenburg'—stems originally from a hybrid between *D. formosa* subsp. *oregana* and *D. peregrina* f. *alba*. Inbreeding of this hybrid in Gothenburg Botanic Garden surprisingly gave rise to a uniform seed strain with a neat habit similar to 'King of Hearts' but with flowers of a clean light pink.

'King of Hearts'—flowers pink, leaves bluish-gray-green, particularly finely cut; resentful of hot-humid climates and sun and best grown in a moist peaty soil; a hybrid of *D. peregrina* × (*D. formosa* subsp. *oregana* × *D. eximia*) created by Marion Ownbey of Washington State.

'Luxuriant'—flowers cherry-red, leaves bluish-green, finely cut; resentful of hot-humid climates and sun; a *D. eximia* × *D. peregrina* hybrid

'Silversmith'—flowers white, flushed pink, leaves green; a Canadian hybrid of *D. formosa* subsp. *oregana* × *D. eximia* bred by Richard Manske.

'Stuart Boothman'—flowers deep pink, leaves gray-green, finely cut; likely a hybrid between *D. formosa* subsp. *oregana* and *D. eximia*.

Key to the Subspecies of *Dicentra formosa*

1a. Leaf blades glaucous beneath, never glaucous but rarely glaucescent above; petals purple-pink to pink, rarely white.............................subsp. *formosa*

1b. Leaf blades distinctly glaucous on both surfaces; petals cream-colored, rarely pale yellow, crest pink...subsp. *oregana*

Dicentra nevadensis Eastwood   PLATE 25
Sierra bleeding heart

Rootstock a stout, elongate rhizome. *Leaves* numerous, glaucous, triangular, 10–30 × 5–18 cm, 2 times pinnately divided; *leaflets* more or less deeply cut into narrow acute teeth or lobes; *petioles* 4–20 cm long. *Inflorescences* 2- to 20-flowered, shorter than to exceeding length of leaves. *Flowers* pendent; *petals* white to pale yellow or rose-tinted; *outer petals* 12–18 mm long, apex reflexed for 3–5 mm long, base pouchlike; *inner petals* 11–17 mm long, crest conspicuous. $2n = 16$.

This species closely resembles the much more widespread *Dicentra formosa*, of which it has been treated as a subspecies by some authors. However, in *D. nevadensis* the flowers are relatively pale and are white to pale yellow or rose-tinted. They are also smaller and narrower and the outer petals less pouchlike at the base. Furthermore, the leaf segments are usually narrower and more sharply toothed. *Dicentra nevadensis* also has a very different habitat preference from *D. formosa*. It is restricted to a few granite balds and sub-alpine forests in California's Sierra Nevada (Plate 15, 25). There it typically grows in open, relatively sunny locations in gritty soils formed from decaying granite at an altitude of 2100 to 3300 m (6,890 to 10,800 ft). *Dicentra formosa*, in contrast, is generally found at much lower altitudes, never reaching the maximum elevation of *D. nevadensis*.

Even though the two species occur within 3–5 kilometers of each other in Sequoia National Park, they are most likely isolated there by their different altitude and habitat preferences and probably do not hybridize. Hybrids have been produced by crossing cultivated plants. Garden hybrids of *Dicentra peregrina* × *D. nevadensis* are grown under the cultivar name 'Tsuneshigo Rokujo'. They are vegetatively similar to D. *nevadensis* but are more compact and have pale pink flowers similar to those of *D. peregrina*.

As a narrow endemic of the high Sierra Nevada *Dicentra nevadensis* is a species of conservation concern. For this reason plants and even seed should not

Dicentra nevadensis. Drawing by Adèle Rossetti Morosini.

be collected from the wild. The species is very rare in cultivation and is only very occasionally offered for sale. The horticultural merit of this species lies mainly in the
foliage. The pale flowers are few in number and barely rise above the leaves. In some
areas in Sweden it is successfully grown outdoors in woodland conditions, but it is
tricky, and to secure survival a treatment like that for *D. peregrina* is recommended.

Dicentra pauciflora S. Watson   PLATES 26, 27
Few-flowered bleeding heart

> *Rootstock* rhizomatous or a cluster of spindle-shaped tubers, often with bulblets
> at base of tubers or along rhizomes. *Leaves* few, green to glaucescent, triangular,
> 7–16 × 3–10 cm, 2 or 3 times pinnately divided; *leaflets* divided into elliptic lobes;
> *petioles* 2–15 cm long. *Inflorescences* 1- to 3-flowered, barely exceeding leaves. *Flow-*
> *ers* nodding; *outer petals* white to pink, 15–25 mm long, apex reflexed for 5–11 mm
> long, base pouchlike; *inner petals* white, 15–24 mm long, crest absent. *2n* = 16.

Preferring relatively high altitudes, the few-flowered bleeding heart, *Dicentra pauci-*
flora, grows in subalpine coniferous forest, usually where the tree cover is just begin-
ning to open up and give way to a mix of dwarf shrubs and low-growing wildflowers, such as shooting stars (*Dodecatheon* spp.) and glacier lilies (*Erythronium*
spp.). Few-flowered bleeding heart is found in the North Coast Ranges of southern
Oregon and northern California, and in a few scattered locations southward in the
Sierra Nevada of California's Plumas and Tulare Counties. Over this range suitable
subalpine forest habitats occur at elevations ranging from 1220 to 2740 m (4000 to
9000 ft). There in open, gravelly soils the species can be locally abundant. In some
favorable sites plants may even spread into less optimum humus-rich soils in relatively shady situations. Populations in marginal habitats are nevertheless often shy
to flower and may well multiply largely via detached tubers and bulbils rather than
by seed. Few-flowered bleeding heart's natural flowering season is from May to
August depending upon both altitude and latitude, but in gardens plants will bloom
in the spring.

Harvard University botanist Serano Watson first described *Dicentra pauciflora*
in 1880 from herbarium material that had been collected in northern California.
The species does not appear to have entered cultivation though until the mid 1900s.

Dicentra pauciflora is vegetatively similar to, and sometimes confused with,
steer's-head, *D. uniflora*. The two species are, nevertheless, readily distinguished
with a minimum of practice. Most noticeably, they differ in the length of the non-
reflexed portion of their outer petals, which is normally 12 mm or longer in *D.*

pauciflora but usually less than 7 mm long in *D. uniflora*. Furthermore, the apical portion of the inner petals is usually narrower (2–3 mm across) and spoon-shaped in *D. pauciflora*, compared to 4–8 mm wide and somewhat triangular in *D. uniflora*. Additionally, while *D. pauciflora* bears one to three flowers per inflorescence, *D. uniflora* consistently only has one flower per inflorescence. The two species can even be distinguished vegetatively since the leaves of *D. uniflora* are usually held almost flat to the ground and usually have obovate to spatula-shaped leaflets, while the leaves of *D. pauciflora* are held more erectly and typically have a much more delicate appearance and elliptic leaflets. The species also differ in the structure of their rootstocks (Plate 27).

In cultivation *Dicentra pauciflora* is a challenge. In most areas the species is best grown in an alpine house given the same treatment as a fritillary and other dwarf bulbs. Some watering during the dormant period is beneficial. Repot in September and keep the plant slightly moist until it goes dormant in May. It can be grown in the open, but its minute size and long dormancy invite a wide range of accidents.

No cultivars of this species are available commercially.

Dicentra peregrina (Rudolph) Makino   PLATE 28

Rootstock a short, erect rhizome. *Stems* 5–15 cm tall. *Leaves* several to numerous, 4–16 × 1–4 cm, glaucous, broadly triangular, 2–4 times pinnately divided; *leaflets* deeply cut into linear lobes; *petioles* 3–12 cm long. *Inflorescences* 1- to 8-flowered, exceeding leaves. *Flowers* nearly erect to usually nodding; *petals* white to purple; *outer petals* 15–25 mm long, apex strongly reflexed for 7–10 mm long, base pouchlike; *inner petals* 15–25 mm long, crest conspicuous. Self-compatible.

Dicentra peregrina, the sole Asian representative of the genus, is easily recognized by its short, upright rhizomes with well-developed fibrous roots, by its glaucous leaves with the segments deeply dissected into linear lobes each less than 1 mm wide, and by its flowers with very strongly reflexed outer petals. The species is distributed in northeastern Siberia, Kamchatka, Sakhalin Island, the Kuriles, and Japan. At one time the Japanese populations were classified as a distinct species, *D. pusilla* Siebold & Zuccarini, under which name, in 1966, the species received a Preliminary Commendation from the Royal Horticultural Society. Subsequent studies have, however, found that the Japanese plants are not morphologically distinct, and accordingly the name *D. pusilla* is now treated as a synonym of *D. peregrina*. The species is highly regarded by Japanese growers and is the symbol of the Tokyo Rock

Garden Club. Both pink- and white-flowered *D. peregrina* have been grown in Great Britain since the early 1960s, at which time the celebrated alpine grower Will Ingwersen writes of them in the *Gardener's Chronicle*. The name *peregrina* is derived from the Latin for emigrant, a name the plant presumably received because it is the only species of *Dicentra* found outside of North America.

Dicentra peregrina is the most challenging to grow of all the dicentras but is nevertheless available from several commercial sources. In most climates it requires alpine house culture and a well-drained, gritty peaty mix, which should never be allowed to dry out completely but which should be kept somewhat drier during autumn and winter. In some areas with cool summers it will, however, grow readily outside and seed around in pure peat.

Dicentra peregrina is usually raised from seed. It is possible to grow flowering sized plants from seed in one year. You can get seeds of this species, even if you have only one plant, by tripping the inner petals so as to disturb the stigmatic surface, triggering the pollen to germinate.

The species has been hybridized both by Japanese and American growers with the larger American species. *Dicentra* 'Tsuneshigo Rokujo', cross between *D. nevadensis* and *D. peregrina* is like a large *D. peregrina* with pale pink flowers. It received a Preliminary Commendation in 1974 when exhibited at the Chelsea Flower Show. *Dicentra* 'Ivory Hearts' and *D.* 'Candy Hearts' are discussed under *D. eximia*, *D.* 'King of Heart' under *D. formosa*. Like *D. peregrina* these hybrids are resentful of hot-humid climates and sun and are best grown in a moist peaty soil, which is never allowed to dry out. They are nevertheless much easier to grow than *D. peregrina*.

Dicentra uniflora Kellogg   PLATES 27, 29
Steer's-head

> *Rootstock* a cluster of club- to spindle-shaped tubers, small bulblets often present at base of tubers. *Stems* 3–10 cm tall. *Leaves* few, usually glaucous, triangular, 4–10 × 1–4 cm, 1–2 times ternately or almost pinnately divided; *leaflets* divided into oblong to spatula-shaped lobes; *petioles* 2–8 cm long. *Inflorescences* 1-flowered, barely exceeding to shorter than leaves. *Flowers* nodding to erect; *petals* pink to white, suffused light brown or purple, inner surfaces of outer petals with a rich purple infusion; *outer petals* 5–20 mm long, apex reflexed for 4–10 mm long, base pouchlike; *inner petals* 11–17 mm long, crest absent. $2n = 16$. Self-compatible.

This species's vernacular name, "steer's-head," is very fitting since its inner petals collectively form a shape very similar to that of a bovine head, while the two strongly reflex outer petals resemble horns. In flower, steer's-head is a pretty plant but not one that is widely, or even readily, grown.

In the wild, *Dicentra uniflora* grows scattered across the Cascade, Sierra Nevada, and Rocky Mountains from southern British Columbia south to Tulare County, California, and east to Wyoming. Throughout its range it grows on rocky slopes and hillsides, often under the protection of coniferous trees but always on gravelly soils. The species prefers life at relatively high altitudes, ranging from 1500 to 3300 m (4920 to 10,800 ft). It is also notable in flowering soon after the snow melts and can often be seen in the wild blooming next to melting snowbanks (Plate 29). In most parts of its range it is the first wildflower to bloom, usually beating even the glacier lilies (*Erythronium* species) famed for their precocious appearance each spring. Depending upon both altitude and latitude, the species's flowering period ranges from very early spring to late summer. Its growing season is also notable in being condensed into a few brief weeks, with the rest of the year being spent underground. Plants produce just a single flower and will apparently skip a year or two without flowering if conditions have been unfavorable the year before.

While readily identified by its single flower with strongly reflexed outer petals, *Dicentra uniflora* has occasionally been confused with *D. pauciflora*; distinguishing features are discussed under that species and are also indicated in the key.

In cultivation *Dicentra uniflora* is a challenge. It requires the same treatment as *D. pauciflora*.

Ehrendorferia   PLATES 30–32
Eardrops

> Biennial or perennial herbs with erect, glaucous stems to 3 m tall. *Leaves* 2–4 times pinnately divided. *Inflorescences* terminal, 5- to many-flowered cymes. *Flowers* erect, sometimes having a slightly pungent odor, more or less heart-shaped; *petals* golden yellow, or cream- to yellowish-white; *outer petals* 10–22 mm long, strongly reflexed, base pouchlike; *inner petals* projecting far beyond outer petals; *nectary* present.

The genus *Ehrendorferia* consists of two species, golden eardrops, *E. chrysantha* (W. J. Hooker & G. Arnott) J. Rylander, and white eardrops, *E. ochroleuca* (G. Engelmann) T. Fukuhara. Both are native to those parts of California with a Mediterranean climate where wildfires occur every few years. The plants inhabit dry gravelly hillsides, gullies, and disturbed areas, and their seeds are triggered to germinate after they have been exposed to smoke. Consequently, these plants are most abundant following a fire, an adaptation that enables them to quickly colonize landscapes from which larger more vigorous plants have been temporarily removed or burnt back. This adaptation also makes them tricky to grow and as a result neither species is common in gardens.

Until 1997 both *Ehrendorferia* species were included in the genus *Dicentra*, where, because of their very distinct appearance, they were classified in their own subgenus. They differ from *Dicentra* and all other genera treated in this chapter by having flowers that point upward, rather than toward the ground, and by the absence of elaiosomes on the seeds. The name *Ehrendorferia* was coined in 1997 and honors Friedrich Ehrendorfer, who from 1970 to 1991 was Director of the Institute of Botany at the University of Vienna. Publication of the name coincided with the celebration of his 70th birthday.

Of the two species, *Ehrendorferia chrysantha* (Plates 30, 31) is the one most often seen in cultivation. As the name *chrysantha* suggests, the plant has golden-yellow flowers. The species is perennial, grows from a stout horizontal almost woody base, and produces glaucous, usually bipinnately compound leaves staggered along a stem that can reach up to 1.5 meters in height. The second species, *E. ochroleuca* (Plates 30, 32), is the largest plant in the family, occasionally reaching a

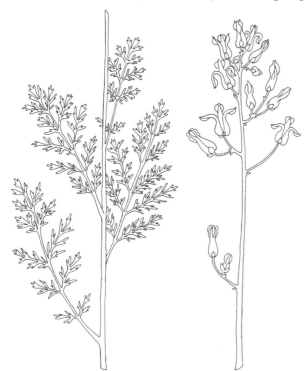

towering 3 meters. It has cream- to yellowish-white flowers and the outer petals are generally larger and thicker than those of *E. chrysantha*, measuring 15–30 mm in length, versus 10–22 mm. These relatively large robust flowers are one of the several features adapting *E. ochroleuca* to hummingbird pollination. In contrast, *E. chrysantha*, with its smaller, yellow flowers is, like other members of the family, insect-pollinated.

Both *Ehrendorferia* species flower from early spring to late summer. *Ehrendorferia chrysantha* has the larger natural distribution and occurs throughout much of western California and parts of northern Baja California, while *E. ochroleuca* is restricted to an area of California roughly from Santa Cruz southward to just below Los Angeles. Neither species is common

Ehrendorferia chrysantha. Drawing by Adèle Rossetti Morosini.

in the wild and both are frequently found as solitary individuals widely separated from each other. However, they may be locally abundant in areas that in recent years have experienced a fire and hence remain free from competing vegetation.

The first of the two *Ehrendorferia* species to be brought into cultivation was not surprisingly the one with the largest natural distribution, *E. chrysantha*. Scottish plant collector David Douglas, while on his 1830 to 1832 expedition to California, was the first European to see it in the wild, but despite introducing many other Californian ornamentals, never introduced it into British gardens. This was left to William Lobb, who a few years later, collecting in the dry coastal mountains of Southern California, sent seed to his employer, the Veitch and Sons Nursery of Exeter. At this famous, but sadly now disbanded, nursery the plants flowered for the first time in September 1852. Golden eardrops has been grown in British Gardens ever since, though it has never been common. This is perhaps because it needs warm summers to set seed and its seeds are then reluctant to germinate unless subjected to smoke. Within the United States, *E. chrysantha* was cultivated in California at least by 1938, at which time it is mentioned in *The Gardener's Chronicle*.

Ehrendorferia ochroleuca is even less frequently seen and doesn't appear to have yet been introduced to gardens outside of the United States. In fact, it is rarely cultivated even in its native California. This is a shame since it is a beautiful plant and being attractive to hummingbirds would especially make a good garden plant where these birds are found. Seed of both species is currently available from less than a handful of commercial sources. A few Californian nurseries, specializing in native flowers, also stock plants of *E. chrysantha*.

The eardrops are best grown in a warm sunny location in a rich but gritty, well-drained soil. Their tall stature, blue-green ferny rosette of leaves, and interesting long-lasting upright heart-shaped flowers make them ideal subjects for the back of an herbaceous border. Propagation is by seed. While these species are short-lived perennials in nature, in cultivation they often die after flowering and are, therefore, usually raised repeatedly from seed. Seed germination is best induced by treatment with commercial smoke extracts.

Ichtyoselmis   PLATE 33
Large-flowered dicentra

> Perennial herb arising from a long rhizome. *Stems* 1 m tall, juicy, erect, few-branched in upper half. *Leaves* 2 or usually 3 times ternately divided, with discrete, ovate, serrate leaflets. *Inflorescences* terminal, 3- to 14-flowered cymes. *Flowers* with two planes of symmetry, fiddle-shaped; sepals entire, lanceolate, 1.3–2 cm

long; *petals* pale-yellow; *outer petals* (3.5–)4–5 cm long, apex not reflexed, base not or very shallowly pouchlike; *inner petals* same length as outer petals; *stamens* free, loosely cohering below the anthers; *nectar* secreted at base of the central stamens.

While rarely seen in gardens, large-flowered dicentra (Plate 33) is commercially available from several specialist nurseries, including some mail-order ones, though invariably the species is sold under the synonymous name *Dicentra macrantha* rather than the currently accepted one, *Ichtyoselmis macrantha* (Oliver) Lidén. That this species is not a *Dicentra* is clearly evident from its tall, leafy stem, its dentate leaves that are reminiscent of those of an *Astilbe*, and its pendent, pale-yellow flowers with fiddle- (or fish-) shaped flowers. The flowers, while often produced sparingly, are the largest in the family, and can measure up to 5 cm long. The name *Ichtyoselmis* is derived from the Greek *ichtyo*, fish, and *selmis*, gallows, a reference to the flower's resemblance to dead hanging fishes, a feature also reflected in the local Sichuan name of goldfish plant. It is also worth noting the speed with which this plant re-emerges from the ground each spring. It is not uncommon for it to achieve its full height in less than a week.

Large-flowered dicentra is native to northern Myanmar (Burma) and western China. It grows locally in woods and glades, at elevations of 1500 to 2700 m (4920 to 8860 ft), and also in disturbed habitats and secondary forest. In 1904 Ernest Wilson found it growing on Mount Emei in China's Sichuan Province and collected seed for his employer Veitch and Sons Nursery. This way the species was introduced to English gardens. Nowadays it is commercially available in the United States, as well as Europe.

In cultivation large-flowered dicentra needs a shady position and moist, humus-rich soil. It is cold-hardy down to –15°C (5°F), but needs protection from cold winds once it is has resumed growth in the spring. Nevertheless, if given a suitably protected site, it is not difficult to grow. It produces flowers in late spring.

Ichtyoselmis macrantha is propagated by division in September or in early spring before growth commences. Seed is often produced and should be sown fresh.

Ichtyoselmis macrantha. Drawing by Adèle Rossetti Morosini.

Lamprocapnos   PLATES 1, 34, 35
Bleeding heart

Perennial herb arising from a rhizome. *Stems* 0.5 to 1 m tall, juicy, erect, sparsely branched, leafy. *Leaves* 2 or almost 3 times ternately or almost pinnately divided; *leaflets* wedge-shaped, more or less deeply divided into broad acute lobes or coarse teeth. *Inflorescences* terminal and axillary from the upper leaves, held almost horizontally, long and loose, 7- to 15-flowered. *Flowers* with two planes of symmetry, more or less heart-shaped, 22–25 mm broad, pendent; *outer petals* pink, or occasionally white, base pouchlike; *inner petals* white, usually with red and yellow markings, about 25 mm long, projecting far beyond the strongly reflexed outer petals, each with a prominent crest; *stamens* free from each other, only shortly fused below the anthers; *nectar* secreted from the base of each central stamen.

Long before it was first seen by Western gardeners, this beautiful Asian plant was cultivated by the Chinese and Japanese. Indeed, so long has bleeding heart been grown in its native land that it is now difficult to determine where it is native and where it is introduced. This confusion has resulted both from the loss of natural populations due to over-collecting and because the species has often escaped from gardens into natural areas where it was not originally present. Nonetheless, natural populations of bleeding heart do, undoubtedly, still occur in northeastern China's Heilongjiang Province and in neighboring parts of Russia and North Korea. In these areas the plant is rare but can be found in moist woodland and on mountains, where it grows in the company of other wonderful garden plants like *Jeffersonia dubia* and *Angelica gigas*.

Lamprocapnos spectabilis (Linnaeus) T. Fukuhara (Plate 1) was one of the first Northeast Asian plants to be introduced to Europe, though at that time it was known as *Dielytra spectabilis*. The currently accepted generic name, *Lamprocapnos*, first appeared in print in 1850, but the specific combination was not validly published until 1997. For one hundred and fifty years bleeding heart has been known as *Dicentra spectabilis* and is indeed still today usually sold under that name. The name *Lamprocapnos* is derived from the Greek *lampro*, bright, and *capnos*, smoke, and is a reference to the showy flowers of this species. An explanation of why this plant is no longer classified in the genus *Dicentra* is given in chapter two.

The first time we have seen this plant mentioned in European literature as a garden plant is in *Vollständige Lexicon der Gärtnerei und Botanik* (Dietrich 1804). This introduction does not appear to have remained in cultivation for more than a few years. According to John Loudon, *Lamprocapnos spectabilis* made its début to

English gardens in 1812 but died out before becoming widely established. The great Scottish plant collector Robert Fortune reintroduced it in 1846. Fortune, a collector for the Royal Horticultural Society, was one of the first plant collectors to visit China when the country was tentatively opening its doors to westerners. He purchased the bleeding heart from a nursery in Shanghai and at the time correctly predicted that it would "become a great favourite in English Gardens." It took several years, however, for the plant to become popular since gardeners at that time knew next to nothing about the cultivation of Chinese plants and wrongly believed them not to be hardy in Britain. Four to five years after the species was introduced to England it was sent to gardens in both continental Europe and North America. So popular has this plant become that today more plants of bleeding heart are likely to be found in our gardens than remain in the wild.

Prior to the species' introduction into European gardens, the Prince of Botany Carl Linnaeus saw a drawing of this species that the Russo-Siberian Alexander de Karamyschew, who studied with Linnaeus at Uppsala, placed at the head of his thesis. Linnaeus was very much taken by it and after seeing a herbarium specimen longed to see a living plant. When his friend Erich Laxmann sent seeds of "*Fumaria spectabilis*" from Sinisopka in Siberia, Linnaeus was delighted. The plants, though, turned out to be "*Corydalis* (syn. *Fumaria*) *nobilis*," a species Linnaeus described as new to science, but not what he had hoped for.

The plant's common name, bleeding heart, refers to its flowers that resemble hearts with drops of (white) blood falling from them. Another descriptive European name is lady in a bath. In Sweden the plant is named löjtnantshjärta, meaning "the heart is hiding," a reference to the resemblance of the dissected flower parts to a woman, a bottle, and a gun, all of which are supposedly found in the heart of a lieutenant. A similar interpretive name is attached to this plant in Canada. The Chinese, however, have a different interpretation and suggest that the individual flowers look like a fish that has a smaller fish in its mouth. Robert Fortune recorded a second Chinese name that translates as "red and white moutan flower." Moutan is Chinese for tree peonies, and the name refers to the similarity between the leaves of bleeding heart and these plants. The distinctive appearance of the plant also inspired Edward Lear, who is better known for his nonsensical limericks, to publish in 1871 a drawing of the fictitious plant "*Manypeeplia up-*

Lamprocapnos spectabilis. Drawing by Paul Harwood.

sidedownia" (see page 170). This nonsense plant is clearly a bleeding heart with little people replacing the flowers. Whichever way the flowers are interpreted *Lamprocapnos spectabilis* must surely be one of our most graceful garden plants. Such is its dramatic appearance and versatility that it has long been a mainstay of both formal perennial borders and more naturalistic woodland gardens.

From the time of its reintroduction in 1846 until the early 1900s *Lamprocapnos spectabilis* was typically grown as a temporary conservatory plant, because it was not widely known to be frost-hardy (even though Fortune had predicted it would be so). The species was in particular grown as a forced pot plant. Plants to be forced were potted up in late summer or autumn after their foliage had died down and brought under glass, starting in December. Grown at a temperature of 10 to 13°C (50 to 55°F) the plants would flower as early as February. Later blooming could be achieved by staggering the time that plants were brought into the heated conservatory. After flowering the plants were hardened off and planted in the open garden in May. Here they were left for at least one year since they were not suitable for immediate forcing. By the late 1930s this practice had largely been abandoned with plants almost exclusively being grown outdoors in the border or woodland garden.

The cultivation of the species in America, while less well documented than in Great Britain, appears to have followed a similar pattern as occurred there. The first record of bleeding heart being grown in North American gardens dates to 1852, when the plant was exhibited at the Pennsylvania Horticultural Society.

Today, in addition to the typical species, two distinct cultivars are widely grown, one with white flowers and the other with gold leaves. White-flowered clones of *Lamprocapnos spectabilis* have been cultivated in English gardens since at least 1887, when Nicholson's mentions one in his *Illustrated Dictionary of Gardening*. However, these must represent a different clone to the ones commonly being grown today, since they were much weaker in their growth than the plants we grow today and their flowers, rather than pure white, were conspicuously tinged with pink. Pure-white-flowered *L. spectabilis* appears to be a mid-20th-century addition to gardens. Today, white-flowered cultivars are sold under two cultivar names, 'Alba' (Plate 34) and 'Pantaloons', though little if anything distinguishes these plants. A third cultivar, 'Gold Heart' (Plate 35), has golden-yellow foliage and the typical pink-and-white flowers of the species. Nori Pope, owner of Hadspen House, a beautiful arts-and-crafts garden in Somerset, England, selected this distinct cultivar in 1993. It is grown primarily for its golden leaves rather than its flowers. To look its best, this cultivar needs a shadier position than the species. 'Gold Heart' is useful for brightening up a dark corner of the garden; otherwise it has the tendency to look rather garish.

In gardens, bleeding heart prefers a partially shady position and a moist, humus-rich soil, and tolerates a wide range of pH. Plants also benefit from fertilizing. The species is hardy to at least –15°C (5°F), but emerging leaves and flowers may be damaged by late frosts unless plants are grown in a sheltered spot. The species flowers from May to June. Propagation is by seed sown in the spring or more usually by division when plants are dormant or have recently emerged. Divided plants can often prove slow to reestablish. Root cuttings may also be taken in the spring and summer but again patience is needed. The leaves reemerge from the ground in early spring and the flowers are produced a few weeks later, lasting from May to June. In regions with cool summers, or if the roots are supplied with plenty of moisture, the leaves will persist until late summer, but in warmer or drier climates the leaves die down shortly after the plant has flowered. This can sometimes leave an unsightly hole in a perennial border, but one that can be filled-in by *Hosta*, ferns, or other late-starting perennials.

5
Corydalis

Annual to perennial herbs. *Stems* soft and juicy, usually hairless. *Leaves* usually alternate, pinnately or ternately divided. *Flowers* in racemes, each subtended by a bract; *corolla* zygomorphic (with one plane of symmetry); upper petal with a nectariferous spur. *Fruit* a usually many-seeded, capsule with a persistent style. *Seeds* black, usually with elaiosomes.

THE GENUS *CORYDALIS* A. P. de Candolle is extremely diverse in morphology, lifeform, and ecology. The remarkable range of life-forms includes tuberous spring ephemerals, annuals of disturbed ground, high alpine scree species, meadow plants, drought-tolerant cushion-forming chasmophytes, rhizomatous forest species, and even some climbers. Still it is easy to recognize a corydalis by its distinctive flower and fruit, and molecular analysis has confirmed the naturalness of the genus in its currently accepted circumscription (that is, after the segregation of *Pseudofumaria*, *Ceratocapnos*, and *Capnoides*—see chapter two).

Κορυδαλλιον (corydallion) is mentioned by Pedacius Dioscorides, surgeon in Nero's army in the first century AD, in his *De Medica Materia Libri VI*, and is—in direct translation—still used for this genus in, for example, Denmark (laerkespore) and Germany (Lerchensporn). In Britain and North America, the epithet larkspur is applied instead to *Delphinium* and *Consolida* in Ranunculaceae, which have similarly spurred flowers. According to Dioscorides the spur of corydalis resembles that of the crested lark.

Of the 450 species in the genus *Corydalis*, a staggering 330 are native to China and Tibet, with several more occurring in neighboring Himalayan countries. Of the currently 35 recognized subgroups (sections), all except the *C. cava* group are represented in China and the Himalaya. Other areas are much less rich. In North America only three sections are represented: the yellow-flowered annuals such as *C. aurea*, two tall purple-flowered species *C. scouleri* and *C. caseana*, and in the subarctic region *C. arctica*. The latter is the only tuberous species found in North America, a contrast to the situation in Europe, Siberia, and West Asia, where tuberous species dominate.

The mountains of West China (notably Central Sichuan) are home to the most spectacular species, a handful of which are starting to become common in cultivation. Here belong, for example, the now well-known *Corydalis flexuosa* along with its relatives, such as *C. omeiana* and *C. pseudobarbisepala*. To see these species together with *Primula*, *Gentiana*, *Meconopsis*, and *Saussurea* in their native screes, cliffs, or forests is a breathtaking experience. Consequently, those natural gardens are becoming more and more popular as destinations for eco-tourism, something which is greatly facilitated by the rapid increase of new roads in areas that were previously difficult to access. The occasional tourist might even stumble on an undescribed species in this mountainous country, as has happened in the past. That more than 150 species have been described only since 1980 gives witness to the potential of new discoveries.

Corydalis in Gardens

Unlike the other genera in Fumariaceae, the genus *Corydalis* is so diverse it is impossible to capture its horticultural profile in a few sentences. The tuberous species that adorn our spring have radically different aspects, uses, and demands than do, for example, the later flowering, non-tuberous, recent introductions from China. Some gardeners may be surprised to learn that, while most cultivated corydalis are tuberous (at least up till the present day), in the wild these species comprise less than one fourth of the total number. Particular cultivation requirements are given in this chapter in each species account, while more general information pertaining to cultivation can be found in chapter one.

Arrangement of the Species

The *Corydalis* treatment that follows is divided into two parts: first treated are the tuberous species, followed by the non-tuberous species. The tuberous species are themselves divided into three groups: section *Corydalis* (*solida* group), section *Leonticoides*, and all the other tuberous sections. Within each of these three groups the most popular or most interesting species are described and discussed in full, while less horticulturally important species and hybrids are briefly referred to under the most similar "main" species. The non-tuberous species are treated under two subheadings: yellow- and cream-flowered plants are treated first, and are followed by white-, blue-, and purple-flowered species The arrangement of the species throughout is taxonomic because this approach allows easy comparison of species by placing related and therefore similar species close to each other.

1. Bleeding heart, *Lamprocapnos spectabilis*, showing bisymmetric flowers. Photo by Henrik Zetterlund.

3. *Hypecoum imberbe* has floral characteristics intermediate between Fumariaceae and Papaveraceae. Photo by Magnus Lidén.

2. *Corydalis maracandica*, showing zygomorphic flowers. Photo by Magnus Lidén.

4. While most members of the bleeding heart family have seedlings with two seed leaves (left) as do most other dicotyledons, some of the geophytic species have lost one of their seed leaves (right), and in this way resemble the distantly related monocotyledons. Photo by Mark C. Tebbitt.

5. *Platycapnos spicata* at Cambridge University Botanic Garden. Photo by Mark C. Tebbitt.

6. Mei Li Snow Mountain, Sichuan Province, China, showing limestone scree habitat, home to numerous *Corydalis* species. Photo by Magnus Lidén.

7. Limestone cliff habitat of *Sarcocapnos pulcherrima* in southern Spain. Photo by Mats Hagberg.

8. Ant dispersing a corydalis seed. Photo by Magnus Lidén.

9. *Adlumia fungosa*, Allegheny vine, an uncommon native of eastern North America. Photo by Mark C. Tebbitt.

10. *Adlumia asiatica*, a rarely cultivated vine from eastern Asia. Photo by Magnus Lidén.

11. Moist rocky woodland on lime-rich soil, New York, typical habitat of *Adlumia fungosa* (lower right). Photo by Mark C. Tebbitt.

12. *Dactylicapnos torulosa*, an annual vine. Photo by Magnus Lidén.

13. Flowers and climbing tendrils of *Dactylicapnos macrocapnos*. Photo by Mark C. Tebbitt.

14. *Dactylicapnos macrocapnos*, a perennial vine, growing interspersed with purple-flowered clematis, at Old Vicarage Garden, Norfolk, England. Photo by Mark C. Tebbitt.

15. Sub-alpine scree habitat of *Dicentra pauciflora* and *D. uniflora* (lower left) and type location of *D. nevadensis* on decaying granite outcrops (center) at Sequoia National Park, California. Photo by Mark C. Tebbitt.

16. *Dicentra canadensis*, squirrel corn, a spring ephemeral found locally in woods in eastern North America. Photo by Magnus Lidén.

17. Comparison of the rootstocks of *Dicentra canadensis* (left) and *D. cucullaria* (right). Photo by Mark C. Tebbitt.

18. *Dicentra cucullaria* is often called Dutchman's breeches on account of its pantaloon-like flowers. Photo by Magnus Lidén.

19. *Dicentra cucullaria* 'Pink Punk', a pink selection of the usually white-flowered species. Photo by Henrik Zetterlund.

21. Comparison of the flowers of *Dicentra formosa* (right) and *D. eximia* (left). Photo by Mark C. Tebbitt.

20. *Dicentra eximia* naturalized in Brooklyn Botanic Garden's native flora garden. Photo by Mark C. Tebbitt.

23. *Dicentra formosa* subsp. *oregana* at Gothenburg Botanic Garden. Photo by Magnus Lidén.

22. Moist rocky woodland habitat of *Dicentra formosa* subsp. *formosa*, at Battle Creek Meadows, Tehama County, California. Photo by Mark C. Tebbitt.

24. *Dicentra* 'King of Hearts' is a stunning and often-grown hybrid cultivar. Photo by Mark C. Tebbitt.

25. *Dicentra nevadensis* is a rarely cultivated high-altitude relative of the more widespread *D. formosa*; here photographed in Sequoia National Park. Photo by Aaron Schusteff.

26. *Dicentra pauciflora*, few-flowered dicentra, inhabits gravelly soils in sub-alpine woodland in the mountains of northern and central California. Photo by Magnus Lidén.

27. Comparison of the rootstocks of *Dicentra pauciflora* (left) and *D. uniflora* (right). Photo by Henrik Zetterlund.

28. The East Asian *Dicentra peregrina* is the only member of its genus found outside of North America. While one of the most beautiful members of the family, this species is often considered a challenge to grow. Photo by Henrik Zetterlund.

29. *Dicentra uniflora* flowering next to a melting snow bank in mid June, at Lassen Volcanic National Park, California. Photo by Mark C. Tebbitt.

30. Comparison of the flowers of *Ehrendorferia ochroleuca* (left) and *E. chrysantha* (right). Photo by Mark C. Tebbitt.

31. *Ehrendorferia chrysantha*, golden eardrops, on a gravelly roadside bank, in Los Padres National Forest, California. Photo by Mark C. Tebbitt.

32. The rare *Ehrendorferia ochroleuca*, white ear-drops, in the Santa Ynes Mountains, California, showing typical post-burn habitat. Photo by Mark C. Tebbitt.

33. *Ichtyoselmis macrantha*, large-flowered dicentra, from northern Myanmar (Burma) and western China has the largest flowers found in the family. Photo by Henrik Zetterlund.

34. *Lamprocapnos spectabilis* 'Alba', a white-flowered cultivar of the more usually pink-flowered bleeding heart. Photo by Mark C. Tebbitt.

35. *Lamprocapnos spectabilis* 'Gold Heart' (left) and the typical green-leaved and pink-flowered variant of the species (right). Photo by Mark C. Tebbitt.

36. *Corydalis vittae* grows locally in limestone meadows in the western Caucasus Mountains. Photo by Henrik Zetterlund.

37. *Corydalis caucasica* subsp. *caucasica* is one of the most garden-worthy members of its genus. Photo by Henrik Zetterlund.

38. *Corydalis malkensis* growing in Gothenburg Botanic Garden's rock garden. Photo by Henrik Zetterlund.

39. The elegant forest species *Corydalis angustifolia* has been grown since the early 1800s but has never been common in cultivation. Photo by Henrik Zetterlund.

40. *Corydalis wendelboi* subsp. *wendelboi* is very common in southwestern Turkey and readily grown in the open garden. Photo by Magnus Lidén.

41. A rare plant in the wild, *Corydalis zetterlundii* is still only known from its type locality. Photo by Henrik Zetterlund.

42. *Corydalis integra* has a beautiful blue cast to its leaves and is an exquisite plant for the rock garden. Photo by Henrik Zetterlund.

43. *Corydalis bracteata* is similar in vegetative characters to the more commonly grown *C. solida* subsp. *solida* but is more robust than that plant, with broader yellow or yellowish lemon-scented flowers. Photo by Henrik Zetterlund.

45. *Corydalis solida* subsp. *incisa* has beautifully incised leaves. Photo by Henrik Zetterlund.

44. *Corydalis bracteata* growing in the rock garden at Gothenburg Botanic Garden. Photo by Henrik Zetterlund.

46. A red variant of *Corydalis solida* growing with crocus. Photo by Henrik Zetterlund.

47. *Corydalis gotlandica*, a Swedish native from the island of Gotland, was described as recently as 1991. Photo by Mark C. Tebbitt.

48. *Corydalis magadanica* has an extremely specialized habitat preference within the vast sphagnum moorlands of eastern Siberia and is consequently found only in a few suitable places near Magadan. Surprisingly, it is not unduly challenging to cultivate. Photo by Henrik Zetterlund.

49. The golden corydalis, *Corydalis gorinensis*, is known only from one granite cliff-face by the Gorin River in eastern Siberia. Photo by Magnus Lidén.

50. In 2000 *Corydalis triternata* received the Award of Garden Merit from the Royal Horticultural Society in recognition of its value as an undemanding garden plant. Photo by Henrik Zetterlund.

51. *Corydalis fumariifolia* subsp. *fumariifolia* is a stunning species that is becoming increasingly popular in gardens. Photo by Henrik Zetterlund.

52. *Corydalis fumariifolia* subsp. *azurea* differs from the typical subspecies by its more triangular flower spurs and usually broader leaflets. Photo by Henrik Zetterlund.

53. In regions with cool climates, *Corydalis lineariloba* is a trouble-free plant for the alpine house or peat wall. Photo by Mark C. Tebbitt.

54. *Corydalis lineariloba* showing tuberous habit of this Japanese species. Photo by Magnus Lidén.

55. Two distinct forms of *Corydalis papilligera* are cultivated, the large-flowered hexaploid shown here, and a much smaller-flowered tetraploid race. Photo by Henrik Zetterlund.

56. *Corydalis repens* is a recent introduction noted for its beautifully spotted leaves. Photo by Magnus Lidén.

57. All cultivated material of the beautiful *Corydalis turtschaninovii* subsp. *turtschaninovii* appears to have originated from Latvian nurseryman Jānis Rukšāns, who received it from a Russian friend in the 1980s. Photo by Magnus Lidén.

59. The stunningly beautiful white form of *Corydalis ornata*. Photo by Henrik Zetterlund.

58. The blue form of *Corydalis ornata* was collected from the same location in southeastern Russia as the white form of the species. Photo by Mark C. Tebbitt.

60. The Central Asian *Corydalis glaucescens* has been introduced into gardens on several occasions. Photo by Henrik Zetterlund.

61. The front third of the otherwise white flowers of *Corydalis nudicaulis* are a beautiful shade of coffee-brown. Photo by Henrik Zetterlund.

62. *Corydalis ruksansii* was first introduced via the famous Latvian bulb nursery of Jānis Rukšāns. Photo by Henrik Zetterlund.

63. *Corydalis schanginii* subsp. *schanginii* grows in rather arid areas of the Altai and Tien Mountains of Central Asia. Photo by Henrik Zetterlund.

64. *Corydalis schanginii* subsp. *ainae* is a better garden plant than subsp. *schanginii*, though less robust in habit. Photo by Henrik Zetterlund.

65. *Corydalis seisumsiana* was first introduced by Arnis Seisums of Salaspils Botanic Garden, Latvia, from Armenia's Zangezur mountain range. Photo by Henrik Zetterlund.

66. Unlike all other species of *Corydalis* the flowers of *C. popovii* develop from the top of the inflorescence downward. Photo by Magnus Lidén.

67. In 2005 *Corydalis sewerzowii* received both an Award of Merit and a Certificate of Cultural Commendation for its value as a show plant. Photo by Henrik Zetterlund.

68. The best forms of *Corydalis nariniana* have a pure white, blackish-purple-keeled front, contrasting a rich deep carmine spur. Photo by Henrik Zetterlund.

69. *Corydalis oppositifolia*, with nectaries and accumulated nectar visible inside the spurs. Photo by Henrik Zetterlund.

70. With its gray-mottled, succulent, hepatica-like leaves, *Corydalis hemidicentra* is difficult to spot in the scree, until it produces its stunning sky-blue flowers. Photo by Magnus Lidén.

71. *Corydalis benecincta*, while difficult and rarely cultivated, is a common plant in high alpine screes in northwestern Yunnan–southwestern Sichuan. Photo by Henrik Zetterlund.

72. A beautiful stand of *Corydalis buschii* in the New England garden of Carol Fyler. Photo by Mark C. Tebbitt.

73. *Corydalis cava* grows wild in a region stretching from Portugal to northern Iran. Shown here is the yellow-flowered tetraploid form from the Crimea that is sometimes given the name *C. marschalliana*. Photo by Henrik Zetterlund.

74. Cliff-dwelling *Corydalis rupestris* is a native of arid regions of Iran, Baluchistan, and Afghanistan. The species is best grown in an alpine house, where, in suitable conditions, it will seed around in the plunge material. Photo by Mark C. Tebbitt.

75. *Corydalis wilsonii* on a tufa wall, needs the protection of an alpine house in colder climates. Photo by Magnus Lidén.

76. *Corydalis cheilanthifolia* showing the evergreen fernlike leaves of this heat-tolerant species. Photo by Mark C. Tebbitt.

77. *Corydalis cheilanthifolia*, growing in the Ernest Wilson Memorial Garden, Chipping Campden, England. Wilson introduced the species from China in the early 1900s. Photo by Mark C. Tebbitt.

78. Habitat of the winter annual *Corydalis aurea*, Professor Valley, Utah. Photo by Mark C. Tebbitt.

79. *Corydalis nobilis*. Photo by Magnus Lidén.

80. *Corydalis nobilis*, growing at Hammarby Estate, north of Stockholm, Sweden, the home of Carl Linnaeus.
Photo by Mark C. Tebbitt.

81. *Corydalis caseana* subsp. *brachycarpa* is a rarity in nature, found only in the Wasatch Mountains near Salt Lake City, Utah. Photo by Mark C. Tebbitt.

82. *Corydalis scouleri*, a widespread native of North America's Pacific Northwest, is a wonderful species for a cool, damp, sheltered position in the woodland garden. Photo by Henrik Zetterlund.

83. *Corydalis sheareri* is proving to be an amenable garden plant, even in areas with hot, humid summers, and has been sold by the Chen Yi nursery under many different names. Photo by Magnus Lidén.

84. The long-pointed petals easily distinguish *Corydalis mucronata*. Photo by Magnus Lidén.

85. First introduced to the United States in 1986 and to the United Kingdom in 1889, *Corydalis flexuosa* is now universally the most commonly grown of all blue-flowered *Corydalis*. Photo by Henrik Zetterlund.

86. *Corydalis flexuosa* in the peat beds at the Royal Botanic Garden Edinburgh, Scotland. Photo by Mark C. Tebbitt.

87. *Corydalis* 'Blue Heron' sold by Heronswood nursery, unlike typical *C. flexuosa*, grows in the wild on wet cliffs and has a more branched habit. Photo by Magnus Lidén.

88. *Corydalis* 'Craigton Blue', a hybrid between *C. omeieana* and *C. flexuosa*, is a better garden plant than either of its parents. Photo by Magnus Lidén.

89. *Corydalis* 'Kingfisher' is a stunning hybrid between *C. cashmeriana* and *C. flexuosa* from the Aberconwy Nursery in North Wales. Photo by Mark C. Tebbitt.

90. *Corydalis flexuosa* 'Purple Leaf'. Photo by Dan Heims, Terra Nova Nurseries.

91. *Corydalis flexuosa* 'China Blue'. Photo by Dan Heims, Terra Nova Nurseries.

92. *Corydalis flexuosa* 'Golden Panda'. Photo by Dan Heims, Terra Nova Nurseries.

93. In gardens *Corydalis omeieana* is usually grown under the name *C. elata* and is easier to cultivate in areas with hot humid summers than *C. flexuosa*. Photo by Henrik Zetterlund.

94. The true *Corydalis elata* is a recent introduction via Chen Yi nursery. Photo by Magnus Lidén.

95. *Corydalis pseudobarbisepala* is grown in many gardens from Chinese imports misidentified as *C. stenantha*. Photo by Magnus Lidén.

97. Another recent introduction from Chen Yi Nursery, *Corydalis mairei* is recognized by its narrow flowers with pointed tips. Photo by Magnus Lidén.

96. Described as recently as 2006, *Corydalis panda* is a stunning relative of *C. elata*. Photo by Magnus Lidén.

98. Ever since *Corydalis cashmeriana* was introduced in the 1930s it has held a position among the most popular and written-about alpine plants. Photo by Henrik Zetterlund.

99. The larger-flowered form of *Corydalis cashmeriana* named 'Kailash', after the holy mountain on which it was collected. Photo by Henrik Zetterlund.

100. *Corydalis pachycentra*, like its close relative *C. cashmeriana*, can sometimes be a challenge to grow; here photographed at Balang Shan, Sichuan. Photo by Magnus Lidén.

102. The flowers of biennial *Corydalis smithiana* have a mysterious musky scent. Photo by Henrik Zetterlund.

101. *Corydalis* 'Blackberry Wine'. Photo by Dan Heims, Terra Nova Nurseries.

103. Like most annual or biennial *Corydalis* species, *C. incisa* is self-fertile, so only a single plant is needed to set seed. Photo by Henrik Zetterlund.

105. *Capnoides sempervirens*, rock-harlequin, is a readily grown annual or biennial suitable for naturalizing in less formal gardens. Photo by Mark C. Tebbitt.

104. This Sichuan biennial, *Corydalis linstowiana*, is now quite common in cultivation. Photo by Magnus Lidén.

106. The widespread weed *Fumaria officinalis* was once used medicinally, as is conveyed in its specific name *officinalis*, which in Latin means "used in medicine." Photo by Magnus Lidén.

107. *Pseudofumaria lutea* will often naturalize on old walls. Here it is growing in brick mortar on a bridge at Helmingham Hall, Suffolk, England. Photo by Mark C. Tebbitt.

108. *Pseudofumaria alba* growing on a stone wall at the Royal Horticultural Society's rock garden at Wisley, England. Photo by Mark C. Tebbitt.

109. *Rupicapnos africana*, being a native of southern Spain and North Africa, in colder climates is best grown in an alpine house. Photo by Magnus Lidén.

110. *Sarcocapnos enneaphylla*, showing fruit-stalk elongating and burying seed in a shady crevice. Photo by Magnus Lidén.

111. *Sarcocapnos enneaphylla* growing on an old wall in Almería, Spain. Photo by Magnus Lidén.

112. *Sarcocapnos pulcherrima* is the largest-flowered member of its genus. Photo by Magnus Lidén.

The Tuberous *Corydalis*

Tuberous species like *Corydalis solida* and *C. cava* have a long history in cultivation, dating back to the herb gardens of European monasteries. Lidén and Zetterlund (1997) described these species in detail. However, since that work is now out of print, we will reproduce and update some of the information relevant to the best and most popular tuberous species now in cultivation.

The tuberous species fall into different categories, both taxonomically and ecologically. Most of them are spring-flowering ephemeral herbs of lower altitudes, adapted—like most geophytes—to a life in summer-dry areas, such as Central Asia, the Middle East, and the East Mediterranean. Those species that occur in wetter climates favor deciduous forests, a habitat that is similarly seasonal in that it is open and brightly lit during the early spring when the corydalis flower, but becomes much drier and darker later on when the tree canopy closes, a time when the corydalis and other spring ephemerals become dormant underground.

One group of tuberous species, section *Dactylotuber*, however, occupies higher altitudes and has a more extended vegetative period. Nevertheless, since the rhizomes of members of this section, such as *Corydalis hemidicentra* and *C. arctica*, have a distinctly tuberlike appearance, they are included here under the tuberous species.

With the recent influx of new species from China, the division into tuberous and non-tuberous species has become harder to uphold. *Corydalis sheareri*, *C. incisa*, and *C. linstowiana* are tuberous or semi-tuberous species that bear little resemblance to the "classic" tuberous sections and are here treated in the non-tuberous part.

Note that in the descriptions of tuberous species, length of stem disregards the thin tapering subterranean stem-base, which may be considerable.

Key to Tuberous Sections of *Corydalis*

1a. Leaves twice pinnately divided, leaflets crenate-toothed; tubers several, stalked, oblong . . . .*C. sheareri*

1b. Leaves 1–3 times ternately divided; tuber not both oblong and stalked 2

2a. Biennial with a tuber shaped like a radish or a carrot, crowned by a leaf rosette . . . .*C. incisa* and *C. linstowiana*

2b. Perennial with a deeply situated tuber and without a leaf rosette 3

3a. Stigma transversely oblong with 4 papillae; seeds keeled, papillose . . . . section *Duplotuber*

3b. Stigma squarish, circular, or obtriangular; seeds neither keeled nor papillose 4

4a. Leaves 2, opposite, usually sessile . . . . .section *Leonticoides*

4b. Leaves not opposite, usually clearly stalked. 5

5a. Stem without scale-leaves (that is, leaves reduced to a bladeless rounded sheathing base) . . . . .section *Radix-cava*

5b. Stem with at least one conspicuous scale-leaf below the ordinary leaves 6

6a. Tuber rounded; stem usually with one scale-leaf and two stem leaves . . . . section *Corydalis*

6b. Tuber often divided below; stem usually with 2–3 scale-leaves and 2–4 stem leaves . . . . section *Dactylotuber*

Section *Corydalis*

Corydalis section *Corydalis* is the largest of the tuberous groups with at least 53 species distributed from Western Europe (*C. solida* and *C. intermedia*) throughout temperate Asia to eastern Siberia (*C. gorodkovii* and *C. ambigua*), Japan and East Central China (*C. kiaotschouensis*), and with an isolated outlier in northern Algeria (*C. densiflora*). The section is immediately recognized by the rounded, rather small tuber and the conspicuous membranous rounded scale that is situated far down the stem, usually at or shortly above the soil surface. With few exceptions the flowering stems carry two alternate leaves.

In the comprehensive list following of the members of this section, species with main entries in the text are given in bold letters. Those with an asterisk (*) are briefly referred to under a similar species.

*alexeenkoana** 83	**gotlandica** 91	*maculata*	**solida** 89
*ambigua** 94	*gracilis** 88	**magadanica** 92	*tarkiensis*
angustifolia 85	*grandicalyx*	**malkensis** 84	*tauricola** 86
bracteata 87	*hallaisanensis*	**nudicaulis** 100	*thasia** 91
caucasica 83	*haussknechtii*	*ohii*	*triternata** 94
caudata	**henrikii** 93	*ornata** 98	**turtschaninovii** 98
*densiflora** 90	*humilis*	*orthoceras*	*ussuriensis*
filistipes	*humosa*	*paczoskii** 85	**vittae** 83
*fukuharae** 96	**integra** 87	*papilligera** 97	*watanabei** 97
fumariifolia 94	*intermedia** 91	*paschei** 86	**wendelboi** 85
*gamosepala** 99	*kiaotschouensis*	*pumila** 90	*yanhusuo** 99
glaucescens 99	*kusnetzovii** 83	**repens** 97	**zetterlundii** 86
*gorinensis** 93	**lineariloba** 96	**ruksansii** 101	
*gorodkovii** 93	*linjiangensis*	**schanginii** 102	

Corydalis vittae Kolakovsky   PLATE 36

Stem suberect, 10–15 cm tall. *Leaves* long-stalked, 3 times ternately divided; *leaf-lets* small, stalked, more or less deeply cleft into obovate lobes. *Racemes* dense, clearly stalked, 6- to 16-flowered; *bracts* entire; *pedicels* 10–15 mm long, not curved backward in fruit. *Flowers* white, or often with a purplish tinge; *outer petals* with broad obtuse limb, often with the margins slightly undulating; *spur* of upper petal curved upward, 13–15 mm long; *inner petals* 10–12 mm long. *Capsule* fusiform, with 5–10 seeds. *2n* = 16. Self-incompatible.

This species was described from Mount Gagra in the Republic of Georgia, where it was found growing on subalpine meadows on limestone at about 2200 m (7200 ft). Plants from the type locality are in cultivation, but the closely related and more widespread *Corydalis kusnetzovii* Khokhrjakov also often appears under the name *C. vittae*.

Corydalis kusnetzovii is a more robust plant. The spur of the upper petal is less ascending or even down-curved. The lower petal usually has a broad saccate claw, and the margins of the limb are not thin and undulate but rather firm and slightly upturned. This species grows in woods in the western part of the main Caucasus range at an altitude of 1000 to 2000 m (3300 to 6560 ft) and is very variable in size and flower color. The corolla can be white to pale yellow and is often suffused with a dirty purple.

Corydalis alexeenkoana N. Busch is a third related species, sharing with the other two a broad stigma and a wrinkled inner fruit epidermis, petty things to which botanists pay attention. The divided bracts make it easy to distinguish from its cousins. To our knowledge it is invariably pale yellow. It hails from Imeretia in southern Armenia at altitudes from 1500 to 2000 m (4920 to 6560 ft).

All three species are easy to grow. Since they have been in circulation for a couple of decades and these plants cross quite freely, plants offered on the market are often of hybrid origin.

Corydalis caucasica A. P. de Candolle   PLATE 37

Stem suberect, 10–20 cm tall. *Leaves* 2 in the lower part of the stem, triangular, almost 2 times ternately divided; *leaflets* entire or cleft into 2–3 obovate lobes. *Inflorescences* loose, 2- to 6-flowered; *bracts* ovate, entire; *pedicels* 4–10 mm long, equaling bracts. *Flowers* lilac, very rarely white; *outer petals* with broad limbs; *spur* 12–16 mm long, hiding a slender long-acuminate nectary about half as long; *inner petals* pale, 9–10 mm long. *Capsule* oblong, 20–25 × 3–4 mm, with 8–15 seeds. *2n* = 16. Self-compatible.

Corydalis caucasica is available from commercial nurseries and is readily grown in a pot as well as in the open garden. It is in the open garden though that this species grows best and where it will even, in a semi-shaded position with an open friable soil, seed around profusely. In spite of being self-compatible, and thus having somewhat shorter-lasting flowers than most related species, it is a most garden-worthy plant with its broad-faced lilac flowers—a decided favorite. Subspecies *caucasica* is a native of the Caucasus Mountains where it grows in open forests and thickets at an altitude of 1000 to 2300 m (3300 to 7550 ft). There is also a western subspecies, *abantensis* Lidén in North West Anatolia, which is very occasionally cultivated, but which lacks the elegance and ease of propagation of subsp. *caucasica*.

Corydalis malkensis Galushko   PLATE 38

Stems 7–20 cm tall, erect, with 1 or 2 branches from the scale-leaf. *Leaves* 1 or 2 times ternately divided; *leaflets* deeply cleft into obovate lobes that may again be shallowly lobed at apex. *Racemes* rather dense, distinctly stalked, about 10-flowered; *bracts* entire, ovate to obovate; *pedicels* 6–10 mm long, equaling bracts. *Flowers* with a yellowish green tint in bud, becoming pure white; *outer petals* very broad, spur of upper petal strongly curved upward, 14–17 mm long; *inner petals* 11–12 mm long. *Capsule* broadly lanceolate, 18–20 × 4–5 mm, with 5–9 seeds. *2n* = 32.

This graceful species has often been considered a white-flowered variant of its close relative *Corydalis caucasica* but differs quite substantially in its denser and clearly stalked raceme, its diminutive sepals, its very broad flowers with upwardly curved spur, and in having twice the number of chromosomes. It grows in cool, damp woods in the upper valleys of the Malka and Kuban Rivers of the North Caucasus. With its pure white broad-lipped flowers it is a splendid, easy-to-grow garden plant that may carpet the ground in a lightly shaded situation and may even be naturalized in grass. It is self-compatible and increases in the garden mainly by seed. *Corydalis malkensis* has been cultivated since at least the 1960s and in 1993 was given the Award of Garden Merit by the Royal Horticultural Society in recognition of it being an outstanding garden plant.

Corydalis angustifolia (Marschall von Bieberstein) A. P. de Candolle   PLATE 39

Stems slender, 8–16 cm tall. *Leaves* green, 2 or 3 times ternately divided; *leaflets* deeply divided into narrow segments. *Racemes* short, 2- to 10-flowered (up to 23-flowered in cultivation), rather one-sided (secund); *bracts* divided into 3–5 linear lobes, or the uppermost bracts entire; *pedicels* 5–10 mm long, equaling bracts, somewhat longer in fruit. *Flowers* usually white, or with a lilac suffusion, or rarely cream, rather narrow; *spur* 9–12 mm long; *inner petals* 12–14 mm long. *Capsule* linear, 23–33 mm long, pendent on slender pedicels, with 10–20 seeds. $2n = 16$. Self-compatible and regularly selfing.

A common species in half-open mountain meadows and scrub from the Elburz Mountains in northern Iran to Caucasus and North East Anatolia, where it may be seen growing with *Anemone blanda, Primula veris*, and *Puschkinia scilloides*. The flowering period is short, as the species is a regular selfer and seed is produced in profusion. The species is suitable for naturalizing in the woodland garden and has even managed to escape to semi-natural habitats on at least one occasion.

The combination of short spur and long inner petals makes *Corydalis angustifolia* an easily recognizable species. It was in cultivation in Europe by the early 1800s, but has never become very common since it is not particularly showy. Today it is only occasionally offered by commercial nurseries.

Corydalis paczoskii N. Busch is a related species from the Crimea, with pink flowers tipped with dark reddish purple, and comparatively longer spurs. Like *C. angustifolia*, it is an easy-to-grow, regular selfer, but it is of little garden merit.

Corydalis wendelboi Lidén   PLATE 40

Stems erect, (5–)10–15(–20) cm tall, usually with a couple of late-developing branches from the scale-leaf axil. *Leaves* 2–4 times ternately divided; *leaflets* cut into narrow obtuse segments. *Racemes* short-stalked, 10- to 25-flowered; *bracts* digitately divided, often with the lobes again divided or toothed; *pedicels* only 3–7 mm long. *Flowers* rather small and narrow, obtuse at apex; *petals* white, maroon, red, pink, or purple; *spur* 9–12 mm long; *inner petals* 9–10 mm long. *Capsule* lanceolate, 10–24 × 3–5 mm, with 4–11 seeds. $2n = 16$. Self-incompatible.

The species is named in honor of the eminent botanist Per Wendelbo, a past director of the Gothenburg Botanic Garden and of Teheran Botanic Garden, who specialized in bulbous and tuberous plants of the Eastern Mediterranean and the Middle

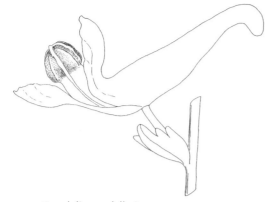

Corydalis wendelboi. Drawing by Adèle Rossetti Morosini.

East, and produced a revision of *Corydalis* for *Flora Iranica*. *Corydalis wendelboi* is common in the mountains throughout Western Anatolia at altitudes from 700 to 2000 m (2300 to 6560 ft). In the north it is represented by subsp. *congesta* Lidén, characterized by broad flowers, very dense racemes, and small capsules. It is from this northern subspecies that the best forms in cultivation have been selected, notably *C. wendelboi* 'Abant Wine', with deep wine-purple flowers.

The species has been introduced on numerous occasions; at one time there were plants in cultivation at Gothenburg Botanic Garden from more than 30 different localities. The first introductions were generally called *Corydalis solida* or *C. densiflora*, even though these two species do not occur in Anatolia.

Toward southeastern Anatolia *Corydalis wendelboi* is replaced by the closely related *C. tauricola* (Cullen & P. H. Davis) Lidén, which differs in having larger flowers, longer pedicels, and longer and narrower capsules. *Corydalis paschei* Lidén is another related, though very distinct, species only known from two small colonies close to Antalya in South West Anatolia. It has a looser and more ascending habit than *C. wendelboi* and is readily distinguished by the clearly separated, much broader leaf lobes and the much broader flowers set on long pedicels subtended by rather small rounded bracts. *Corydalis wendelboi*, as well as its two close relatives, is suitable for growing in the rock garden in addition to the alpine house.

Corydalis zetterlundii Lidén   PLATE 41

Stems ascending, 8–15 cm tall (to 25 cm tall in cultivation). *Leaves* 2, closely set toward the base of the stem, short-stalked and rather small, 2 times ternately divided; *leaflets* deeply divided into narrow lobes. *Racemes* long, short-stalked, 10- to 12-flowered (to 25-flowered in cultivation), rising high above the leaves; *bracts* with 1–3 long teeth or narrow laciniate on each side; *pedicels* shorter than bracts, 3–6 mm long (up to 10 mm long in cultivation), lengthening and becoming reflexed in fruit. *Flowers* white or usually variegated with muddy purple; *outer petals* with narrow eroded-toothed limbs; *spur* 11–14 mm long; *inner petals* 10–11 mm long. *Capsule* narrowly lanceolate, 20–25 × 3 mm, with 6–10 seeds. $2n = 16$. Self-incompatible.

This species, which has no close relatives, was discovered as late as 1988, and is still only known from the type locality, a wooded mountain slope in Macedonia. *Corydalis zetterlundii* has been commercially available since 1992. The flowers are nicely presented well above the foliage and with their pleasant spicy fragrance make this a choice plant for the rock garden or alpine house.

Corydalis integra Barbey & Forsyth-Major   PLATE 42

Stem suberect, rather robust, 10–20 cm tall (to 35 cm tall in cultivation) with 1–3 branches from the scale-leaf. *Leaves* very glaucous, 2 times ternately divided; *leaflets* more or less divided into obovate to oblong segments. *Racemes* rather loose, 5- to 20-flowered; *bracts* broadly elliptic, entire or the lower ones often divided into 2–5 segments. *Flowers* pale pink to almost white, with the inner petals tipped with blackish purple; *spur* 12–13 mm long; *inner petals* 9–12 mm long. *Capsule* linear to narrowly lanceolate, angular in cross section, 15–20(–27) × 2–3 mm, with 5–8(–14) seeds. *2n* = 16. Self-incompatible.

This is a very variable species with several scattered occurrences on mountains in the Aegean region. For example, it grows in Greece on Mount Athos, the center of Eastern Christian Orthodox Monasticism and the only region of Europe where women (and the female sex of other mammals) are forbidden. It may also be found on Mount Cholomon, on the higher Aegean islands of Naxos, Sámos, and Chios, and on Kaz Dagh in northwestern Anatolia. It is a splendid, readily grown rock garden plant, which, being from the mountains, is frost-hardy. It is currently offered for sale by only a few nurseries.

Corydalis bracteata (Willdenow) Persoon   PLATES 43, 44

Stems erect, 15–30 cm tall (to 40 cm tall in cultivation), unbranched or usually with a single late developing branch from the scale-leaf. *Leaves* thin, 1–3 times ternately divided; *leaflets* divided into narrowly obovate lobes; *petioles* long. *Racemes* 5- to 13- (to 20-) flowered; *bracts* cleft into 4–7 narrow lobes; *pedicels* 10–15 mm long, becoming patent to slightly arcuate in fruit. *Flowers* large, broadly winged, cream to yellow, rarely white; *spur* of upper petal 12–15 mm long; *lower petal* with a broad saccate claw abruptly dilated into an emarginate limb 9–15 mm broad; *inner petals* 11–14 mm long. *Capsule* elliptic, 15–18 × 5 mm, with a very short style and 5–10 seeds. *2n* = 16. Self-incompatible.

Corydalis bracteata. Drawing by Adèle Rossetti Morosini.

Corydalis bracteata is similar in appearance to the ubiquitous *C. solida*, but is more robust and has much broader, lemon-scented flowers. However, it is the difference in flower color that most readily distinguishes the two species: *C. bracteata* has yellow flowers, while those of *C. solida* are purple, red, or white.

Corydalis bracteata has been in cultivation since 1823, but has never been very common. Being a plant of continental climate—it is native to Central Siberia in the upper reaches of the Ob River—the species is not always cooperative in the mild unreliable winters of Western Europe, where it tends to come up too early, before the frosts are past. *Corydalis bracteata* will occasionally establish self-perpetuating colonies outside the flowerbed and merits as one of the best tuberous species. It has long been naturalized in the lawns of the botanic gardens of St. Petersburg and Moscow, and recently in a couple of places in Stockholm. In Gothenburg it has been planted in the north face of a peat wall and in this relatively cool niche is slower to emerge in the spring and hence less likely to be damaged by frost. Consequently, the plants have thrived and now seed around into large mats.

A few named cultivars and hybrids of *Corydalis bracteata* are commercially available. *Corydalis bracteata* 'Marina' is a very pale yellow form selected from nature and sold by Latvian nurseryman Jānis Rukšāns.

Corydalis 'Allenii' is a hybrid of garden origin, widely distributed as *C.* ×*allenii* Irwing (an invalid name since it postdates the publication of a different plant that Fedde named as *C. allenii*), with *C. bracteata* and *C. solida* as parents. This hybrid is rather like *C. bracteata* but has creamy white, pink-veined flowers. It is a vigorous grower with tubers that regularly multiply and require division every few years. However, it is completely sterile and never sets seed. Interestingly, the hybrid will, on occasion, form spontaneously when the parents meet in gardens.

The related *Corydalis gracilis* N. Busch grows in the upper Jenisei area of Sibe-

ria (to the east of *C. bracteata*'s range) together with *C. solida* subsp. *subremota*. It is
very similar to *C. bracteata* but is more delicate with fewer and often broader flowers.
The main difference, however, lies in the
tubers, since *C. gracilis* uniquely produces
an accessory tuber in the scale-leaf. The
species has similar cultural needs to *C.
bracteata* and as a consequence of producing accessory tubers is readily multiplied
vegetatively. Nevertheless, this species is,
as yet, even less common in cultivation
than *C. bracteata*.

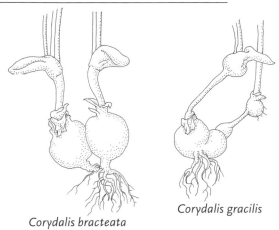

Corydalis gracilis

Corydalis bracteata

Corydalis tubers. Drawing by Adèle Rossetti
Morosini.

Corydalis solida (Linnaeus) Clairville   PLATES 45, 46

Stems erect, 6–25 cm tall, usually with a late-developing branch from the scale-
leaf. *Leaves* 1–4 times ternately divided, ultimate lobes obtuse, usually narrow, but
sometimes very broad, glaucous below. *Racemes* rather dense, somewhat elongating in fruit, 5- to 22-flowered; *bracts* usually longer than broad, apically more or
less deeply divided; *pedicels* slender, 5–15(–20) mm long, more or less curved
backward in fruit. *Flowers* purple, red, or white; *outer petals* broadly winged and
usually emarginate at apex, often with a shallowly toothed margin; *spur* straight or
apically curved backward, 8–15 mm long; *nectary* tapering, at least half as long as
the spur; *inner petals* 9–13 mm long. *Capsule* broadly lanceolate to elliptic, dorsiventrally flattened, pendent. *2n* = 16. Self-incompatible.

In the wild, *Corydalis solida* has a large distribution and is composed of distinct
geographical races. Subspecies *solida* grows in Central and Eastern Europe. It is
replaced in the Balkan Mountains by subsp. *incisa* Lidén and further east in the upper Jenisei region of Russia by subsp. *subremota* Popov ex Lidén & Zetterlund, the
latter a rather insignificant plant with small blue or purplish blue flowers. In continental Europe, subsp. *solida* is often seen naturalized in parks and gardens, and
because it has been in cultivation for hundreds of years, it can be difficult to dis-
criminate natural occurrences from ancient garden escapes.

Both subsp. *solida* and subsp. *incisa* (Plate 45) are common in cultivation, and
many cultivars have been named. Subspecies *solida* is a more lowland species (for
example, in the Baltic it is predominantly coastal), while subsp. *incisa* is a mountain

plant. These two subspecies are readily distinguished in most cases, but intermediates are found where the subspecies meet. Subspecies *incisa* is altogether a shorter and stouter plant with narrower leaf-lobes, longer and less distinctly stalked racemes, and much more divided bracts where the primary lobes are again divided or toothed. It is a good all-round garden plant, as testified by it being given an Award of Garden Merit by the Royal Horticultural Society in 2000.

Subspecies *solida* is currently the most widespread of all cultivated *Corydalis*. The most common variant in cultivation has flowers of a not particularly attractive grayish purple and can be found in parks all over Central and Northern Europe. This variant can be aggressive in the rock garden and will often overtake choicer plants, but since it goes dormant in a fortnight this is not usually a problem. Used as a naturalized plant in a larger landscape it is, however, quite charming, especially if associated with other spring flowers in light woodland. When European nurseries offer plain *C. solida*, this is the plant that you should expect to receive.

Several red-flowered selections of *Corydalis solida* have been grown over the years, most of them having at least part of their origin from Transylvania. The Van Tubergen Nurseries offered "*C. solida transilvanica rubra*" in its 1925 catalog, but their original clones may have possibly vanished from cultivation. A second introduction was made by Josef Kupeç and Milan Prasil in 1972, from which further selections were made, often grown under the incorrect names *C. transsilvanica* and *C. transsylvanica*. In 1977, in an attempt to alleviate the problem of these incorrect names, the cultivar name 'George Baker' was applied to these red-flowered plants. This, however, caused further confusion since the name was, in subsequent years, used for more than one clone, including some with pink flowers.

Corydalis solida 'Zwanenburg' is probably the best of the named red clones but is still rare in cultivation. Many new cultivars appeared in the 1990s. Some good pink and reds from various British gardeners and an outstanding selection in every possible color is offered by Jānis Rukšāns. In the late 1990s the Royal Horticultural Society grew several tuberous species and their cultivars in the Society's trial garden at Wisley. Of the *C. solida* cultivars tested, 'Dieter Schacht' (with deep pink flowers) and 'George Baker' performed best, and accordingly were given the Award of Garden Merit. Brian Mathew gives more details of this trial in a March 2001 article in *The Garden*, appropriately titled "Earning Their Spurs."

Subspecies *incisa* is a stouter plant with more divided leaves and bracts, and usually paler or even white flowers (though there are also dark purple clones in circulation). It has been in cultivation since the late 1800s, usually under the name *Corydalis densiflora*.

Corydalis pumila (Host) Reichenbach and *C. densiflora* J. Presl & C. Presl are related to *C. solida* but differ in several characters. Both are self-compatible, with smaller flowers, comparatively broader bracts, shorter pedicels that are more erect in fruit, and have a different coloration of the corolla with paler outer petals that are only darker along the outer margins of the limb. *Corydalis pumila* is known from central Sweden southward to northern Greece. It produces partly fertile hybrids with *C. solida,* especially in parks and gardens in east central Sweden. *Corydalis densiflora* grows in southern Italy, Sicily, and northern Algeria. Although similar, *C. pumila* is clearly distinct from *C. densiflora* in its much smaller size, nodding racemes, and in being a regular selfer. Both are sometimes cultivated, but more as collectors' items than as ornamentals.

A third related species, *Corydalis thasia* (Stojanov & Kitanov) Stojanov & Kitanov (syn. *C. solida* subsp. *longicarpa* Lidén), is of greater promise. The flowers are larger and broader than in *C. solida* and set in loose few-flowered racemes. *Corydalis thasia* is restricted to the high Aegean islands of Thásos and Ándros, and is not known to be in cultivation.

Corydalis gotlandica Lidén   PLATE 47

A rather stocky plant, 7–15(–20) cm tall. *Leaves* strongly glaucous, especially below, 2 times ternately divided; *leaflets* divided. *Racemes* very dense, short-stalked, slightly nodding in flower, but becoming erect in fruit, 5- to 15-flowered; *bracts* broad, entire, or the lowermost bracts usually divided; *pedicels* stout, much shorter than the bracts. *Flowers* reddish purple, almost closed, with mouth facing upward; *spur* straight, directed upward, 10–13 mm long; *outer petals* sharply emarginate with acute lateral tips; *inner petals* 9–10 mm long. *Capsule* very broad, rather abruptly tapering to a prominent style, with 3–6 seeds. $2n = 32$. Self-compatible.

Corydalis gotlandica is one of very few plants with a distribution restricted to Scandinavia. It is only known from the Baltic limestone island of Gotland, but seems to thrive there in man-made habitats such as gardens and lawns and is currently expanding its range. It has even become a weed in "the garden of the bathing friends" in the seaport of Visby.

Corydalis gotlandica is very similar to *C. intermedia* (Linnaeus) Mérat, a widespread European species, but can boast of having twice the number of chromosomes. As such, it is a tetraploid instead of a diploid like most other species in the genus. The normal way for a tetraploid species to form is by chromosome doubling of an initial hybrid plant. If this event happened in the not-too-distant past, we could also trace the parental species by means of DNA patterns. In this way we have shown that *C. gotlandica* is a chromosome-doubled derivate of a primary hybrid between *C. solida* and *C. intermedia*, with *C. solida* as the pollen parent. This may have happened as recently as a century ago and certainly less than 10,000 years ago when the ice cap retreated from Scandinavia. The primary hybrid can still be found on extremely rare occasions where the two species meet.

This kind of species formation, namely, hybridization followed by chromosome doubling (alloploidy), is a common phenomenon in plants but is very rare in animals. Our common bread wheat, *Triticum aestivum*, for example, is the result of two such events, with the intermediate stage represented by spaghetti wheat *T. durum*. Next time you eat pasta, consider that it has only 28 chromosomes in each cell, while the bun has 42.

Corydalis magadanica A. P. Khokhrjakov   PLATE 48

Stems 10–20 cm tall, much branched from the scale-leaf, usually with branches from the axils of the lower stem leaves. *Leaves* 2–4, triangular, 2 times ternately divided; *leaflets* deeply divided into narrow lobes. *Racemes* 7- to 16-flowered; *bracts* rather small, entire; *pedicels* 10–20(–30) mm long, much longer than bracts. *Flowers* with a firm texture, white, usually with a greenish-yellow suffusion in bud and often a dirty pink tint when mature; *spur* 9–12(–16) mm long; *inner petals* 10–12 mm long; *outer petals* with broad rounded entire limbs. *Capsule* narrowly oblong, square in cross section, 15–30 mm long, with 4–15 seeds. Self-incompatible.

This species is known from just a few places on the Siberian east coast. It is apparently a very rare plant in the wild, occurring only in a handful of suitable places near the port city of Magadan. However, since its distribution area is difficult to access, particularly in the late spring when *Corydalis magadanica* is in flower and the ground is no longer frozen, the distribution of the species may well be larger than we know it today.

The species was introduced into cultivation by a Baltic expedition in 1993. The area in which it grows is cold and humid, and most of the vegetation consists of sphagnum moorland with little soluble nutrients, favoring plants like *Pinus pumila*, *Rhododendron aureum*, and *Cassiope redowskii*. On the few rocky outcrops the nutrient level is slightly higher, so beautiful stands of *Betula ermanii* can gain a foothold and enrich the soil with their leaves. At the margins of these groves, plants of *C. magadanica* grow along with other beauties including *Clematis ochotensis*, *Fritillaria camschatcensis*, and *Pulsatilla magadanensis*.

As a garden plant in western Sweden, *Corydalis magadanica* has a surprisingly short dormancy for a species of section *Corydalis*, starting to root in July, and sometimes producing leaves by late autumn. It is therefore wise to repot it soon after it has died down in early summer.

Corydalis magadanica is available from specialist nurseries (though beware as some nurseries sell *C. heterocarpa* under this name). It is currently the most widely cultivated representative of a peculiar group from Siberia which comprises only three species: *C. magadanica*, *C. gorodkovii* Karavaev, and *C. gorinensis* V. M. Van (Plate 49). All three of these plants are characterized by the frequent occurrence of 2 or even 3 scale-leaves, branches from the axils of the stem leaves, small entire bracts, long pedicels, and rather firm flowers with rounded entire outer petal limbs. The species of this group are best grown in a peaty but rich humusy soil. A protective cover of peat, needles, or leaves may be advisable in regions where late winters are unpredictably interspersed with warm spells, causing the plants to emerge too early. Of the triad, *C. magadanica* is the most amenable, still it is not easy. In Northern Europe it is most successful in a cool part of the garden in a mix of equal parts of peat, grit, and leaf mold. *Corydalis gorinensis* is the most beautiful, but difficult. In Gothenburg Botanic Garden it survives best in the alpine house, where it is treated like other choice bulbs and kept "slightly moist" during dormancy.

Corydalis gorodkovii has a rather wide distribution in the mountains north of Magadan and has been distributed by Magadan collectors. We have no idea how it performs in cultivation. It is very similar to *C. magadanica* in flower, but is a shorter plant with considerably smaller leaves.

Corydalis gorinensis is a particularly desirable species with golden yellow flowers set on long reddish stalks. It was introduced by the same expedition that brought us *C. magadanica*. It occurs in a remote part of Siberia along the Gorin River, home to the cannabis-smoking Nanai tribe. The Gorin is flanked there by the taiga and the underlying bedrock only surfaces in three cliff-faces ("byk") that provide suitable habitat for *C. gorinensis*, as well as a second species, the equally beautiful *C. turtschaninovii*.

Corydalis henrikii Lidén

Stems rather weak and slender, 15–18 cm tall (or much more in greenhouse-grown plants), with 1–2 branches from the scale-leaf axil. *Leaves* long-stalked, 3 or 4 times ternately divided; *leaflets* deeply cleft into narrow lobes. *Racemes* 7- to 13-flowered (10- to 20-flowered and rather loose in cultivation); *bracts* divided into about 5 segments, which are often again divided or toothed; *pedicels* thin, 5–11(–30) mm long, slightly curved backward in fruit. *Flowers* usually pale pur-

plish pink, rarely white, tips of the inner petals dark; *outer petals* with rather narrow limbs, 4–6 mm broad; *spur* 15–22 mm long, very slender, tapering; *nectary*
very short, acute; *inner petals* about 10 mm long. *Capsule* lanceolate, 15–22 ×
4 mm, with 6–10 seeds. *2n* = 16. Self-incompatible.

The long thin flowers and finely divided leaves of *Corydalis henrikii* give it an elegant appearance, despite the species's tendency to be a bit floppy in habit when
grown under glass. The species behaves better outside in the rock garden, where it
gets brighter light and its start is delayed. It was brought into cultivation in 1990 as
a new species by the KPPZ-expedition that encountered it in a few places in Kartal
Dagh in the Gaziantep province of southern Turkey. In this region it grows on
north-facing limestone scree and on limestone outcrops in cultivated areas at
around 1000 m (3300 ft) in altitude, along with *Bongardia chrysogonum*, *Helleborus
vesicarius*, and *Iris histrio*.

    Corydalis henrikii is very closely related to *C. triternata* Zuccarini (Plate 50),
which occurs more to the south in Lebanon, Israel, Syria, and the extreme southern
tip of Turkey. Together they form a pair of vicariant species. *Corydalis triternata* differs by its less divided leaves and bracts, nodding flowers, somewhat coarser spur,
and in details of its stigma and seed. It is a good garden plant of easy disposition
that is suitable for cultivation either in the alpine house or the rock garden.

Corydalis fumariifolia C. J. Maximowicz   PLATES 51, 52

Stems simple or usually with one branch, 8–20(–28) cm tall. *Leaves* ternately divided, rather thin, green. *Racemes* 5- to 12- (to 25-) flowered; *bracts* entire to comb-
like toothed or divided in the shape of a fan; *pedicels* slender, erecto-patent, not or
only slightly curved in fruit. *Flowers* pale to bright blue or purplish blue, rarely purple or white, usually with the broad wings of the outer petals darker, and the inner
petals contrastingly white; *spur* straight, sometimes slightly curved backward at
apex, 8–11 mm long; *nectary* very shortly acuminate, up to one-third as long as the
spur; *outer petals* rather broadly winged with a clearly emarginate limb; *inner petals*
pale, 8–13 mm long. *Capsule* linear, dorsiventrally flattened with thin valves and a
more or less undulate marginal rim, often streaked with reddish brown when mature, (15–)20–25(–30) × 2.5–3 mm, with 5–15 seeds. *2n* = 16. Self-incompatible.

The elegant blue-flowered *Corydalis fumariifolia* is an extremely variable species,
here divided into two subspecies. Subspecies *azurea* Lidén is the most commonly
cultivated. It was first recognized in garden literature in 1970 as *C. ambigua* and is

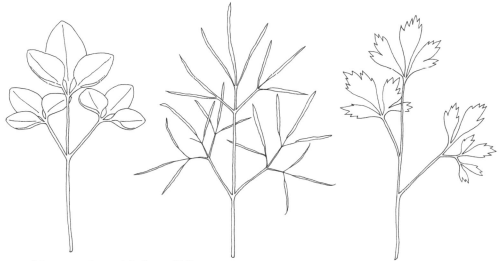

Leaf diversity of *Corydalis fumariifolia*. Drawing by Adèle Rossetti Morosini.

characterized by its broad leaf lobes being nearly always entire, by its lanceolate entire bracts, and by its rather tubby flowers with stout triangular spurs. It is native to Japan's Hokkaido Prefecture and to the Russian island of Sakhalin, where in springtime it can form dense carpets in deciduous woods together with *Dodecatheon frigidum*—a magnificent sight. If you buy this plant and want the really fabulous clear blue forms, vegetatively propagated material of known origin will spare you disappointment.

Subspecies *fumariifolia* (Plate 51) is widespread in lowland forests on both sides of the Russia-China border in East Asia. It is extremely variable in the degree of division of the leaves and bracts, as well as in the size and shape of its flowers. All variations may be found within a single population, so there is a wide scope for selection. Generally, it can be distinguished from subsp. *azurea* (Plate 52) by its narrower leaf lobes, divided bracts, and narrower flowers. Several forms have entered cultivation via the mail-order nursery of Jānis Rukšāns. The species was first collected and described as a new species by Carl Maximowicz, a past curator of St. Petersburg botanic herbarium.

Corydalis fumariifolia is perhaps best grown in a peat bed and given a cool rootrun. In the open garden it should be planted in a cool spot, hidden from the forcing rays of spring sun. It is very liable to appear above ground when there is still risk of frost. A peaty-woodsy loam is preferred. Some years it will flower before the frosts are over, and may, as a result, suffer unless protected with a cover of leaves or evergreen sprigs.

Corydalis fumariifolia is often wrongly identified in cultivation as *C. ambigua*

A. von Chamisso & D. F. L. von Schlechtendal, a similar but tetraploid species native to Kamchatka, which to our knowledge is not in cultivation. That species is distinguished by smaller and more glaucous leaves and a broadly saccate lower petal.

Corydalis fukuharae Lidén is a closely related species from Japan's Honshu Prefecture, distinguished by the longer and narrower spur, the presence of a distinct spurlet on the lower petal, and a different stigma. It is very rare in cultivation but is a beautiful species with cultural needs similar to *C. fumariifolia*.

Corydalis lineariloba Siebold & Zuccarini   PLATES 53, 54

> *Stems* strongly geniculate at the nodes, forming an angle of almost 180° with the lowermost leaf, 7–14(–20) cm tall, nearly always with an accessory tuber in the scale-leaf. *Leaves* 2–4 times ternately divided, very variable in size, degree of division, and width of leaflets. *Racemes* dense or loose, 2- to 6- (to 15-) flowered; *bracts* obovate to ovate with narrow acute teeth, sometimes more deeply divided into linear lobes, rarely entire; *pedicels* slender, (5–)10–15(–20) mm long, longer than bracts, straight in fruit. *Flowers* greenish in bud, pale to bright blue at anthesis, rarely purple, 15–25 mm long; *spur* straight, 7–14 mm long; *inner petals* 7–10 mm long, excluding the protruding dorsal wings. *Capsule* fusiform, 12–18 × 4–5 mm, with 4–10 seeds. *2n* = 32, 48, 64. Self-incompatible.

Blue-flowered *Corydalis lineariloba* is a very variable species including a number of geographical and chromosomal races. It is found on the mountains of the Japanese Prefectures of Honshu, Kyushu, and Shikoku in woods and meadows. It is a lovely garden plant, quickly spreading into a lace carpet adorned by good-sized short-scaped flowers, though its small size necessitates a raised position of the plant or kneeling adoration by the spectator. The pale to bright blue flowers, however, are reasonably large.

Corydalis lineariloba was first introduced to European gardens in the 1980s but is not widely available from commercial sources. Most forms of the species multiply rapidly by adventitious tubers formed in the scale-leaves. In this way it may produce quite large uniform patches both in the wild and in the garden.

Corydalis lineariloba 'Rokujo' is a very distinctive clone with incised, bright green foliage and large sky-blue flowers in a compact inflorescence.

The species is suitable for growing in the alpine house or in a cool position outdoors in a lightly shaded, gritty soil.

The similar *Corydalis papilligera* Ohwi (Plate 55) is also in cultivation but is uncommon. It can be readily distinguished from *C. lineariloba* by its toothed lower petal, which is strongly gibbous at the base, shorter inner petals, comparatively longer spur, broad flat fruit, seeds covered with tiny spines, and tough tuber skin. It is a particularly fine plant in its large-flowered hexaploid form. As with *C. lineariloba* the pale dorsal crests of the inner petals protrude beyond the apical junction of the petals.

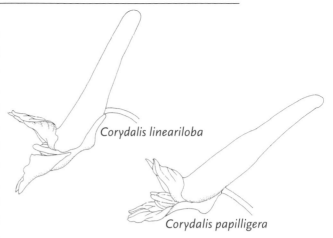

Corydalis flowers. Drawing by Adèle Rossetti Morosini.

Corydalis repens Mandl & Mühldorf   PLATE 56

Stems suberect, 10–15 cm tall, rather weak and juicy, branched from the scale-leaf. *Leaves* green to grayish green, usually mottled with whitish markings, 1 or 2 times ternately divided; *leaflets* rounded and well-separated. *Racemes* rather loose, 4- to 14-flowered; *bracts* entire; *pedicels* about 10 mm long, lengthening to up to 20 mm long in fruit. *Flowers* white to pale blue or pale pink throughout, with broad deeply emarginate limbs; *spur* of upper petal straight, obtuse, subtriangular, slightly directed upward, 8–9 mm long; *inner petals* 7–9 mm long. *Capsule* broadly elliptic, with 4–6 seeds. Probably self-incompatible.

Corydalis repens from southeast Siberia, Manchuria and Korea is a very recent addition to cultivation, but one currently offered by both Jānis Rukšāns and Chen Yi. The flowers are similar to those of *C. fumariifolia* subsp. *azurea*, but smaller and paler. The spotted leaves add to the attraction of this humble species.

The closely related *Corydalis watanabei* Kitagawa has a similar distribution but is still very rare in cultivation. It has previously been considered a variant of *C. repens*. The flower shape is unique, however. The outer petals are very broad at the apex with a very deep narrow cleft. The inner ones are even more peculiar with the dorsal crest prolonged much

Corydalis watanabei. Drawing by Adèle Rossetti Morosini.

beyond the apex in two long acute appendages, like a beetle's antennae. It is an altogether daintier plant with small pale blue to pale purple flowers in few-flowered racemes. Cultivation of both species is as for *C. fumariifolia*.

Corydalis turtschaninovii Besser   PLATE 57

Stems erect, 10–25 cm tall. *Leaves* glaucous, somewhat fleshy, 2 or 3 times ternately divided, very variable in the shape of the ultimate lobe; lowermost leaf somewhat sheathing at base. *Racemes* rather dense, 6- to 20- (to 30-) flowered; *bracts* divided into few to several acute lobes; *pedicels* 5–10 mm long, equaling the bracts, lengthening to 10–20 mm long in fruit. *Flowers* blue or purplish blue; *outer petals* with emarginate usually toothed limbs with a conspicuous mucro in the notch; *spur* slightly curved backward at apex, 10–14 mm long; *nectary* obtuse, about half as long as spur; *inner petals* 9–12 mm long. *Capsule* linear, 16–26 mm long, somewhat torulose. $2n = 16$. Self-incompatible.

Corydalis turtschaninovii is widespread in open forests in East Asia. It occurs in Siberian Russia from Lake Baikal (the world's deepest lake) to Vladivostok, as well as in Korea and the Manchuria region of northeastern China. The species name honors Nikolai Turtschaninov who botanized in the Lake Baikal area. Jānis Rukšāns introduced the species to cultivation, having received it from a Russian friend in the 1980s, and now offers several named cultivars. Many plants, however, have been sold under the synonymous name *C. remota*, as well as *C. repens*. Although easily identified, *C. turtschaninovii* is a very variable species, and often individuals exhibiting the extremes of leaf shape (narrow versus broad lobes, serrate versus entire margin) grow side by side in a population, something it shares with *C. fumariifolia*, which is often found in the same localities. Because *C. turtschaninovii* comes later into flower than most forms of *C. fumariifolia* and is just as pure blue in its best forms, it is bound to become at least as widespread as a garden plant.

Corydalis ornata. Drawing by Adèle Rossetti Morosini.

The closely related *Corydalis ornata* Lidén & Zetterlund (Plate 58) is even more garden-worthy. Several clones are in cultivation (broad-lobed, narrow-lobed, blue-flowered, purple-flowered), but the narrow-lobed form with reddish pedicel and pure white flowers with a crenulate lip thinly lined with blue "lipstick" catches most of the praise (Plate 59). *Corydalis ornata* can be distinguished from *C. turtschaninovii* by the shorter more triangular spur, the very short subacute nectary, and twice the number of chromosomes.

Further south in China are found two more related species: *Corydalis yanhusuo* (Y. H. Chou & C. C. Xu) W. T. Wang ex Z. Y. Su & C. Y. Wu and *C. gamosepala* C. J. Maximowicz. *Corydalis yanhusuo* is today by far the most important medicinal plant in the genus and one of the primary painkillers in traditional Chinese medicine. It is sold as boiled and dried tubers in large quantities at Chinese town markets and increasingly on the internet in the United States. Among the numerous alkaloids found in this plant, the most important are tetrahydropalmatine and bulbocapnine, also found in, for example, *C. cava* and *Dicentra* species. Because "yanhusuo" is also tranquilizing and reduces spasms, it is used for treatment of Parkinson's disease.

Corydalis glaucescens Regel   PLATE 60

Stems ascending to suberect, 10–25 cm long, usually with several branches from the scale-leaf. *Leaves* glaucous, long-stalked, 2 times ternately divided; *leaflets* stalked. *Racemes* long and loose, 5- to 12- (to 22-) flowered; *bracts* entire, lanceolate; *pedicels* thin, 5–14(–22) mm long, equaling or longer than bracts. *Flowers* gracefully nodding, pale pink to white with dark purple to greenish keels, broadly winged and emarginate at apex; *spur* of upper petal 10–14(–17) mm long; *nectary* only about 1.5 mm long, obtuse; *lower petal* with a broad limb and a short claw with a pronounced gibbosity; *inner petals* short, 7–9 mm long, pale. *Capsule* broadly lanceolate, 11–17 × 4 mm. *2n* = 16. Self-incompatible.

This elegant plant is easily distinguished from all other species of the genus because, unlike most tuberous species, it produces several ascending branches from the scale-leaf situated at ground level. The rather small flowers that are loosely arranged in long racemes do not make for one of the showier species, but, nonetheless, *Corydalis glaucescens* is a gem for the connoisseur. Furthermore, it is readily cultivated as long as the summers are dry or the plant is protected under glass. *Corydalis glaucescens* is native to Central Asia, East Kazakhstan, Kyrgyzstan, and the Xinjiang Autonomous Region of China, and is apparently locally common at altitudes from 1000 to 2000 m (3300 to 6560 ft).

Several introductions of *Corydalis glaucescens* have been made, and the species is now widely available from specialist nurseries. Albert Regel first introduced it to cultivation in 1877, while working for St. Petersburg botanic garden. It was, in fact, one of several *Corydalis* species that he introduced from Central Asia. The species was introduced to the United Kingdom in 1879 and pictured in *Curtis's Botanical Magazine* (plate 6925, as *C. kolpakowskiana*). Rather oddly, it has recently been offered for sale as *C. kaschgarica*, an unrelated, non-tuberous, never cultivated xerophyte.

Three named selections of *Corydalis glaucescens* are offered commercially: *C. glaucescens* 'Cream Beauty', was collected in the vicinity of Bishkek (formerly Frunze), the capital of Kyrgyzstan, by Latvian nurseryman Jānis Rukšāns. It is a rather compact plant with a creamy touch to the flowers. *Corydalis glaucescens* 'Medeo' was also introduced by Rukšāns, this time from near the high altitude skating rink at Medeo in Kazakhstan. It is vigorous and has pinkish flowers. The third cultivar, *C. glaucescens* 'Pink Beauty', is an early flowering form with cream flowers offered by a few nurseries.

Corydalis nudicaulis Regel   PLATE 61

> *Stems* erect, 15–20 cm tall (often more in garden situations), with a membranous scale-leaf close to the tuber. *Leaves* 2 or occasionally 3 times ternately divided; *leaflets* lanceolate to obovate, with a clear pink tip. *Racemes* long and loose, 10- to 20-flowered (up to 40-flowered in cultivation); *bracts* entire; *pedicels* straight, 5–15(–20) mm long, equaling or longer than bracts. *Flowers* white to creamy white with a dark brown coloration toward the front and with purple-tipped inner petals; *spur* of upper petal upwardly directed, tapering, 11–15 mm long, sometimes slightly bent downward at apex; *nectary* very short, obtuse; *outer petals* with a narrow rim; *inner petals* 9–11 mm long. *Capsule* lanceolate, 18–22 × 3–4 mm, with about 20 small seeds. *2n* = ca. 16. Self-incompatible.

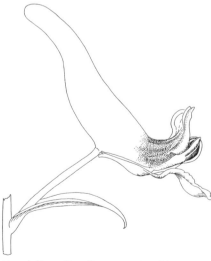

Corydalis nudicaulis is native to Tajikistan, in the western Pamir-Alai Mountains at altitudes of 1000 to 2000 m (3300 to 6560 ft). There it grows in humus-rich soils near streams and among shrubs, always seeking the moisture of north-facing slopes. Its closest relatives are *C. ruksansii* and *C. schanginii*, with which it shares a short obtuse nectary and dark-tipped inner petals. However, in some previous literature, including *Flora of the USSR*, this species was placed close to *C. cava*, but regarded as a transition to the *C. solida* group. This is because the scale-

Corydalis nudicaulis. Drawing by Adèle Rossetti Morosini.

leaf is situated closer to the tuber and is less durable in this species than in its relatives, and therefore may be absent from herbarium specimens.

Corydalis nudicaulis has been in cultivation at least since 1987, when plants collected by Arnis Seisums were grown in the Gothenburg Botanic Garden. It is a very elegant plant, with erect stems and white flowers with a coffee-brown front third. The species is sometimes given the colloquial name coffee and cream, a reference to its two-toned flowers. It is best admired in a pot in the alpine house, since it is too modest to compete for attention outside.

Corydalis ruksansii Lidén   PLATE 62

Stems 10–15(–20) cm tall, suberect to ascending. *Leaves* 2 times ternately divided; *leaflets* deeply divided, ultimate lobes often markedly unequal in size, elliptic to obovate, acute to obtuse. *Racemes* loose, 7- to 20-flowered; *bracts* ovate to lanceolate, entire; *pedicels* 7–14(–22) mm long, straight, erecto-patent, equaling or longer than bracts. *Flowers* narrow, whitish, with purplish-pink midveins to the outer petals; *spur* of upper petal curved upward, straight or slightly curved backward at tip, 12–13 mm long with a short obtuse nectary; *inner petals* about 10 mm long, tipped with dark purple. *Capsule* linear, 12–17 × 2–3 mm, with 2–5 seeds. *2n* = ca. 16. Self-incompatible.

Corydalis ruksansii often does not live up to expectations when grown in the greenhouse, especially following a mild winter, a situation that will lead to the leaves becoming chlorotic and the flowers deformed. In the open garden, however, the plant will be more compact and produce healthy flowering racemes. You need to look quite closely, nevertheless, to unravel this species's charms, especially since the flowers are quite small. If you do take the time, you will discover the fine pink line formed by the mid-vein of the upper petal—exquisite.

Jānis Rukšāns, after whom the plant is named, made the first verified introduction of this species in 1980 under the name *Corydalis glaucescens* 'C. D. Brickell'. This is one of many *Corydalis* species introduced via Rukšāns nursery, a wonderful mail-order source of rare and interesting bulbs. Importantly, all his plants are nursery grown, alleviating pressure on the wild populations. In the wild, *C. ruksansii* is restricted to the mountains of northwestern Tajikistan and northeastern Uzbekistan at altitudes of 1500 to 2500 m (4920 to 8200 ft), where it grows in humus-rich soils.

Latvian botanist Arnis Seisums has recently selected a new hybrid cultivar, *Corydalis* 'New Contender', from open-pollinated *C. ruksansii*, with the presumed pollen parent being *C. schanginii*. The cultivar has whitish flowers with pink veins, which are larger than those of *C. ruksansii*.

Corydalis schanginii (Pallas) B. Fedtschenko   PLATES 63, 64

Rootstock a large tuber, up to 3 cm in diameter when mature. *Stems* 10–40 cm long, ascending to suberect, and rather thick. *Leaves* glaucous, 2 times ternately divided; *leaflets* entire or deeply incised, ultimate lobes ovate to lanceolate, usually acute. *Racemes* long, 5- to 25-flowered (up to 30-flowered in cultivation), rising high above the leaves; *bracts* lanceolate, entire; *pedicels* 5–15 mm long, equaling bracts. *Flowers* long and narrow; *spur* 21–28 mm long, tapering, straight or usually gently curved downward at apex; *outer petals* narrow and acute; *inner petals* narrowly crested, conspicuously tipped with chocolate purple, 14–16(–18) mm long; *nectary* short, obtuse. *Capsule* linear, 18–25 × 2–3 mm, with 4–8 seeds. *2n* = 16. Self-incompatible.

Corydalis schanginii is widely distributed from the westernmost corner of Mongolia almost to the Black Sea. It is found there in summer-dry areas, from an altitude of 500 to 2000 m (1640 to 6560 ft). Two variants of this species are recognized as subspecies: subsp. *schanginii* (Plate 63) has rosy purple flowers with a distinct but narrow rim bordering the lower petal, while subsp. *ainae* Rukšāns ex Lidén (Plate 64) has a yellow front to the flower, lacks the rim, and is a slenderer plant with looser racemes. When crossed, the two subspecies form perfectly fertile intermediate offspring. The much more garden-worthy subsp. *ainae* is only known with certainty from the Kara-Tau Mountains in Kazakhstan, where Jānis Rukšāns discovered it in 1977, but it is possible that it also occurs further west.

Both subspecies do far better in the open garden than in a greenhouse, where they emerge too early, become etiolated, and develop pale flowers. In wetter climates, however, they perform best if protected from excessive summer rain, so a dry spot is recommended. Cold winters, though, are never a problem.

Subspecies *schanginii* is pictured as *Corydalis longiflora* in *Curtis's Botanical Magazine* 1833 (plate 3230). It is mentioned in *Vollständige Lexicon der Gärtnerei und Botanik* Dietrich 1804) as being in cultivation ("kommt in unser Gärten gut fort"), suggesting that it was introduced already by Peter Pallas to St. Petersburg in the 1770s. It is easy to grow and very frost-hardy. Subspecies *ainae* is a much more recent introduction to gardens, not having been discovered until 1977.

Section *Leonticoides*

This group of species is more of a challenge to grow than the species of section *Corydalis*, but successful growers will be highly rewarded with some of the most beautiful as well as the strangest plants in the genus. They are found from Crete and Anatolia eastward to western Nepal and the Xinjiang Autonomous Region of China. Most grow in mountainous areas with cold winters and hot dry summers, where they come into flower when the snow retreats. Twenty-one species are recognized. The eight species described here were selected because they are commercially available and not too prone to etiolation in cultivation.

The species of section *Leonticoides* can be immediately recognized from the other tuberous groups since they have two opposite leaves on the stem and a large perennial tuber. Like *Corydalis cava*, they produce both stems and leaves from the tuber, and there is no scale on the stem, as found in the section *Corydalis*. The lower part of the stems and of the petioles of radical leaves (that is, the leaves originating from the tuber) is thin and dwindles down in the soil or scree to the often deep-seated tuber. The stem leaves of nearly all species are sessile, but each is divided into three-stalked leaflets. This may give the impression of six leaves set in a ring.

In nature most species grow in scree or in low scrub on steep slopes. The tuber is deeply situated (15–40 cm) and extremely difficult to collect, so you can be sure that commercial material is from cultivated stock.

In cultivation these species are mainly grown in pots in the alpine house or in a bulb frame. Their natural deep seating is difficult to achieve and it is an art to grow a perfect pot specimen. To make a good attempt one needs Long Tom pots and a gritty but leaf-rich compost. Plants should be started (that is, watered) in late November. If you are then blessed with a cold January and February, the result can be pleasure in the earliest spring. If the winter is mild, however, plants will appear in the dark January and produce sprawling, leggy, etiolated specimens.

The best site for these plants is the bulb frame, where they can be planted deep (40 cm) in a rich well-drained loam. They should be kept dry from June to November and slightly moist during the active season. Some species, like *Corydalis diphylla*, *C. ledebouriana*, and *C. maracandica*, have also proven reliable in dry borders.

In the comprehensive list below, species with main entries in the text are in bold letters. Those with an asterisk (*) are briefly referred to under a similar species.

afghanica	*erdelii** 108	*maracandica** 107	*seisumsiana** 105
aitchisonii* 106	*griffithii*	**nariniana** 108	**sewerzowii** 106
chionophila	*hyrcana** 109	*oppositifolia** 108	*uniflora*
cyrtocentra	**ledebouriana** 106	*podlechii*	**verticillaris** 108
darwasica 104	*lydica** 108	**popovii** 105	
diphylla 104	**macrocentra** 107	*rutifolia*	

Corydalis diphylla Wallich

Stems erect, 6–15 cm tall. *Leaves* shortly stalked, slightly glaucous, (1–)2–3(–4) times ternately divided, ultimate lobes very unequal in size. *Racemes* loose, 3- to 11-flowered; *bracts* 6–12 mm long, entire; *pedicels* 5–30 mm long in flower, slightly elongating and becoming strongly reflexed in fruit. *Flowers* white or cream with the tips of the inner petals and the wings of the outer petals purple; *outer petals* widely divergent, exposing the purple limbs; *spur* broad at base, curved upward, 8–13 mm long, curved backward at apex. $2n = 16$. Self-incompatible.

Corydalis diphylla grows in open forests in the West Himalaya eastward to western Nepal at altitudes from 2000 to 4100 m (6560 to 13,450 ft). Nathaniel Wallich, superintendent of Calcutta botanic garden from 1817 to 1846, first discovered the species growing in Kumaon, India. The West Himalayan subsp. *occidentalis* Lidén has been available from specialist nurseries in the United Kingdom in the past, although it is not listed in the *RHS Plant Finder* of 2007 to 2008. It can be immediately distinguished from all other species in section *Leonticoides* by the stalked leaves and the loose few-flowered raceme of long-stalked, broad-lipped flowers. Its flowers vary in size and color, and in the finest forms have very broad deep purple lips with a contrasting white spur, making for a striking show-plant.

Corydalis darwasica Prain

Stems relatively firm and erect, projecting 5–10(–15) cm above the ground. *Leaves* very glaucous, sessile, ternately divided; *primary leaflets* long-stalked, pinnately divided; *secondary leaflets* deeply divided into overlapping lobes. *Racemes* dense, 4- to 10- (to 13-) flowered; *bracts* 8–14 mm long, entire; *pedicels* 10–15(–20) mm long. *Flowers* white to cream or with a pinkish suffusion, the reflexed part of the lower petal with a dark purple blotch; *spur* 10–12 mm long; *inner petals* about 10 mm long. $2n = 16$. Self-incompatible.

Corydalis darwasica grows in screes in western Tajikistan, northeastern Uzbekistan, and southeastern Kazakhstan at an altitude of 1000 to 3200 m (3300 to 10,500 ft). The species was first collected in Darwaz, which today is in Tajikistan but at that time belonged to the Bukhara emirate. The cream flowers with the purple blotch across the lower lip are distinctive and together with the much-dissected, bluish foliage make for a choice plant. The species is firmly established in cultivation, even though it is rarely offered commercially.

Corydalis darwasica is superficially similar to *C. seisumsiana* Lidén (Plate 65) from southern Armenia and northern Iran. The latter is occasionally offered for sale and can be distinguished from *C. darwasica* by its narrower leaf lobes and the longer and thinner spur (13–19 mm long instead of 10–12 mm). Unfortunately, it becomes rather floppy if grown under glass.

Corydalis popovii Nevski ex Popov   PLATE 66

> *Stems* erect, 8–15(–25) cm tall. *Leaves* 2 or 3 times ternately divided. *Racemes* loose, 2- to 8-flowered, rising high above the leaves, developing from the top downward; *bracts* entire; *pedicels* erect (3–)5–10(–25) mm long. *Flowers* usually pale pink to purplish pink, rarely white, with dark purple apical parts, facing upward; *outer petals* laterally compressed at apices, truncate, but with a distinct mucro; *inner petals* 14–16(–18) mm long, with a broad conspicuous triangular notch; *spur* 18–34 mm long, tapering toward the strongly curved apex. *2n* = 32. Self-incompatible.

Corydalis popovii is one of the more striking species in the genus with large flowers that open upward to face the sky. It has a unique reversed flower development. In no other *Corydalis* species do the flowers open from the top of the raceme downward. The sharp triangular notch of the apices of the unusually broad inner petals is also unique in the genus. In addition, it has a strong odor, a heavy mix of jasmine and horse manure.

Corydalis popovii occurs on mountain slopes of the western Pamir-Alai (western Tajikistan, southeastern Turkmenistan, southeastern Uzbekistan) at altitudes of 600 to 1900 m (1970 to 6200 ft), on clay-rich soils.

Corydalis popovii. Drawing by Adèle Rossetti Morosini.

As far as the section *Leonticoides* goes, *Corydalis popovii* is a relatively easy species to grow and is available from a few commercial nurseries. Nevertheless, it is best suited to cultivation in an alpine house.

Corydalis sewerzowii Regel   PLATE 67

Stems ascending to erect, 5–10(–15) cm tall. *Leaves* glaucous, 2 or 3 times ternately divided; *leaflets* entire to shallowly incised. *Racemes* 4- to 10-flowered; *bracts* obovate, entire, 10–15 mm long; *pedicels* 5–10(–15) mm long. *Flowers* golden yellow; *spur* 23–30 mm long, curved backward at apex; *outer petals* subacute to obtuse at apex, with a distinct rim; *inner petals* 13–15 mm long. $2n = 16$. Self-incompatible.

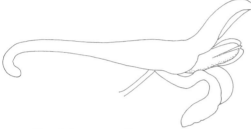

Corydalis sewerzowii. Drawing by Adèle Rossetti Morosini.

A striking species with a rather small distribution in southeastern Kazakhstan, northwestern Tajikistan, and eastern Uzbekistan, where it is found at altitudes from 500 to 1700 m (1640 to 5575 ft). Introduced by Albert Regel who collected it in the mountains around Angren in eastern Uzbekistan. The plants in circulation today, though, hail from Mogul Tou in northwestern Tajikistan. *Corydalis sewerzowii* has a compact habit and large vibrantly golden flowers in dense racemes that shortly emerge above the intensely glaucous foliage.

Corydalis sewerzowii is sometimes confused with *C. aitchisonii* Popov since both species have large yellow flowers with long slender spurs. They are not, however, very closely related. Apart from "botanical" details of stigma and seeds, *C. aitchisonii* differs in having fewer and more clearly separated and more rounded leaflets, and much longer pedicels. It is also occasionally grown by alpine enthusiasts, but is much more prone to etiolation than *C. sewerzowii* and will never look as attractive under glass. It has a rather wide distribution in Central Asia from northeastern Iran and southern Turkmenistan through northern Afghanistan to Tajikistan.

Corydalis ledebouriana Karelin & Kirilov

Stems suberect, 5–20 cm tall. *Leaves* 2 or 3 times ternately divided, ultimate lobes very unequal in size. *Racemes* long, 5- to 10- (to 14-) flowered; *bracts* entire; *pedicels* 2–9(–12) mm long. *Flowers* with a purplish violet apex, spur pale pink or almost white, rarely reddish purple or white; *outer petals* acute to acuminate, very narrowly winged; *spur* 9–15(–18) mm long, never apically curved backward, often strongly curved upward and inflated toward the apex, but forms with slender and/ or straighter flowers also occur; *nectary* much shorter than spur, turned upward; *inner petals* 9–11 mm long. $2n = 32$. Self-incompatible.

Corydalis ledebouriana is quite widespread in the mountains of Central Asia, occurring from the Tarbagatay Mountains on the Kazakhstan-Xinjiang border south to central Afghanistan. The name honors Carl Friedrich von Ledebour (1785–1851), professor of botany in Tartu and author of a Russian flora. The species is very variable in color, but is easily recognizable by its comparatively short upturned nectary. In all other species of the section the nectary reaches almost to the tip of the spur (easily seen if you hold a flower to the light). Other characters to note are the narrow acute flowers and short pedicels. Albert Regel of St. Petersburg apparently introduced the species into British gardens in 1879. The species is completely frost-hardy despite its rather delicate, succulent appearance.

The related *Corydalis maracandica* M. Mikhaïlov (Plate 2) was discovered in 1971 by Marina Mikhaïlov in the western Zeravshan Range in Tajikistan and is now quite widespread in cultivation, sometimes being offered by specialist nurseries. Except for the long nectary, it is very similar to *C. ledebouriana*. It is usually yellow flowered, but pink-flowered forms do occur in the wild.

Corydalis macrocentra Regel

Rootstock a tuber, often very large. *Stems* 4–10 cm tall, usually branched, more or less covered with small, rough protuberances. *Leaves* very glaucous; *primary leaflets* 2 times pinnately divided with acute conspicuously red-tipped lobes. *Racemes* 2- to 6-flowered; *bracts* with undulate margins, apically divided; *pedicels* 12–20 (–25) mm long, strongly curved backward in fruit. *Flowers* yellow, often flushed reddish brown, with acute 3-lobed limbs to the outer petals; *spur* long and slender, 24–30 mm long. $2n = 16$. Self-incompatible.

In the wild this rare species is known from Tajikistan and northern Afghanistan, where it grows on sandy slopes on dry hills at an altitude of roughly 1000 m (3300 ft). It is quite different from all the other species in this section in having divided bracts, branched stems, and a somewhat longer flowering period.

Corydalis macrocentra must be protected from summer moisture and will feel most at home in a continental climate with cold winters and hot dry summers. The species is only occasionally offered for sale. The name *macrocentra* is Latin for long spur, a reference to the fact that this plant has one of the longest spurs in the genus.

Corydalis nariniana Fedorov   PLATE 68

Stems erect, 5–15 cm tall. *Leaves* 2 times ternately divided; *leaflets* divided into elliptic subacute unequally sized lobes. *Racemes* 5- to 10-flowered; *bracts* entire. *Flowers* firm, either distinctly bicolored with a rich carmine or purple spur, blackish purple narrowly crested keels toward the apices of the outer petals, and pure white inner petals, and middle parts and wings of outer petals, or rarely white all over, 10–12 mm long; *spur* broad, obtuse, 12–18 mm long, straight, curved backward at apex. *2n* = 16. Self-incompatible.

This very handsome species is restricted to Armenia and the northeastern extreme corner of Turkey. It was introduced into cultivation from the Sevan Lake area by Czech collectors in the 1980s as *Corydalis persica* and is still persisting, despite only being occasionally offered by specialist nurseries. The best forms have a pure white, blackish-purple-keeled front, contrasting a rich deep carmine spur. In 1986 it was awarded a Preliminary Commendation when exhibited by D. J. Cobb as *C. persica*, under which name it may still be found in catalogs. This name, however, is a synonym of *C. verticillaris*.

   Corydalis nariniana is part of a species complex of mainly Anatolian species. It is distinguished from *C. erdelii* Zuccarini (southern Anatolia) by the larger flowers with the limbs of the outer petals with distinct spreading margins, from *C. oppositifolia* A. P. de Candolle (eastern Anatolia) (Plate 69) by details of the stigma and form and coloration of the corolla, and from both by the narrow dorsal crests of the outer petals. A third related species, *C. lydica* Lidén from West Anatolia, has creamy white corollas (only turning pink after fertilization) set on long stiff pedicels. These are all occasionally offered in plant catalogs or on the internet. None of them, however, can compete with *C. nariniana* in beauty.

Corydalis verticillaris A. P. de Candolle

Stems weak, 4–10 cm tall. *Leaves* sessile, ternately divided; *leaflets* 2 or almost 3 times pinnately divided into small ultimate lobes. *Racemes* 2- to 8-flowered; *bracts* entire; *pedicels* shorter than the bracts in early flowering, lengthening considerably and becoming strongly reflexed in fruit. *Flowers* white, usually with a purple spur and dark purplish keels to the outer petals, rarely wholly pinkish purple, usually turning more reddish after pollination; *spur* of upper petal long and thin, usually gracefully curved upward and turn down at the very tip, 16–28 mm long; *inner petals* 10–12 mm long. Self-incompatible.

This extremely variable taxon is related to *Corydalis seisumsiana* (see under *C. darwasica*) and *C. oppositifolia*. Three subspecies are recognized. Subspecies *verticillaris* is widely distributed in the Iranian mountain chains: Elburz and central Zagros. In the southern Zagros Mountains it is replaced by the small-flowered subsp. *parviflora* Lidén, and in the northern Iranian province Azerbaijan by subsp. *boissieri* (Prain) Wendelbo. The latter is particularly attractive with its very strongly curved flowers and small leaves with comparatively few and broad leaf divisions, but unlike the other two subspecies it is regrettably not in cultivation.

Subspecies *verticillaris* was first introduced from the type locality Mount Alwand (Elvend) by E. K. Balls in 1932 and was pictured in *Curtis's Botanical Magazine* in 1937 (plate 9486), after receiving an RHS Award of Merit in 1934. It has lately been reintroduced into cultivation by several expeditions and from several places (mainly as a byproduct of *Dionysia* collecting trips). However, it is not offered by any commercial source and is likely to remain a plant for the corydalis connoisseur.

In the alpine house *Corydalis verticillaris* needs good light and protection from high temperatures so that it does not get too weak and sprawling. In nature it grows on open slopes and fine-grained screes, from 1500 to at least 3300 m (4,920 to 10,800 ft). It can be seen on Mount Tochal on an easy outing in spring a few hours' walk from Teheran city, along a path lined with cake shops and water-pipe merchants.

Lidén and Zetterlund (1997) tentatively included *Corydalis hyrcana* Wendelbo in the synonymy of *C. verticillaris*, something we now know is not the case. This very distinctive species is currently known from four places in the wooded northern slopes of the Elburz chain. Being a plant of deciduous forests distinguishes it from all other species of this section, and it is only logical that its habit is similar to that of *C. cava*. *Corydalis verticillaris* made a brief visit into cultivation in the late 1990s.

Other Tuberous Species

Corydalis arctica Popov
Section *Dactylotuber*

> *Rootstock* an elongated tuber more or less branched below. *Stems* erect, (4–)
> 10–15(–25) cm tall, simple or with 1 or 2 weak, late-developing branches, usually

with 2 scale-leaves on the lower part of the stem, and 2–4 ordinary leaves. *Leaves* glaucous, ternately divided; *leaflets* deeply cut into 3–5 lanceolate obtuse segments. *Racemes* very dense, 2- to 7-flowered, on peduncles 3–10 cm long; *bracts* obovate, entire; *pedicels* 3–5 mm long, elongating to 6–16 mm long and remaining erect in fruit. *Flowers* white, pale blue, purple, or violet, held with the spur pointing almost straight upward and forming a very acute angle with the pedicel; *spur* 8–15 mm long; *outer petals* acute, often shortly crested; *inner petals* 8–10 mm long. *Capsule* pendent from erect pedicels, explosively dehiscent. *2n* = 16.

Corydalis arctica is one of the most widespread species in the genus, occurring from the Mackenzie District of western Canada through Alaska and into Siberia almost to the lower Jenisei. It is also found in Kamchatka and on some of the islands south of the Bering Straight. No other species of *Corydalis* grows this far north, and travelers in arctic Siberia have expressed delight in how the species' clear blue flowers brighten the permafrost vegetation.

Corydalis arctica belongs to section *Dactylotuber,* which is otherwise distributed in Asia from Caucasus to Mongolia and southwestern China. This species is often called *C. pauciflora* in American floras, but that species is restricted to northern Mongolia and south central Siberia. *Corydalis arctica* is easily distinguished from it, for example, by the vertically held flowers and the lack of a pouch on the lower petal. It is rare in cultivation and requires a cool climate. It is probably best planted on a north-facing peat wall in the open garden.

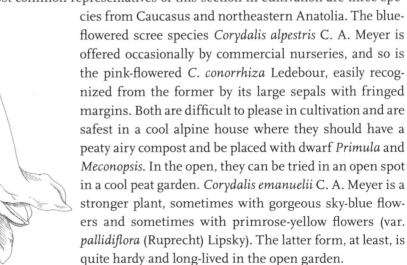

The most common representatives of this section in cultivation are three species from Caucasus and northeastern Anatolia. The blue-flowered scree species *Corydalis alpestris* C. A. Meyer is offered occasionally by commercial nurseries, and so is the pink-flowered *C. conorrhiza* Ledebour, easily recognized from the former by its large sepals with fringed margins. Both are difficult to please in cultivation and are safest in a cool alpine house where they should have a peaty airy compost and be placed with dwarf *Primula* and *Meconopsis*. In the open, they can be tried in an open spot in a cool peat garden. *Corydalis emanuelii* C. A. Meyer is a stronger plant, sometimes with gorgeous sky-blue flowers and sometimes with primrose-yellow flowers (var. *pallidiflora* (Ruprecht) Lipsky). The latter form, at least, is quite hardy and long-lived in the open garden.

Corydalis arctica. Drawing by Adèle Rossetti Morosini.

Corydalis hemidicentra Handel-Mazzetti   PLATE 70
Section *Dactylotuber*

> *Rootstock* a long, cylindrical tuber. *Stems* slender, ascending, usually branched,
> basally (below ground) with 2–3 scale-leaves. *Leaves* divided into 3 sessile rounded
> fleshy wax-covered leaflets, variegated in greenish gray and reddish brown; *peti-*
> *oles* long. *Racemes* very condensed, 3- to 9-flowered, long-stalked; *bracts* small,
> entire; *pedicels* 7–30 mm long, straight and suberect. *Flowers* bright blue or some-
> times purplish blue; *outer petals* acute, crested; *spur* straight or upcurved, 12–15
> mm long; *inner petals* 10–13 mm long. Self-incompatible.

In northwestern Yunnan and adjacent Tibet *Corydalis hemidicentra* is a characteristic plant of rough alpine screes, a habitat it shares with several other *Corydalis*
species, as well as *Fritillaria delavayi*. One of the more striking of all *Corydalis*, this
beautiful, as well as unusual, species with sky-blue-flowers has been repeatedly introduced into cultivation. However, it has proven to be difficult to keep alive and has
never been available from nursery-propagated stock. In native screes, the tubers are
often deeply situated and the stems and leaves have to find their way to the surface
through a thick layer of silt and pebbles—a situation almost impossible to duplicate
in cultivation. The name *hemidicentra* translates as "half dicentra," an epithet that
equally applies to each and every species of *Corydalis*.

The Austrian Heinrich Handel-Mazzetti spent five very fruitful years collecting plants in southwestern China from 1914 to 1919, prevented by the outbreak of
the world war from returning home. This eminent plant geographer and system-
atist did not introduce any plants in cultivation but is responsible for the discovery
and description of no less than 10 species of *Corydalis*, along with several other
plants. Eventually he became keeper of the Natural History Museum in Vienna. His
account of his travels in China has been recently translated into English.

The leaves of *Corydalis hemidicen-*
tra are remarkably similar to those of
C. benecincta W. W. Smith (in section
Benecinctae) (Plate 71), which sometimes grows in the same screes; both
have three rounded fleshy leaflets mottled in gray, green, and brown. They
look very similar to a lichen-covered
pebble and presumably have evolved as
a defense against herbivores. The two

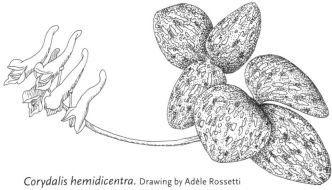

Corydalis hemidicentra. Drawing by Adèle Rossetti
Morosini.

species differ substantially in floral details, as well as in their method of seed dispersal, and are not particularly closely related. In *C. benecincta* the pedicels curve downward at maturity so as to bury the seeds, whereas in *C. hemidicentra*, as in *C. arctica*, the capsules are set on erect pedicels and are explosively dehiscent. *Corydalis benecincta* has been offered on Chen Yi's Web site as "*C. trifoliata*."

Corydalis buschii Nakai   PLATE 72
Section *Duplotuber*

> Rootstock a small tuber, formed as a swelling on the tip of stolonlike outgrowths
> from the old tuber. *Stems* erect, 10–20(–30) cm tall, slender and not very stiff, with
> 1–3 scale-leaves on the lower part of the stem and 2–4 ordinary leaves. *Leaves* thin,
> 2 times ternately divided; *leaflets* deeply divided, ultimate lobes small, lanceolate;
> *petioles* long. *Racemes* short and dense, 5- to 15-flowered; *bracts* broad, apically
> toothed or divided into acute lobules; *pedicels* short, thin, 3–5 mm long, equaling
> the bracts. *Flowers* purple to pinkish, rounded-emarginate at apex, rather small;
> *spur* 10 mm long; *inner petals* pale, 7–8 mm long. $2n = 16$. Self-incompatible.

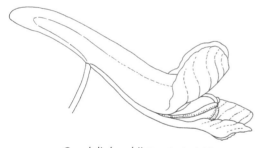

Corydalis buschii. Drawing by Adèle Rossetti Morosini.

Corydalis buschii is found in northeastern North Korea and closely adjacent parts of China and Russia in wet meadows and forest glades. It is a relative of *C. decumbens* (see following), but has an erect habit and denser, more floriferous racemes. It is also much more widely grown today, being available from several commercial nurseries. The species thrives and multiplies outside in a rich, lightly shaded woodland spot, but is not suitable for the alpine house. In optimal conditions, it will spread into a carpet. The flowers are rather late to bloom compared to other tuberous corydalis, opening in the middle of May in the northeastern United States. Jānis Rukšāns first introduced *C. buschii* into cultivation from near Vladivostok and still offers it for sale. The name honors the Russian botanist and explorer Nicolaĭ Busch.

Corydalis decumbens (Thunberg) Persoon
Section *Duplotuber*

> Rootstock a small, rounded tuber with one to a few new tubers formed annually
> directly on the old tuber; *radical leaves* with long thin partly underground petioles.

Stems usually several, decumbent to ascending, 10–25 cm long, weak and slender with very thin bases. *Leaves* 2, 2 times ternately divided; *leaflets* usually deeply cut. *Racemes* loose, 3- to 10-flowered; *bracts* entire; *pedicels* 10–12 mm long, thin, much longer than bracts. *Flowers* whitish to pale pink, often with pale blue markings; *outer petals* rather broad, emarginate; *spur* 7–10 mm long; *inner petals* about 11 mm long. *2n* = 16. Most strains are self-compatible.

The species is classified in a group with *Corydalis buschii* (see above) and *C. ternata* (Nakai) Nakai, defined by their peculiar stigma and seed characters.

Corydalis decumbens was described (as *Fumaria decumbens*) by Carl Peter Thunberg, Linnaeus's most famous student and eventually his successor in Uppsala as professor in medicine and botany. During his stay in Japan, when he collected this species, Thunberg was mainly restricted to Deshima, an artificial island close to Nagasaki, and was only allowed to make one short trip to the shogun in the capital Edo (now Tokyo) with a Dutch delegation. By the help of Japanese acquaintances, by collections during the Edo trip, and by searching through the hay brought from the mainland for the cattle, he managed nevertheless to describe a substantial fraction of the Japanese flora. In addition to southern Japan, *C. decumbens* also occurs in eastern China.

Known as Xiatianwu, this species is, next to *Corydalis yanhusuo*, the most important medicinal plant in the genus and used for treatment of central nervous system diseases.

Corydalis decumbens has been in cultivation for a long time from a Japanese collection. It is easy to grow and multiplies through the production of lots of accessory tubers. The weak decumbent stems and few-flowered racemes prevent it from making any bigger immediate impression, but take your time to sniff the flowers and you will note a really pleasant smell, like that of *Viola odorata*.

Corydalis cava (Linnaeus) Schweigger & Körte   PLATE 73
Section *Radix-cava*

A perennial herb from a tuber, with roots scattered over the surface, becoming large and hollow, and eventually falling apart in old individuals. *Stems* 10–30 cm tall (excluding subterranean part), often several from each tuber, with 2 alternate leaves on the stem (unlike the species of section *Corydalis*, *C. cava* also produces leaves from the tuber). *Leaves* 2 times ternately divided; *leaflets* cut into subacute to obtuse lobes. *Racemes* stalked, 6- to 16- (to 23-) flowered; *bracts* entire, ovate, 10–20(–30) mm long; *pedicels* shorter than bracts. *Flowers* white, purple, red, or yellow; *outer petals* broadly winged, emarginate, rather straight, spur of upper petal 10–14 mm long; *inner petals* 11–12 mm long. *Capsule* oblong, 18–24 × 5 mm, with 5–10 seeds. *2n* = 16, 24, 32.

Corydalis cava is a valuable horticultural plant since it is readily grown in the garden, especially in a shady location. In most garden situations the species will eventually form clumps but is never overly aggressive. It is a suitable plant for a perennial border, north-facing rock garden, peat wall, or woodland garden. As an added bonus, the flowers are fragrant. Not surprisingly, the species is widely available from commercial nurseries.

As a native wildflower, *Corydalis cava* is widespread in deciduous forests from northern Iran to Portugal, with its northernmost occurrences in southern Sweden. It flowers from February to late May, depending on latitude, altitude, and seasonal temperatures. In the Central and Northern European populations one commonly encounters red, white, and purple individuals growing intermixed. In the Balkans, uniformly white- or pale yellow-flowered populations are also found. A yellow-flowered tetraploid form from the Crimea is sometimes recognized as *C. marschalliana* (Willdenow) Persoon and is occasionally cultivated (Plate 73). Since there are several intermediates, and as the characters said to distinguish this taxon have a reticulate pattern if seen over the whole distribution area, this species is not recognized here.

Corydalis cava has been cultivated at least since the 15th century. The northernmost occurrences in central Sweden, for example, are all tied to old monasteries and castles, where the plant was grown not only for its beauty, but also for its medical properties. Like most members of the bleeding heart and poppy families, it contains poisonous alkaloids. The most important substance among the various alkaloids in the crude extract is bulbocapnine, which inhibits the reflex and motor activities of striated muscle. *Corydalis cava* was once widely used in the treatment of muscular tremors, and according to John Gerard's herbal of 1633 is also useful for treating swollen hemorrhoids and tonsils. From other sources we learn that the dried and powdered tuber is the medicine of choice for bone rot. Cattle fed with this plant in large doses can suffer neurotoxic effects with agitation and convulsions. Today though, this species is of little importance as a drug, especially compared to *C. yanhusuo*. Nevertheless, when purified, the main components of *C. cava*, bulbocapnine and corydaline, have sedative, hypnotic, and narcotic effects, while tetrahydropalmatine shows analgesic and sedative effect. Accordingly, *Corydalis* extract has been used to make sedative tea mixtures (Dorm Tea®) and other sleep-inducing phytopharmaca (for example, Salusdorm® and Neurapas®).

The hollow tuber of this species is reflected in many of its vernacular names like hålrot and hollow root, and indeed in its Latin specific epithet *cava*.

As testified by ancient tradition, as well as more recent Spanish witchcraft, if picked during Valpurgis Night (April 30th), this plant will have enhanced magical properties and can be used to exorcise evil spirits from your home, stables, and livestock. We have sprayed an infusion of *Corydalis cava* in and around our homes according to this prescription and not a single evil spirit has appeared since.

Single-colored stands may be produced in the garden by selectively breeding individuals with a desired flower color and isolating these plants from individuals with other flower colors. In the woodland garden, where the species is best suited and perhaps best displayed, pure stands of white-flowered individuals can look particularly attractive, especially when seen at dusk. That said, we are also fond of the deepest yellow as well as the darkest purple forms.

The other species in the section *Radix-cava*, *Corydalis blanda* Schott, is much less commonly seen in cultivation and is only occasionally available from commercial nurseries. It is shorter (sometimes only 5 cm tall) with very glaucous leaves, which usually have acute lobes. It also flowers considerably later than *C. cava*, and the pedicels are stouter and red-colored, while the corolla is pale, finely freckled with dull purplish pigmentation. Furthermore, the tuber is very different, being flatter and more irregular than that of *C. cava*. *Corydalis blanda* is endemic to the Balkan Peninsula, where it is found in alpine meadows and screes, often where snow has lingered. It flowers from May to early July. Four subspecies are recognized, each endemic to one mountain area. The most distinctive and elegant is subsp. *oxelmannii* Lidén, endemic to Mount Chelmos on the Peloponnese Peninsula.

The tubers of both *Corydalis cava* and *C. blanda* are rather similar to those of section *Leonticoides* but not as drought resistant. They should be handled and traded like erythroniums—in peat and plastic. They should be planted fairly deep (20 cm) in a fertile garden loam. They do not mind lime. Of the two, *C. blanda* is best in an open position in the rock garden, whereas *C. cava* is perfect in the woodland garden and will seed around prolifically when conditions are right.

Non-tuberous Species with Yellow and Cream Flowers

Corydalis rupestris Boissier PLATE 74

Cushion-forming cliff-dweller. *Leaves* 2 times pinnately divided, heavily glaucous, fleshy and somewhat fragile. *Racemes* several, dense, 8- to 30-flowered; *bracts* small, linear; *pedicels* very short. *Flowers* evenly golden yellow; *outer petals* with rounded extreme tips often bent outward; *spur* 2–3 mm long, rounded; *inner petals* 15–17 mm long. *Capsule* ovate, tapering to a long stiff style, many-seeded. *2n* = 16. Self-compatible.

Corydalis rupestris is a spectacular and unusual plant for the alpine house, producing dense racemes of golden yellow flowers throughout the spring and early summer. It is a common plant in the mountains of Iran, Baluchistan, and parts of Afghanistan. The species grows in crevices of steep cliffs, both in hard limestone and in the peculiar soft Bazoft conglomerate at low to intermediate altitudes. It is often to be seen growing next to *Dionysia* species, as well as with other cliff-dwellers. Its name is Latin for "rock-loving," a reference to its habitat preference. Given its origin it should not be surprising that this species can survive outdoors only in warm and dry continental climates.

As *Corydalis rupestris* produces plenty of seeds through selfing, and the seeds readily germinate and can tolerate dry storage for a couple of years, this species is widespread in botanic gardens and is also grown in the alpine houses of enthusiasts. In the right circumstances, the plant will often escape pot culture and seed around in the plunge material of the alpine house. It is perfectly frost-hardy, but detests winter wet. In the open garden it is best grown in a trough, preferably in a piece of tufa. Should the original plant die, it will often be replaced by self-sown seedlings. Surprisingly, it is rarely available commercially.

The closely related *Corydalis macrocalyx* Litvinov, characterized by huge, pale entire sepals and much broader bracts, replaces it in northeastern Iran and Turkistan. This species has yet to enter cultivation.

Corydalis wilsonii N. E. Brown   PLATE 75

Perennial herb forming a dense rosette. *Leaves* very glaucous, oblong, 2 times pinnately divided; *leaflets* neat and rounded. *Racemes* long and dense, 10- to 25-flowered; *bracts* small, entire. *Flowers* yellow, acute to acuminate; *outer petals* not crested, but the tips often conspicuously curved outward, spur 5–6 mm long; *inner petals* about 15 mm long, with broad dorsal rounded wings. *Capsule* narrowly linear, many-seeded, on a sharply reflexed very short pedicel. *2n* = 16. Self-compatible.

Corydalis wilsonii is similar to *C. rupestris* even in the profile of its flowers. It may be distinguished most readily from that species by its more discrete rosettes, rounded leaflets, and long linear sharply reflexed capsules. Furthermore, unlike *C. rupestris*, it has a strong, sweet, nauseating fragrance, similar to that of *Narcissus tazetta*.

Corydalis wilsonii starts flowering in early spring (sometimes as early as January) and continues through the summer. It is much commoner than *C. rupestris* as an alpine house plant. Unfortunately, it is not hardy. The species is perfect, though, for a tufa wall inside an alpine house kept above freezing in the winter. Given such a position it will often self-sow. Despite its flashy advertising, *C. wilsonii* does not need pollinators to set seed in abundance. It was originally introduced by Ernest Wilson from Hubei Province in Central China and first flowered in cultivation in England in 1903.

Corydalis tomentella Franchet is a closely related species but with looser, up to 30-flowered racemes and smaller flowers more rounded at their apex. It is unique in the genus in that short hairs completely cover the plant except for the flowers. The species is naturally distributed in the Chinese provinces of Hubei, Sichuan, and Shanxi, and was introduced to Europe by Maurice de Vilmorin in about 1894, and again by Ernest Wilson in 1902. It is widely cultivated in botanic gardens, and like its relative produces plenty of seed through selfing. In the wild it grows upon limestone cliffs.

A third species that has long been cultivated in botanic gardens is the wonderful limestone-loving *Corydalis saxicola* Bunting (syn. *C. thalictrifolia* Franchet). It is a looser, more upright plant with greener, larger, less divided leaves and looser racemes with larger flowers. It is as yet rare and seldom offered despite being first introduced as seed by Ernest Wilson as long ago as 1900. The species owes its rarity in cultivation to the fact that it is not frost-hardy. Hybrids between *C. saxicola* and *C. wilsonii* are sometimes seen and are most similar to *C. wilsonii*, but larger in all their parts. We suspect that the recently launched *C.* 'Canary Feathers' was selected among such hybrids.

Corydalis ophiocarpa J. D. Hooker & Thomson

Biennial herb, forming a large grayish-glaucous rosette the first year, followed by leafy, branched, erect stems 30–50 cm tall. *Leaves* ovate-lanceolate, 2 times pinnately divided; *petioles* winged with wings continuing along the stem. *Racemes* sessile, spikelike, 15- to 40-flowered; *bracts* small, lanceolate, entire. *Flowers* cream-colored, usually with the inner petals tipped purple; *spur* short and rounded, 3–4 mm long; *inner petals* about 9 mm long. *Capsules* long and linear, strongly contorted. $2n = 16$. Self-compatible.

Despite having rather insignificant flowers, this species from the eastern Himalaya and China is widespread in gardens and is frequently offered by nurseries in both

Corydalis ophiocarpa. Drawing by Adèle Rossetti Morosini.

the United Kingdom and North America. No doubt this is because the species is easy to grow in almost all gardens and once established will seed itself around with abandon, sometimes becoming a minor weed in the process. The species's name *ophiocarpa* is Greek for "snakelike fruit" and refers to the plant's long, thin strongly contorted capsules. The species flowers from May to June, but it is the leaf-rosettes that are the main feature, sort of translucent gray-green, with an attractive coppery tint in the fall.

Corydalis cheilanthifolia W. Hemsley   PLATES 76, 77

A densely tufted subscapose perennial herb, forming a rosette. *Leaves* elliptic-acuminate, 2 times pinnately divided, fernlike, 15–25 cm long, on stalks 1–10 cm long. *Racemes* several, spikelike, 10- to 28-flowered; *bracts* small, linear; *pedicels* short, reflexed. *Flowers* yellow; *spur* short and rounded, 4–6 mm long; *inner petals* 9–11 mm long; sometimes flowers cleistogamous and lacking a spur. *Capsule* linear, with many small seeds. $2n = 16$. Self-compatible.

Corydalis cheilanthifolia is closely related to *Corydalis ophiocarpa*, but is lower-growing with green elliptic leaves and much brighter flowers. It is a charming, easy-to-grow garden plant, suitable for a wide range of situations. It is equally at home in the rock garden, peat wall, or woodland border and can even be used as a low ground cover. The great botanical explorer Ernest Wilson first introduced the species in 1904, while collecting in China for Veitch and Sons Nursery. In fact, it was one of four *Corydalis* species that Wilson was to successfully introduce from China for this once great nursery, the other three being *C. saxicola*, *C. tomentella*, and *C. wilsonii*. All of these species, unusually for *Corydalis*, have long-lived, drought-resistant seeds. Particularly dense stands of this species may be seen at the E. H. Wilson Memorial Garden in Chipping Camden in the English Midlands (Plate 77). In this small but charming garden situated close to Wilson's birthplace are displayed many of the plants that he introduced to cultivation, including such favorites as *Acer griseum*, *Davidia involucrata*, *Lilium regale*, and *Magnolia wilsonii*.

Corydalis cheilanthifolia. Drawing by Adèle Rossetti Morosini.

Corydalis cheilanthifolia occurs in Central China in the provinces of Hubei, Guizhou, eastern Sichuan, and southeastern Yunnan, where it grows amid stones on streambanks at intermediate altitudes. Because it is a plant of relatively low altitudes, *C. cheilanthifolia* is unusually tolerant of hot, humid summers, and for this reason will grow in gardens where most other *Corydalis* fear to tread, such as in the hot, humid southeastern United States. It is also frost-hardy.

The plant will form numerous spikes of clear yellow flowers, some years as early as March, and these may, given cool temperatures, continue to be produced into July. The dark green foliage is also attractive, especially since it attains a rusty flush late in the season and persists through the winter. At that time *Corydalis cheilanthifolia* most resembles a fern of the genus *Cheilanthes*, after which it is named. A word of caution, though: in shady situations, under stress, or late in the season, it may disappoint you with small cleistogamous flowers, which lack a spur.

Corydalis cheilanthifolia is easy to propagate both by seeds and by division. When established it spreads efficiently by seed, often appearing next to a rock. The seeds, unlike those of most corydalis, will even survive long-term storage, a factor that has contributed to widespread cultivation.

Corydalis aurea Willdenow   PLATE 78
Golden fumewort, golden smoke

Winter annual, much-branched from the base. *Leaves* 2 times pinnately divided. *Racemes* several, 10- to 20- (to 30-) flowered, shorter than or slightly exceeding the leaves; bracts entire, ovate, pointed; *pedicels* short, 5–10 mm long. *Flowers* yellow, 13–16 mm long, including the 4- to 5-mm-long straight or slightly incurved spur. *Capsules* linear, often torulose, not explosively dehiscent. $2n = 16$. Self-compatible.

Corydalis aurea is the most widespread member of a group of six similar yellow-flowered winter annuals from North America. A key to these six species follows. These plants are close cousins to the Asian *C. pallida* group and have much the same appearance, demands, and uses in the garden. All the North American species are winter annuals since they produce their seed in May and June but it does not germinate until autumn, allowing these plants to overwinter as seedlings and thus begin flowering the next spring as soon as the soil begins to warm. As garden plants some of them are quite attractive, albeit in a modest way and most, if not all, have been cultivated in Europe, as well as in North America, at one time or another. These species like a dry, gravelly site where they can self-sow and are fully self-compatible and hence produce plenty of seeds. The seeds will survive dry storage for at least a year or two, though data suggest that they are not very long-lived in the natural seed bank. *Corydalis curvisiliqua*, *C. crystallina*, and *C. montana* have slightly larger flowers than the other three species of this group and for this reason are more garden-worthy. However, they are less likely than *C. aurea* to be self-perpetuating in colder climates.

Corydalis aurea occurs almost throughout the United States (except the Far West and Southeast) and is also found in southern and western Canada and southeastern Alaska. In nature, the species grows on loose, gravelly soils on talus slopes, rocky hillsides, and other similar open habitats (Plate 78). It flowers from spring to late summer. From a gardener's perspective, *C. aurea* is not the showiest member of the group. As an accessory self-seeder it is, nevertheless, a welcome addition in the wildflower garden and is more frost-hardy than the other members of the group, so will self-seed even in northern gardens. The species does not appear to currently be available from commercial sources, though it has been grown on and off in the United Kingdom since as long ago as 1683.

Corydalis micrantha (Engelmann ex A. Gray) A. Gray (scrambled eggs, slender fumewort) is an inconspicuous close relative of *C. aurea*, with narrow flowers and very small seeds. It is distributed with three subspecies in the central and southern United States. All three subspecies usually grow on disturbed sandy soils and flower in the spring. In poor light or under other kinds of stress the species often produces cleistogamous flowers. It does not appear to be available commercially or even cultivated, at least not intentionally.

Corydalis montana Engelmann ex A. Gray is endemic to west central United

States and a small part of neighboring Mexico. It is sometimes treated as *C. aurea* subsp. *occidentalis* as, for example, in the *Flora of North America*, which states that the two intergrade but usually can be distinguished when fruiting. *Corydalis montana* has erect, stout capsules and seeds that have a narrow marginal ring, while the capsules of *C. aurea* are not held erectly and are slender. Further, the seeds of *C. aurea* lack a marginal ring. In the flowering state, the longer racemes clearly overtopping the leaves and the larger flowers with straight to upturned rather long spurs usually render the two taxa distinct. The plant does not appear to be available commercially.

Corydalis curvisiliqua Engelmann ex A. Gray (curvepod fumewort) is distinguished from its relatives by its comparatively large, curved flowers, each with a long upturned spur and short high crests. It is a much rarer species than the other five, confined to disturbed,

Corydalis aurea. Drawing by Adèle Rossetti Morosini.

sandy soils in Illinois, Iowa, Kansas, Oklahoma, and Texas. Two subspecies are recognized. Subspecies *curvisiliqua* is restricted to central and southern Texas. The more northern subspecies *grandibracteata* (Fedde) G. B. Ownbey is in cultivation in Illinois at Rivendell Botanic Garden. The species flowers from early to late spring.

Corydalis crystallina Engelmann ex A. Gray (mealy fumewort) is an attractive plant, very similar in appearance to *C. curvisiliqua*, but with shortly hairy capsules. It is found in nature from southwestern Missouri to central Texas in prairies, fields, open woods, and wasteland, but does not appear to be available commercially. It flowers from mid to late spring.

Corydalis flavula A. P. de Candolle (yellow fumewort) is a rather diffuse plant with small flowers in few-flowered racemes and is not particularly showy. Nevertheless, it would make a welcome addition to the naturalistic garden, where, given a convenient rock outcrop, it could perhaps be planted close to eye level. The species does not appear to be currently available commercially. Carol and Jerry Baskin of the University of Kentucky have, however, developed a protocol for the commercial production of this annual in containers, suggesting that its release into commerce may be imminent. Certainly with native plant gardening currently being fashion-

Corydalis flavula. Drawing by Adèle Rossetti Morosini.

able in the United States, the commercial introduction of the species seems likely in that country. *Corydalis flavula* stands out from the other North American yellow-flowered annuals in having a few-flowered inflorescence, very short spur, and long pedicels. The species is endemic to eastern North America, where it occurs from Michigan and the extreme south of Ontario south to Louisiana and west to far eastern Nebraska, Kansas, and Oklahoma. The species is only abundant, however, in the Virginias, Pennsylvania, and the Carolinas. In the wild *C. flavula* is found on calcareous to neutral, mineral-rich soils in moist floodplains, wooded slopes, and rock outcrops. Its altitude preference ranges from sea level to 650 m (2100 ft). It flowers in early to late spring.

Key to the *Corydalis aurea* Complex

1a. Flowers short; inner petals 5–7 mm long, spur about 2 mm long, pedicels 6–16 mm long . . . . *C. flavula*

1b. Flowers longer; inner petals 7–12 mm long, spur 4–8 mm long (except in cleistogamous flowers, which may be smaller), pedicels 1–6(–10) mm long 2

2a. Capsules covered with fine, short, white hairs. . . . .*C. crystallina*

2b. Capsules hairless. 3

3a. Seeds very small, less than 1.5 mm long . . . . *C. micrantha*

3b. Seeds larger, about 2 mm long. 4

4a. Pedicels 1–3 mm long; seed surface rough (when magnified) . . . .*C. curvisiliqua*

4b. Pedicels 5–10 mm long; seed surface smooth (when magnified) 5

5a. Plant erect to ascending with racemes much overtopping the leaves; flowers distinctly crested; seeds with a marginal ring . . . . *C. montana*

5b. Plant ascending with racemes not much exceeding the leaves; flowers usually hardly crested; seeds lacking a marginal ring . . . . *C. aurea*

Corydalis heterocarpa Siebold & Zuccarini

Biennial herb, forming a dense wide rosette in late summer. *Stems* leafy, branched, 15–30 cm tall. *Leaves* distinctly stalked, green or slightly glaucous, triangular to triangular-oblong, 2 times pinnately divided; *leaflets* cut into subacute lobes or coarse teeth. *Racemes* few to several, spikelike, 10- to 20-flowered; *bracts* small, entire; *pedicels* 3–5 mm long. *Flowers* pale to bright yellow, usually with a grayish purple suffusion toward the apex of the outer petals, not crested, rather narrow and acute, with a short obtuse spur. *Capsule* oblong, not sharply constricted between the seeds. *Seeds* rounded, flattened, obtusely keeled, covered with short spines (densely so toward the margin), with a large membranous elaiosome folded back over the seed. *2n* = 16. Self-compatible.

Highly praised by some nurseries and certainly quite spectacular in its early flowering, this highly selfing biennial has become rather widespread in recent years and is now being distributed under different names, for example, as *Corydalis magadanica* and *C. nobilis*. The species is found in Korea and southern Japan, and has been collected just once in eastern China. It grows in open, often disturbed habitats. The most common seed strain in circulation is probably of Japanese origin.

In the garden, *Corydalis heterocarpa* starts flowering in spring and continues well into summer, and sometimes even into autumn. Plants germinate in early May and will rarely flower the first year.

Several of *Corydalis heterocarpa*'s close relatives have also been cultivated from time to time. *Corydalis orthopoda* Hayata, a native of Taiwan and the Japanese islands of Ryukyu and Bonin, is very similar, only with grayer foliage, paler flowers in looser racemes, and fewer tubercles on the seed. A few nurseries in Europe sell the species under the name *Corydalis* "Yushan," most probably from a seed introduction from Taiwan.

Corydalis speciosa Maximowicz from East Asia (eastern Siberia, Japan, Korea, northeastern China) was first introduced by Carl Maximowicz and cultivated by Albert Regel in St. Petersburg in the late 1850s. According to Regel it is a splendid garden plant that "rivals *C. nobilis* in beauty" (*speciosa* is Latin for showy). Its leaves are oblong and more finely divided, the flowers are broadly winged at apex, the capsule is constricted between the seeds like a string of beads, and the seed is pear-shaped and smooth. It is a variable species. A distinct Japanese form has been described as *C. pterophora* Ohwi. It has very broad acuminate limbs to the outer petals and green leaves.

Similar to *Corydalis speciosa* but far less attractive is the Japanese *C. pallida*

Corydalis speciosa.
Drawing by Adèle Rossetti
Morosini.

(Thunberg) Persoon, distinguished by its looser habit, short-lasting flowers, and small rounded keeled seeds covered with minute acute spines in concentric rings. Although easy to grow, these two species seem not to be currently on the market. *Corydalis pallida* was first introduced to the United Kingdom as long ago as 1884 but is today rarely seen.

Corydalis wilfordii Regel, widespread in eastern China and South Korea, has seeds similar to those of *C. heterocarpa* but with denser and longer spines. The fruits are narrow and constricted between the seeds, like those of *C. speciosa* and *C. pallida*.

These Asian yellow-flowered annual and biennial species are closely related to the *Corydalis aurea* group of North America but are better garden plants (especially *C. speciosa*), having larger, showier flowers. All look their best in spring and will thrive in slight shade in a woodland border. Since these plants are annuals, they are suitable for growing in areas with hot, humid summers, like the eastern United States.

Corydalis chaerophylla A. P. de Candolle

Perennial herb with a stout *rootstock*. *Stems* firm, 60–130 cm long, naked below, leafy and branched above. *Basal leaves* long-stalked with much divided triangular lamina; *stem leaves* like the basal, but smaller and more shortly stalked. *Racemes* very dense, simple or often branched, 6- to 40-flowered; *bracts* small, entire; *pedicels* 4–5 mm long, curved backward in fruit. *Flowers* pale yellow, narrow, 16–25 mm long, including a 10- to 15-mm-long spur. *Capsule* obovoid, small, explosively dehiscent, with several small seeds. $2n = 16$. Self-compatible.

Corydalis chaerophylla is a common plant in the Himalaya, where it is found in wet woods. It is a coarse plant with leaves reminiscent of many umbellifers, such as sweet cicely, *Myrrhis odorata*. The ancient Greek *chaerephyllon* has via Latin *cerefolium* become our "chervil." In the garden, it is suitable for naturalizing in a woodland setting. The dense foliage of this plant usually dominates, however, and when the pale yellow flowers eventually make an appearance in late summer, they often fail to attract attention, despite being numerous. The species is only occasionally offered for sale by specialist nurseries.

Corydalis chaerophylla was first collected by Nathaniel Wallich and described by

Augustin Pyramus de Candolle, a Swiss botanist, who was a prolific author of new plants. In particular he is known for his contribution to *Prodromus Systematis Naturalis Regni Vegetabilis* (published between 1823 and 1873), which remains to this day the most recent monograph of several groups of plants.

Corydalis davidii Franchet

Perennial herb from a short rhizome with several long wiry roots. *Stems* slender, leafy, branched, rather weakly angular, 40–80 cm long. *Leaves* long-stalked with green triangular lamina thrice cut into threes; *leaflets* rounded, entire, well-separated. *Racemes* spikelike, 5- to 20-flowered, conspicuously one-sided; *bracts* small, entire; *pedicels* 3–4 mm long. *Flowers* pale to bright yellow, sometimes with a muddy tinge toward the keels of the tips of the outer petals; *spur* straight, tapering, 15–20 mm long; *inner petals* 8–11 mm long.

This is a common species in southern Sichuan, where it is found in secondary forests, roadsides, and along fences and walls from 1000 up to about 3000 m (3300 to 9840 ft). Tourists to Mount Emei cannot miss it, as it grows here and there in disturbed glades along roads and paths, often with *Corydalis omeiana*. Though it can tolerate rather deep shade, it will look a lot better and less lanky in a well-lit situation. *Corydalis davidii* has been cultivated in Europe since 1995 and is still available only from specialist nurseries.

The species's name honors Armand David (also known as Père David) who from 1862 to 1874 traveled widely in northern, central, and western China, as well as Mongolia and Tibet. He discovered the dove tree (*Davidia involucrata*) and Père David's deer (*Elaphurus davidianus*). Despite mainly being an ornithologist, he collected many new species of *Corydalis*, all of them described by Adrien Franchet who worked at the Museum of Natural History, Paris.

Corydalis nobilis (Linnaeus) Persoon   PLATES 79, 80

Perennial with a swollen irregularly lobed fragile rootstock that often becomes hollow with age. *Stem* erect, hollow, rather thick and juicy, 30–50 cm tall, with sharp ridges. *Leaves* 3–5 in the upper half of the stem and from the rootstock, 2 times pinnately divided; *leaflets* fan-shaped, coarsely toothed; *basal leaves* large with lamina up to 20 cm long; *stem leaves* smaller, and rapidly decreasing in size toward the inflorescence. *Racemes* 20- to 35-flowered, very dense and almost globular at first, elongating in fruit; *lower bracts* large, deeply cut into linear segments; *upper bracts* much smaller, entire. Flowers cream, golden yellow toward the tip, inner petals with dark tips; *spur* 6–8 mm long, obtuse; inner petals 13–15 mm long. *Capsule* elliptic, 14–19 × 6–7 mm. *2n* = 16. Self-compatible, but probably requires insect visits (or other mechanical disturbance of the stigma) to set seed.

Spring at Linnaeus's garden in Uppsala or at his summer residence at Hammarby southeast of the city is highlighted by dense mats of *Corydalis nobilis* (Siberian corydalis) (Plate 80), one of the few species of the genus that was known to this great taxonomist. Since its introduction to Sweden in 1765 the species has even managed to spread around the city and is today a welcome naturalized weed in hedges, along fences of fashionable villas, and in city parks and cemeteries. Linnaeus received the plant from his student Erich Laxmann. The seed had been collected on the Siberian mountain Sinisopka in the northwesternmost part of the Altai range.

Corydalis nobilis is a wonderful plant with large globular golden flower heads and an intoxicating spicy scent. In continental climates it is readily cultivated and is very cold-hardy. Linnaeus predicted a great horticultural future for this plant. Sadly, it is as yet not widely known outside of Finland and Sweden, though it is now, at last, offered by several nurseries in the United Kingdom and North America. Only in the late 20th century was a second introduction made, but this has not spread outside of specialist gardens. The species was originally introduced to England from Linnaeus's stock via the Royal Botanic Gardens, Kew in 1783, but it has never been widely grown in the British Isles. This is no doubt because it resents turbulent springs in which mild spells are followed by freezing temperatures. It is much more suited to regions where cold winters give way predictably to warmer springs, as they do in areas with more continental climates, such as those situated further from the coast or on the eastern side of large land masses.

Siberian corydalis may be propagated by seed or by division in September when new roots are forming. It can be considered semi-tuberous, and, though coming later into flower than the tuberous species, dies down after flowering and becomes dormant. Likewise, it thrives best in a place that is reasonably dry in summer, and hence readily establishes itself in hedges and in parks under deciduous trees. It is self-compatible, but produces more and healthier seeds following cross-pollination, and under such circumstances can be rather aggressive and not easily weeded out.

Corydalis ellipticarpa C. Y. Wu & Z. Y. Su

Glabrous perennial herb from a stout rhizome, crowned by a conspicuous rosette of extremely swollen leaf bases. *Stems* suberect to erect, 30–50 cm tall, simple, with 2–4 leaves in the upper half. *Basal leaves* long-stalked with triangular lamina 2–3 times cut into threes; *leaflets* deeply divided into obtuse or acute lobes. *Stem leaves* stalked, like the basal but smaller and less divided, glaucous, sometimes with whitish veins. *Racemes* dense, 8- to 15-flowered, considerably elongating in fruit; *bracts* ovate to obovate, deeply serrate-toothed; *pedicels* straight, more or less erect, 10–20 mm long, equaling bracts. *Flowers* yellow, turning brownish with age, more or less broadly crested, rarely lacking a crest; *spur* curved downward, tapering toward the apex, 16–18 mm long; *lower petal* broadly and conspicuously saccate; *inner petals* 14–16 mm long. *Capsule* obovate to elliptic, pendent, explosively dehiscent. Self-incompatible.

The species grows in open woods in the Woolong Panda Preserve area in Central Sichuan, where it is seen growing with, for example, the purple-flowered *Corydalis anthriscifolia*. Except for the yellow flowers, it is very similar to *C. brunneovaginata* Fedde and *C. quantmeyeriana* Fedde. The latter species is probably also in cultivation. This species complex is still poorly understood.

It is sold (misidentified as, for example, *Corydalis nigroapiculata*) by the Chinese internet firm Chen Yi and has lately been propagated in cultivation in the West and sold as "*Corydalis* sp." Its requirements in cultivation are similar to those of *C. flexuosa* and *C. anthriscifolia*.

The authors of this species, Wu Cheng-Yi and Su Zhi-Yun at the Kunming department of botany, have together with Zhuang Xuan discovered and described numerous species of *Corydalis* from China. Professor Wu is one of the most productive Chinese botanists. He has co-edited, and written several treatments in the *Flora Republicae Popularis Sinicae*. For a non-Chinese speaking audience, this work is now appearing in an English version, *Flora of China*, revised to include the latest scientific achievements. *Flora of China* is also available on the World Wide Web.

Non-tuberous Species with Blue, Purple, Pink, and/or White Flowers

Corydalis caseana A. Gray   PLATE 81

Glabrous perennial herb from a thick rootstock. *Stems* 50–220 cm high, erect, terete, thick, and hollow, with 3–6 leaves spread along the stem. *Leaves* 3–4(–6) times pinnately divided, with rounded membranous stipules at the base of the petioles. *Racemes* spikelike, simple or branched, 30- to 200-flowered. *Flowers* 15–25 mm long, white to pinkish purple, with the inner petals tipped with blackish purple; *petals* broad or narrow, with or without crests. *Capsules* thick-walled, ob-ovate, explosively dehiscent, sharply reflexed on straight pedicels. Self-compatible to some degree, but normally cross-pollinated.

No other *Corydalis* (except possibly *C. gigantea* Trautvetter & Meyer from East Asia) grows to such astonishing proportions as *C. caseana*, which can reach heights of almost 2.4 m. First cultivated in 1886, this species has never received the interest it deserves as a garden plant. In the wild, it is widely distributed in the mountains of the western United States but has a very patchy distribution, being comprised of six geographically isolated subspecies. Individual populations often contain several individuals but are typically widely separated and are largely restricted to sites in or near running water, on rich mineral soils, at altitudes of 370 to 3400 m (1200 to 11,150 ft)—a rather precise habitat preference.

Corydalis caseana subsp. *brandegei* (Watson) G. B. Ownbey (Brandegee's fume-wort; New Mexico, Colorado) and subsp. *cusicki* (Watson) G. B. Ownbey (Cusick's fumewort; Idaho, northeastern Oregon) are the tallest and largest-flowered of the six subspecies, and are particularly garden-worthy. In Gothenburg they are culti-vated in an open woodland as well as by the edge of a pond, where they flower in early June. The soil is like that typically found in a rich woodland site but mixed with coarse sand. The much daintier subsp. *aquae-gelidae* (Peck & Wilson) Lidén & Zetterlund (coldwater fumewort; Oregon, Washington) grows at lower elevations and prefers a shadier, less windy, habitat. It has more finely cut leaves and smaller flowers. Subspecies *caseana* (sierra fumewort, California), subsp. *brachycarpa* (Ryd-berg) G. B. Ownbey (Utah), and subsp. *hastata* (Rydberg) G. B. Ownbey (northern Idaho) are horticulturally less interesting. Subspecies *brachycarpa* (Plate 81) is prob-ably the rarest of the subspecies in the wild, although only subsp. *aquae-gelidae* is red-listed, probably because it has previously been attributed specific status. *Flora of North America* reports that *C. caseana* is poisonous to both cattle and sheep, which eat it despite the plant's toxicity.

As with most other species of *Corydalis*, it is not uncommon to find the spurs pierced by nectar thieves (that is, insects that do not perform pollination but still drink the nectar). However, it seems as if fruit-set is only marginally affected by robbers, and pollination biologist Joan Maloof suggested that they might even be beneficial, because a depleted nectar source may cause the legitimate pollinators to shorten their visits to an inflorescence and to fly longer distances.

In the Amur region of East Asia are found two closely related species but only one of them, *Corydalis gigantea* Trautvetter & Meyer, is cultivated, albeit infre-quently. The section *Archaeocapnos* to which these and *C. caseana* belong is distinguished by rounded membranous stipules and also includes the American *C. scouleri* (see below) and a few Chinese species.

Corydalis scouleri W. J. Hooker   PLATE 82

A large stoloniferous perennial, 50–120 cm tall. *Stems* rounded, hollow, usually with 3 leaves at or above the middle of the stem. *Leaves* (as in all members of the section *Archaeocapnos*) with rounded membranous stipules, 3 or occasionally 4 times pinnately divided, green above, glaucous beneath. *Racemes* simple or branched, narrow, usually with fewer than 25 flowers, but occasionally up to 35. *Flowers* held almost vertically, pale to deep purplish pink; *outer petals* lacking a rim but with conspicuous entire apical crests; spur 14–20 mm long; *inner petals* 9–10 mm long. *Capsule* strongly reflexed, obovate, explosively dehiscent. *2n* = ca. 130–150. Self-compatible to some degree, but normally cross-pollinated.

Corydalis scouleri is easily distinguished from its close relative *C. caseana* by its leaves that are held in one plane, its uniformly pink flowers, which are almost vertically held and which have very broad entire crests, its slender far-reaching underground rhizomes, and its large seeds (about 3.5 mm in diameter versus 2–2.5 mm in diameter). A very peculiar thing about *C. scouleri* is that it has three times as many chromosomes as any other species of *Corydalis*—around 140. In the wild it is distributed from the southern tip of Vancouver Island southward to Oregon's lush Siuslaw National Forest. Like *C. caseana* it is confined to cool, wet habitats. However, *C. scouleri* inhabits the forest understory and is found on humus-rich soils at lower altitudes from near sea level to 1100 m (3600 ft). As such, the two species rarely come into contact in the wild, and when they do, as at Tanner Creek in northern Oregon, they apparently do not hybridize.

Corydalis scouleri is named in honor of John Scouler, who at age 20

Corydalis scouleri. Drawing by Adèle Rossetti Morosini.

collected the plant while working as the surgeon and naturalist on the 1824 to 1825 expedition to the Columbia River. William Hooker, who first described the species, later worked at the University of Glasgow where Scouler was professor of geology.

Corydalis scouleri is a much under-valued garden plant that was first grown at the Royal Botanic Gardens, Kew, but today is available from only a few specialist nurseries. As early as 1898, evaluations and cultural instructions by plantsman Sam Arnott, of snowdrop fame, appear in *The Garden*: "charming foliage . . . and pretty flowers . . . a position sheltered from strong winds . . . that destroy the tender leafage and shrivel it up as by fire." The species is prone to start into growth too early in the season and thus get cut down by spring frosts. Given a sheltered woodland site and a cool summer climate, *C. scouleri* makes a wonderful garden plant.

Corydalis scouleri is easy to propagate from pieces of the fleshy horizontal rhizome. It can increase to form a beautiful raised floor of leaves, overtopped by narrow violet flower spikes. Indeed, displayed this way the species may be seen carpeting the floor under many of the larger rhododendrons at the Royal Botanic Garden, Edinburgh. The species flowers from April to June.

Corydalis anthriscifolia Franchet

Rootstock thick, with fibrous remnants. *Stems* erect, branched above, 50–80 cm tall with 3–5 leaves in the upper half. *Basal leaves* very large with a stalk up to 35 cm long, green, triangular, 2 or almost 3 times pinnately divided; *leaflets* more or less deeply divided, coarsely toothed, acute; *upper leaves* much smaller and less divided, sessile. *Racemes* dense, sometimes simple but more often wide and much branched, 10- to 15-flowered. *Bracts* small and linear. *Pedicels* erect, thin, 4–10 mm long. *Sepals* large, entire, shieldlike, early falling. *Corolla* bluish to reddish purple, usually paler toward the apex; *spur* gracefully tapering, upwardly directed, 18–25 mm long; *lower petal* usually much paler than the upper, boat-shaped; *inner petals* 9–10 mm long. *Capsule* narrowly obovate, thick-walled.

Corydalis anthriscifolia is a native of Central Sichuan, where it grows in the Woolong Panda Reserve in open woods. It is superficially similar to *C. mucronata*, but the foliage and rootstock are quite different, the sepals are large and early falling, and the outer petals are not beaked. It is also reminiscent of the American *C. scouleri*, but the foliage is similar to that of the common European cow parsley, *Anthriscus sylvestris*, after which it is named.

The species has, since about 2000, been introduced via Chen Yi, misidentified as *Corydalis jingyuanensis*. Plants sold as *C. anthriscifolia*, however, have turned out to be *C. quantmeyeriana* Fedde. For good measure, plants labeled as *C. quantmeyer-iana* were *C. mucronata* Franchet, while plants offered as *C. mucronata* have been *C. sheareri* S. Moore, all according to the pictures on Chen Yi's Web site in 2006.

Corydalis longicalcarata C. Chuang & Z. Y. Su

> *Rhizome* stout, more or less vertical. *Stems* one to few, erect to suberect, 20–35 cm tall, with 2–3 leaves in the upper half. *Basal leaves* stalked, 2 or almost 3 times pinnately divided; *leaflets* small, discrete, rounded, entire; *stem leaves* like the basal, but much smaller and less divided. *Racemes* dense, 2- to 5-flowered; *lower-most bract* frequently ternately divided with rounded sessile leaflets; *upper bracts* ovate, entire; *pedicels* 4–8 mm long, erect. *Flowers* similar to those of *Corydalis anthriscifolia*; *sepals* large (4 × 2–3 mm), whitish, shieldlike, and entire, early fall-ing; *outer petals* without crests and without a spreading margin; *spur* 17–26 mm long, straight and tapering, upwardly directed, claw of lower petal with a very large pouch; *inner petals* 9–12 mm long. *Capsule* obovate, pendent.

This species from Mounts Emei and Wawu in western Sichuan is another Chen Yi introduction. It is related to *Corydalis anthriscifolia* and shares with this species the same type of rootstock as well as membranous stipules, large early-falling sepals, and a subvertically held long-spurred corolla that lacks a crest. The foliage, how-ever, is unique in the genus and the main attraction. Like its relative, *Corydalis lon-gicalcarata* prefers deep humus-rich soils and a woodland setting.

Corydalis sheareri S. Moore   PLATE 83

> *Rootstock* tuberous, elliptic, 1–4 × 0.5–1.5 cm, producing slender underground rhizomes with several daughter tubers. *Stems* few, suberect, 20–50 cm long, with 2–4 stalked leaves, sparingly branched above, sometimes papillose-hairy above. *Leaves* 2 or occasionally 3 times pinnately divided, triangular, with discrete cre-nately toothed or shallowly lobed rather unequally sized leaflets. *Racemes* 5- to 20-flowered, rather dense at first, elongating in fruit; *lower bracts* broad and often deeply cut into ovate lobes, as long as or longer than the erecto-patent 4- to 10-mm-long pedicels; *uppermost bracts* smaller and entire. *Flowers* pale bluish pur-ple to pink, much darker toward the apex, shortly crested apically; *spur* 13–17 mm long, evenly tapering toward the pointed apex, straight or curved downward; *inner petals* 11–13 mm long, often with a dark tip. *Capsule* linear, with seeds in one row. *Seeds* with sparse papillae. Self-incompatible.

Common in central and southern China, *Corydalis sheareri* is a recent introduction to horticulture. This spring-flowering species is unmistakable with its obtusely crenate leaflets, acute spur, and papillose seeds. *Corydalis sheareri* 'Silver Spectre' is becoming particularly widespread, though usually sold under the incorrect name *C. leucanthema*. This clone was originally collected by Dan Hinkley in 1996 from "a creek bank in Sichuan" at 1950 m (6400 ft) and has diffuse pale gray patterns along the veins of the leaflets, a feature not uncommonly seen in *C. sheareri* as a whole. *Corydalis sheareri* (both with and without spots) is also offered from the Chen Yi Web site and certain other nurseries under various names, including *C. aquilegioides*, *C. jingyuanensis*, *C. mucronata*, and *C. stenantha*, although other species have also been received under these names.

The underground system of this species is similar to that of *Helianthus tuberosus*, the common Jerusalem artichoke. When the plant goes dormant the tubers can be easily separated, so the species is readily propagated. Forma *bulbillifera* produces elongate bulbils in the axils of cauline leaves. The closely related *Corydalis esquirolii* H. Léveillé has stems with numerous small bractlike leaves below the inflorescence, each subtending an easily detached small bulbil.

Corydalis temulifolia Franchet has some resemblance to *C. sheareri* in the dentate leaflets and the pale pinkish flowers with spur evenly tapering toward the apex. It is, however, a more robust plant with a short rhizome, large fleshy leaf-bases, fewer, larger, more acute, and more regularly toothed leaflets, and fewer and broader flowers in the raceme. It has been in cultivation for several years in specialist's collections. *Corydalis temulifolia* 'Chocolate Stars', remarkable for its dark brown foliage in early stages of growth, has recently been released on the internet market under the incorrect species name "*quantmeyeriana*."

Corydalis mucronata Franchet   PLATE 84

Rhizome elongate, knotty because of the presence of densely set fleshy rounded scales or leaf base remnants. *Stems* ascending to erect, juicy and brittle, 20–60 cm, sparsely leafy and branched above; *basal leaves* few, long-stalked, in a loose rosette. *Leaves* triangular, 2 or occasionally 3 times pinnately divided; *leaflets* crenately toothed to shallowly lobed. *Racemes* long and loose, 10- to 20-flowered; *bracts* much shorter than the thin 7- to 14-mm-long pedicels, lower bracts divided, upper bracts entire. *Flowers* pale rosy purple with contrasting dark purplish red, irregularly cleft sepals; *outer petals* long-mucronate, not crested; *spur* 23–27 mm long, straight or usually gracefully curved upward, evenly tapering to a thin apex; *inner petals* pale, 10–11 mm long. *Capsules* broadly ovate.

Corydalis mucronata is a very graceful and unusual species, with beautiful, downward-pointing flowers that open pale purple and then fade to buff. The name *mucronata* refers to the long mucronate, or beaked, outer petals of the species. The closely related *C. pseudomucronata* C. Y. Wu, Z. Y. Su & Lidén is almost identical but for its slightly smaller flowers and a different stigma shape. Both species are rare in cultivation. *Corydalis mucronata* is pictured in volume one of *Perennials* by Phillips and Rix (1991) as *C. sheareri* and has been distributed by Chen Yi under the name *C. quantmeyeriana*. It is a native of West Central Sichuan, flowering in May at altitudes of 1100 to 2000 m (3600 to 6560 ft).

Corydalis flexuosa Franchet   PLATES 85, 86

Rootstock elongate, densely set with thick fleshy scales, sometimes producing runners with only a few distant scales. *Stems* 20–40 cm long, with 3–5 leaves, not or sparingly branched above. *Leaves* rather small, dark green, 3 times ternately divided into rather narrow obtuse lobes. *Racemes* dense, about 10-flowered, often conspicuously arranged on one side; *lower bracts* often much divided; *upper bracts* small and entire; *pedicels* erecto-patent. *Flowers* clear blue or with a purplish tinge, rarely white, not crested; *spur* straight, sometimes slightly upwardly directed, 12–17 mm long; *upper outer petal* acute at apex; *lower outer petal* with a narrow claw abruptly widened into a rounded limb; *inner petals* pale, 14–16 mm long. *Capsule* linear, pendent, with several small seeds. Self-incompatible.

Corydalis flexuosa is part of an intricate complex of species that is not fully understood taxonomically, but which is recognized from, for example, the *C. elata* group by its linear many-seeded fruits. *Corydalis flexuosa* sensu stricto (Plates 85, 86) is an erect herb, growing on rich slopes in open woods in the Woolong and Baoxing Valleys of China's Sichuan Province, at altitudes from 1800 to 2800 m (5900 to 9200 ft). It flowers in spring and usually dies down during the summer. Late in the season new leaves develop that will survive until next spring, and sometimes a second flush of flowers is produced in autumn.

Nowhere is the genus more diverse than in the "Hengduan Mountains hotspot" of western China, the home of *Corydalis flexuosa* and its closest relatives. This area, consisting of western Sichuan and adjacent parts of neighboring provinces, is recognized as the most species-rich area in the world outside of the trop-

Corydalis flexuosa. Drawing by Paul Harwood.

ics. It has an extremely jagged topography with high rainfall and north-south flowing rivers dividing mountain chains that reach high above the tree line, thus allowing for a great diversity of ecological niches. Not unexpectedly, most species in such a country have very restricted distributions; many are known only from one mountain chain, a single mountain, or even a single cliff face. Western China has not been severely affected by the latest glaciations and, during climatic fluctuations, populations have had the possibility to move up or downhill or north-south along the rivers, factors promoting a low rate of extinction.

Corydalis 'Blue Heron' (Plate 87) is a shorter, more branched and spreading plant than *C. flexuosa* sensu stricto and has darker green clearly glaucous foliage that does not die down in summer, broader bracts, and clear azure-blue flowers. The flowers are very similar to the normal form of *C. flexuosa*, but with a sweeter fragrance. 'Blue Heron' was collected by plantsman Dan Hinkley in 1996, who found it "in wet seeps with *Epimedium davidii* . . . near the Woolong Panda Preserve" at ca. 1700 m (5575 ft). The different ecology and growth habit may indicate that it should possibly be treated as a species distinct from *C. flexuosa*. It is noteworthy that several narrow endemics in this section of the genus share the same habitat. *Corydalis* 'Blue Heron' starts flowering in early summer and may continue with the occasional flowering raceme well into September. It was first distributed as *C. curviflora* (then later as *C. pachycentra*) 'Blue Heron' by Heronswood Nursery, wisely with a question mark for the specific determination.

Higher up on open slopes in Balang Shan west of the Woolong Valley, at altitudes from 3000 to 4000 m (9840 to 13,000 ft), *Corydalis flexuosa* is replaced by *C. calycosa* H. Chuang (syn. *C. flexuosa* subsp. *kuanhsiensis* C. Y. Wu). This has much shorter and less fleshy rhizomes and stiff erect stems with (in the best forms) an impressive cylindric cluster of 10 to 30 very broadly crested flowers. It flowers much later, well into August and is rare in cultivation, but has been sold by Chen Yi under the name *C. nemoralis*.

However, if one wants beauty, hardiness, and flower longevity, none of these species can compete with the hybrid *Corydalis flexuosa* × *C. omeiana*, a real breakthrough in *Corydalis* breeding, combining the ease of cultivation of *C. omeiana* with the beauty of *C. flexuosa*, and with a much extended flowering period. This cross was first noted by Ian Young and has been named *C.* 'Craigton Blue' (Plate 88).

Another excellent cultivar is *Corydalis* 'Kingfisher' (Plate 89), a sterile hybrid between *C. flexuosa* and *C. cashmeriana* that was introduced by Keith Lever of Aberconwy Nursery, North Wales. It has electric-blue flowers, much like those of *C. cashmeriana* in its best forms but considerably larger. The inner petals tend to be dark purple toward the apex, which may indicate that the Kailash form of *C. cash-*

meriana was a parent. The plant approaches *C. flexuosa* in size and its flowering season surpasses that of either parent—a lovely plant. It is interesting to note that the presumed parents of this hybrid come from what are considered separate sections of the genus, namely, sections *Elatae* and *Fasciculatae*. Recent molecular studies have shown, however, that these two sections may be less distant than previously thought.

Numerous cultivars of *Corydalis flexuosa* now exist, and more continue to be released each year. Washington State nurseryman Reuben Hatch was the first to introduce *C. flexuosa* to gardens in 1986. Such was its immediate popularity that it was soon produced on a large scale via micropropagation, as it is to this day. This clone was subsequently brought to the United Kingdom around 1991 under the cultivar name 'Blue Panda'. Meanwhile, self-sown seedlings of this plant from Heronswood Nursery in Washington State were named 'Purple Panda' for their blue flowers tinged with purple. In 1989 further clones were introduced from China by British botanists James Compton, John d'Arcy, and Martyn Rix, and were given the cultivar names 'Purple Leaf' (syn. 'Blue Dragon'), 'Père David', and 'China Blue'. Chris Grey-Wilson in 1993 introduced an additional clone—'Balang Mist'. All of these cultivars are rather similar but differ somewhat in behavior. 'Purple Leaf' (Plate 90) has purplish blue flowers, reddish-purple leaves, and may continue flowering well into summer; 'Père David' has clear blue flowers, glaucous foliage with red markings on and near the main vein, and is more prone than the other cultivars to produce stolons; 'China Blue' (Plate 91) has bright blue flowers, which are prone to turn purple in cold weather, and green foliage; and lastly, 'Balang Mist' is clump forming and has flowers that are white with a hint of blue. 'China Blue' is the most heat- and humidity-tolerant of all the cultivars. 'Golden Panda' (Plate 92) has golden-yellow leaves with red markings on and near the main vein, pale blue flowers, and was discovered in a flask of tissue-cultured *C.* 'Blue Panda' at Terra Nova Nursery in Oregon in 2000. 'Nightshade', a seedling of 'Père David' introduced in 1996, has purplish flowers and green leaves that are blotched with purple. Finally, we should mention 'Tory MP', which is now widely available in the United Kingdom and was given its name by nurseryman Nick Macer because "it's true blue and tends to go on and on [flowering]."

Corydalis flexuosa, as well as the other taxa discussed here, is best grown in a slightly acidic to neutral soil and is hardy to −15°C (5°F). Summer heat will cause the plants to become dormant, but leaves (and sometimes additional flowers) should reemerge when temperatures cool in the autumn. Division is best done at this time. If seeds are required, more than one clone will be needed since *C. flexuosa* is self-incompatible.

Corydalis omeiana (C. Y. Wu) Lidén   PLATE 93

Rootstock elongate, densely set with thick fleshy scales. *Stems* 30–50 cm long with 3–6 leaves, not or sparingly branched. *Basal leaves* green, 2 or 3 times ternately divided into obovate obtuse lobes, frequently with red spots at the incisions; *upper leaves* smaller and less divided. *Racemes* dense, about 10-flowered, often conspicuously one-sided; *lower bracts* often much divided; *upper bracts* small and entire; *pedicels* erecto-patent. *Flowers* clear blue or with a purplish tinge, not crested; *sepals* 2–2.5 × 1.5–2 mm, wrinkled, early falling; *spur* straight, sometimes slightly downwardly directed, 14–18 mm long; *upper outer petal* acute at apex; *lower outer petal* with a narrow claw abruptly widened into a rounded limb; *inner petals* pale, 12–14 mm long. *Capsule* linear, pendent, with several small seeds. Self-incompatible.

This species was first noted botanically as *Corydalis flexuosa* var. *omeiana* C. Y. Wu. It has been in cultivation since the 1990s, mistaken for *C. elata*, which it approaches in the rather broad claw to the lower petal and the elliptic fruit. Vegetatively, however, it tends more toward *C. flexuosa* in, for example, the more pronounced rhizome, more subordinate bright green foliage, and denser inflorescence. The flowers of *C. omeiana* are very elegant with a narrow straight or down-curved spur. The lower petal has a broad undulate limb that almost encloses the upper petal in bud and lacks the basal gibbosity of *C. elata*. The sepals are also quite different. In *C. elata* they are very small, thin, and deeply toothed, whereas in *C. omeiana* they are up to 4 mm long, finely toothed, thickish, uneven, and early falling. *Corydalis omeiana* grows plentiful on Mount Emei in West Central Sichuan, from 2500 to 2900 m (8200 to 9500 ft), where it flowers in early summer. It is one of the few endemics that is happy with the intense exploitation of the summit area since it became appointed a World Heritage Site.

Corydalis omeiana is available, under the name *C. elata*, from many nurseries in the United Kingdom and North America, and has proven amenable to regions with warm summers, like, for example, the eastern United States. Also in the South of England it is a much easier species to grow than *C. flexuosa*. Some gardeners, however, note that its rather weak stems have a tendency to fall over and need supporting with pea sticks.

Corydalis omeiana flowers later than *C. flexuosa*, being at its best in late June, and unlike that species, its leaves do not die down in summer. In milder climates the leaves are even semi-evergreen during winter.

Corydalis elata Bureau & Franchet   PLATE 94

Rootstock a short rhizome with fleshy scales. *Stems* erect, one to several, 35–50 cm long, leafy, sparingly branched above. *Leaves* green above, paler beneath, tri-angular, 2 times ternately divided; *leaflets* obovate, coarsely lobed; *basal leaves* rather long-stalked; *upper stem leaves* sessile, much smaller, and less divided. *Racemes* rather loose, 10- to 25-flowered, with flowers all round; *lower bracts* often rather large and divided; *upper bracts* small and entire; *pedicels* straight, erecto-patent, 13–20 mm long, longer than the bracts. *Flowers* blue to purple; *outer petals* acuminate or almost beaked, sometimes toothed; *spur* straight or curved, 13–16 mm long; *lower outer petal* usually with a pronounced gibbosity at the base; *inner petals* pale, 10–11 mm long. *Capsule* broadly fusiform, pendent, explosively dehiscent, with a few large seeds.

Corydalis elata sensu stricto is a newcomer to cultivation, plants having arrived in gardens via Chen Yi. This species with purplish blue to blue flowers is vigorous and easily propagated. It is one of several related species with a very restricted distribution in Central Sichuan, where it grows in humid forests and glades and sub-alpine shrub.

Corydalis elata is easily distinguished from *C. flexuosa* in its coarser foliage, much longer and looser and not one-sided racemes, and a lower petal with a broader claw, which often has a pronounced gibbosity at its base. It is likewise different from *C. omeiana* in its long-stalked lower leaves, small sepals, and a more pointed corolla. The stock in cultivation is variable. Most plants have rather dull purplish-blue flowers. The occasional bright blue individuals are also grown, though rarely do these have as clear blue flowers as the best form of *C. flexuosa*. In all three species small red spots are not uncommon at the junction of the leaf-lobes.

Corydalis elata will thrive in cultivation in semi-shade, in a well-drained, yet water-retentive, humus-rich soil on the acid side that should never be allowed to completely dry out. Seed can be set plentifully, at least when two or more clones are planted together. We suspect that the species may also self, although this remains to be proven. An added bonus with this species and some of its relatives, including *C. flexuosa*, is their exquisite fragrance like *Gardenia* with a distinct touch of *Cocos*. As a garden plant, *C. elata* cannot compete with *C. flexuosa* or its hybrids. Being a plant from higher altitudes, we expect, however, that it will prove to be hardier.

Corydalis pseudobarbisepala Fedde   PLATE 95

Rhizome elongate, with many long thick roots. *Stems* few to several, 10–25 cm long, erect or ascending, simple or very rarely with a single branch. *Basal leaves* rather long-stalked with small rounded lamina, 1–2 times ternately divided; *leaflets* shallowly to deeply cut into rounded lobes, glaucous. *Stem leaves* 2–4, subsessile, rounded, like the basal, but less divided. *Racemes* 10- to 15-flowered, very dense in flower, considerably elongating in fruit; *lower bracts* very broad and divided, *upper bracts* entire, obovate; *pedicels* erecto-patent, longer than the bracts. *Flowers* blue, sometimes with a violet tinge; *inner petals* 10–14 mm long, darker toward the apex, but usually white at the extreme tip; *outer petals* broadly crested; *spur* very broad, slightly curved, 10–13 mm long; *lower outer petal* broadly saccate, usually with a diminutive spur or gibbosity at the very base. *Capsule* broadly obovate, pendent.

Corydalis pseudobarbisepala is locally common in Sichuan's Balang Shan at altitudes of 3500 to 4000 m (11,500 to 13,000 ft), growing on slopes along the roadside, and, at higher altitudes, also in the rough alpine screes, where it is found with *Meconopsis punicea* and other alpine gems. The higher-altitude forms tend to have shorter, ascending stems. Surprisingly, even though this is a low alpine plant, *C. pseudobarbisepala* will respond well in cultivation with the same treatment as the woodlander *C. flexuosa*. Being a newcomer to cultivation it is still rare in gardens, though this is likely to change in the future.

The sturdy flowers and sessile broad-lobed stem-leaves make it impossible to confuse this species with anything else, though it has been sold as *Corydalis stenantha* (a very different species from Yunnan) through the Chen Yi Web site. Some forms in cultivation have variegated leaves.

Corydalis panda Y. W. Wang & Lidén   PLATE 96

Glabrous perennial with a rather short rhizome with fleshy scales and long thickish roots. *Stems* few to several, often reddish, 8–15(–25) cm long, suberect or ascending, often with 1–3 branches. *Basal leaves* long-stalked with small ovate lamina deeply cut into narrow lobes. *Stem leaves* 2–4, scattered along the stem, like the basal but the upper leaves very shortly stalked. *Racemes* dense, 8- to 15-flowered; *lower bracts* leaflike, *upper bracts* progressively smaller and less divided; *pedicels* slender, longer than the bracts, erecto-patent. *Flowers* blue, sometimes with a purplish tinge; *outer petals* narrowly crested; *spur* narrow, 11–13 mm long, often strongly curved downward; *lower outer petal* not saccate; *inner petals* 8–10 mm long. *Capsules* narrowly oblong, pendent.

Corydalis panda is a plant of astounding beauty. On some select slopes of Balang Shan the vividly blue flowers cannot fail to attract the attention of passersby, and, we suspect, may have even caused more than one traffic accident. This conspicuous species was discovered only in 2004 by Beijing botanists exploring along a new highway and was described as recently as 2006. It is only known from the type locality, where it is plentiful. Imagine our surprise when we discovered a picture on a Web site, proving that, well before it was scientifically noted, it was in cultivation in northern Norway as *C. flaccida*. This is yet another result of the Chen Yi exports. The plant pictured as *C. flaccida* on her Web site (2006), however, is *C. pseudoflumi-nicola* Fedde. In gardens the species is later flowering than most other blue-flowered corydalis, with blooms being produced from July to September.

In the type locality *Corydalis panda* grows together with *C. pseudobarbisepala* at altitudes from 3800 to 4200 m (12,500 to 13,650 ft), attaining and even surpassing the tree line. It is readily distinguished from *C. pseudobarbisepala* in its narrow leaf-lobes, much narrower flowers, and narrow capsules.

Corydalis mairei H. Léveillé   PLATE 97

Stems much-branched from the base, erect, themselves frequently branched, 30–50 cm high. *Leaves* dark green, often paler along the veins, 2 or 3 times ter-nately divided; *leaflets* cut into acute lobes. *Racemes* several, 6- to 20-flowered, rather dense in flower, but becoming much looser in fruit; *bracts* much divided into acute lobes, or the uppermost bract sometimes entire; *pedicels* patent. *Flow-ers* pale blue to purplish blue, lacking a terminal crest, sharply acute at apex; *spur* long, narrow, curved, 11–14 mm long; *inner petals* 10–12 mm long. *Capsules* linear-oblong, pendent.

Like *Corydalis elata*, this is a recent introduction from Chen Yi. It can hardly be con-fused with any other cultivated species. The narrow elegant pointed blue flowers are produced in profusion, and because the plant branches freely, the flowering season is quite long. The species is still rare, but seems easy to propagate and often sets seed in cultivation. It hails from the mountains of South Sichuan.

The species's name honors Ernest Maire, a French missionary who collected plants in eastern Yunnan from 1905 to 1916.

Corydalis cashmeriana Royle   PLATES 98, 99

Rhizome small, with a tight bundle (fascicle) of spindle-shaped storage roots and small "bulblets," seated firmly below ground level. *Radical leaves* and flowering stems have weak slender bases that become more robust once above soil level. *Stems* about 10 cm long, simple, with 1 or 2 sessile digitately divided leaves. *Racemes* corymbose, 2- to 8-flowered, slightly elongating in fruit; *bracts* deeply cut into lanceolate segments; *pedicels* 15 to 30 mm long, longer than bracts, suberect and straight. *Flowers* clear blue, sometimes with a violet tinge; *upper outer petal* acute at apex, with or without a dorsal crest; *spur* 8–13 mm long; *lower outer petal* with a broad diamond-shaped limb; *inner petals* 9–11 mm long, pale, or (in an elegant form from the Tibetan holy mountain Kailash) darker toward the apex. *Capsules* narrowly oblong, pendent, explosively dehiscent. *2n* = 16. Self-incompatible.

A real classic, *Corydalis cashmeriana* has been in cultivation since botanical explorers Frank Ludlow and George Sherriff introduced it via seed in 1933. Never failing to attract admiration and desire, the species was awarded a Certificate of Merit from the Royal Horticultural Society on its premiere at a flower show the following May, and an Award of Merit a few years later, in 1938.

While highly desirable, *Corydalis cashmeriana* is a challenge in many gardens, especially since it requires a cool root-run in the summer. Scotland, with its cool climate, is famous for its large colonies, and in western Scandinavia the plant is also readily grown. In slightly warmer climates, as in the south of England, *C. cashmeriana* will survive in gardens but will never perform as spectacularly nor have as vivid blue flowers as it does in cooler, more northerly climates. The species is best grown in a peaty, water-retentive but well-drained soil; a raised peat bed is excellent. In a pot it usually fares less well but even so, given a cool root-run, it should survive. Just as importantly, the soil must never be allowed to dry out nor should it become overly wet. In northern regions *C. cashmeriana* will grow in an open sunny situation, but in warmer climates it will require a little shade during the afternoon, the hottest time of day. If properly situated, *C. cashmeriana* will increase in size and then has to be regularly divided, preferably in late August. Take care when you separate the plants so the storage roots from individual rhizomes keep attached where they belong. A top dressing of fine leaf mold and grit and some bonemeal should also be applied each autumn.

Corydalis cashmeriana is in the wild a variable species with a wide distribution in the Himalaya, from Kashmir to Bhutan, growing in alpine grass turf and rarely in more open gravels. A cultivated form named 'Kailash' (Plate 99) is a delightful dwarf version with rather large flowers that are darker toward the apex than in most other forms of the species. Its cultivar name suggests that it was collected near the holy mountain Kailash, where the immortal Shiva spends his time practicing Yogic austerities, making joyous love, and smoking marijuana.

At high altitudes toward the northeast, *Corydalis cashmeriana* is replaced by the much smaller *C. jigmei* C. E. C. Fischer & Kaul. In

Corydalis cashmeriana. Drawing by Adèle Rossetti Morosini.

the wetter eastern part of the species's distribution area grows *C. ecristata* (Prain) D. G. Long. This species is sometimes confused with *C. cashmeriana* but is immediately recognizable by its small size, narrower leaf lobes, a very broad truncate lower petal limb, and shorter flowers. Both these related plants are occasionally grown in specialist gardens. *Corydalis* 'Kingfisher' is a wonderful hybrid between *C. flexuosa* and *C. cashmeriana* discussed under *C. flexuosa*.

Corydalis pachycentra Franchet   PLATE 100

Storage roots narrowly fusiform. *Radical leaves* few with a thin tapering base and a small rounded deeply cut lamina. *Stems* few, suberect, slender, 6–18 cm long, with 1 or 2 sessile leaves deeply cut into lanceolate lobes. *Racemes* short, elongating in fruit; *bracts* lanceolate, usually entire; *pedicels* erecto-patent, about as long as the bracts. *Flowers* obtuse, usually bright azure blue, sometimes with white markings at the apex; *spur* turned upward, thick and obtuse, 8–11 mm long; *inner petals* about 8 mm long. *Capsules* pendent from erect pedicels.

Corydalis pachycentra is similar to the more widely grown *C. cashmeriana,* but is readily distinguished by its tubby flowers with broad upward-curved spur, and by its undivided bracts. It grows in northwestern Yunnan up to Central Sichuan (Balang Shan) and is very common on alpine meadow slopes from 3500 to 5000 m (11,500 to 16,400 ft) in altitude. It especially occurs where there is a mosaic of grass turf and open soil. More rarely it is found in screes.

Many forms of this delightful plant have been introduced over the last decades. They show a surprisingly wide range of variation in plant and flower size. Some forms have thin underground stolons, whereas others are clump forming. In Yunnan the species flowers in early summer, in Central Sichuan in August. As botanists often say, "more research is needed."

The very similar *Corydalis curviflora* Maximowicz has a more northerly distribution and may also be in cultivation, though we have not seen it. The shape of the storage roots readily distinguishes the two species. In *C. pachycentra* they are narrowly fusiform and gradually narrowed toward the point of attachment, whereas in *C. curviflora* they are cylindrical. Several relatives of these species occur in western China and eastern Tibet, some with the same brilliantly blue flowers, others with yellow, cream, or purple flowers.

Corydalis taliensis Franchet

Perennial with a short contorted rootstock, much branched from the base. *Stems* leafy, branched throughout, usually decumbent to ascending, 20–60 cm long. *Leaves* long-stalked (except the uppermost), sheathing at base, thin, 2 times ternately divided; *leaflets* shallowly cut into broad obtuse lobes. *Racemes* dense, 7- to 20-flowered, considerably elongating in fruit; *bracts* rather small, divided or entire; *pedicels* 5- to 10-mm long, equaling the bracts. *Flowers* purple, spur and inner petals paler; *outer petals* with long entire crests that reach beyond the apex; *spur* 9–11 mm long; *inner petals* 10–13 mm long. *Capsule* pendent, narrowly linear, terete. Self-incompatible.

Corydalis taliensis is a native of warm-temperate regions of Yunnan and Sichuan from Tali to Lijiang and Muli. Three vicariant subspecies are recognized. Subspecies *taliensis* seems to be nitrophilous (preferring nitrogen-rich soils), and grows on walls and by ditches at rather low altitudes of 2000 to 2500 m (6560 to 8200 ft) in and around the old city of Dali in Yunnan. Jean Marie Delavay, a French missionary and botanist, first collected it there in the 1880s.

Corydalis taliensis is similar to *C. smithiana*, but is a perennial (rather than a biennial) and is more robust with longer branches, broader and obtuse leaf-lobes, less divided bracts, shorter pedicels, denser racemes, flowers with larger entire crests, and narrower capsules. Unlike *C. smithiana*, it does not set seed spontaneously, and because of this and the fact that it is only marginally frost-hardy, it is rarer in cultivation. Nevertheless, a few nurseries in the United Kingdom offer it.

Corydalis taliensis can be increased vegetatively, since the nodes of the plant often root when they come into contact with the substrate. It is a charming plant suited to a frost-free alpine house or, in milder regions, a spot in the rock garden.

Corydalis shihmienensis C. Y. Wu & H. Chuang is similar to *C. taliensis*, but the flowers are acute at apex and the straight spur tapers smoothly into a fine apex. It is native to Central Sichuan. The cultivar 'Blackberry Wine' (Plate 101) is offered by several nurseries in the United States and can take colder climates than *C. taliensis*. In the wild, *C. shihmienensis* seems to be usually annual or biennial, but despite this the cultivar is propagated by in vitro culture. A chlorotic sport of such a plant has recently been commercially released under the name *C.* 'Berry Exciting'.

Corydalis smithiana Fedde PLATE 102

Biennial herb, forming a rather small rosette the first year, which does not persist through the winter. *Stems* angular, suberect to ascending, usually several, 15–30 cm tall, leafy and branched. *Leaves* triangular, dark green, 2 times ternately divided; *leaflets* deeply cut into acute lobes; *petioles* rather long, basally sheathing, even upper leaves with distinct stalks. *Racemes* very loose, especially below, 5- to 10-flowered; *lower bracts* leaflike with distinct stalks; *upper bracts* becoming progressively smaller and less divided; *pedicels* 8–20 mm long, patent to slightly curved backward in fruit. *Flowers* pale purplish-red; *outer petals* shortly crested toward the subacute rather broad mucronate apex; *spur* straight or slightly curved, hardly tapering, 10–13 mm long; *inner petals* 10–12 mm long. *Capsule* pendent, narrowly oblong, slightly flattened, rather thin-walled.

Corydalis smithiana was introduced several times in the 1990s and is worth growing for its undemanding nature and purplish-red flowers that have a pleasant musky fragrance. It is best suited to the rock garden, where it will thrive among rocks or in peat, in a not too shady location. Much seed is set and unusually for a *Corydalis* survives dry storage and requires one or two cold periods to germinate.

Corydalis smithiana grows in stony places, including roadsides, from southern Sichuan to northern Yunnan. The species is particularly common in open gravelly situations around the Zhongdian ("Shangri-La") plateau in northwestern Yunnan, from an altitude of 2800 to 3600 m (9200 to 11,800 ft).

The species's name honors William Wright Smith (1875–1956), who was Regius Keeper of the Royal Botanic Garden, Edinburgh, and described several of George Forrest's plant collections from Yunnan.

Corydalis incisa Persoon PLATE 103

Biennial or rarely annual herb; if biennial, forming in the first year a small rosette and a rounded storage root similar to a pale radish. *Stems* 1 to several, sharply ridged, erect, 15–50 cm long, leafy throughout, sparingly branched. *Leaves* stalked, triangular, bright green, 2 times pinnately divided with acutely serrate leaflets, or sometimes rather deeply divided. *Racemes* dense, 10- to 20-flowered; *bracts* sharply toothed; *pedicels* straight, erecto-patent, 10–20 mm long, longer than the bracts. *Flowers* pale pink (rarely white), often with a bluish tint in the middle and darker reddish purple toward the apex; *sepals* small, cut to the base into narrow lobes; *outer petals* with toothed limbs and with short high toothed dorsal crests; *spur* oblong, very slightly curved, obtuse, 8–10 mm long; *nectary* very short; *lower outer petal* with rather broad claw and a pronounced swelling at the base; *inner petals* pale, 10–11 mm long. *Capsule* pendent from straight suberect pedicels, oblong, explosively dehiscent. *2n* = 16. Self-compatible.

Corydalis incisa leaf. Drawing by Adèle Rossetti Morosini.

Corydalis incisa is a startling biennial. The sharply toothed leaflets and the dense racemes of shortly crested reddish-purple flowers make it easily distinguishable. Seed germinates in spring and builds up small green rosettes. In the summer the plant withdraws to a small radishlike root to continue growth in the autumn. The rosette remains green through the winter and in the following spring produces compact racemes of dramatically colored flowers.

Corydalis incisa is widespread and common in Japan (where it is called murasa-kike-man), Korea, Taiwan, and eastern China. It grows in a wide variety of open and semi-open habitats, often by the edge of rice paddies. We have seen the species naturalized along the Bronx River in New York City. It flowers in the spring and early summer. There appear to be annual as well as biennial forms of this species.

According to Duke and Ayensu's *Medicinal Plants of China* (1984), the dried, powdered flowers of *Corydalis incisa* are used locally to treat rectal collapse. During famine the young plants, though slightly toxic, have also been cooked and eaten. A few specialist nurseries occasionally offer the species.

Corydalis linstowiana Fedde   PLATE 104

Biennial herb with a root like a small pale carrot. *Stems* much-branched from the base, ascending, leafy, 8–25 cm long. *Leaves* long-stalked, triangular, dark bluish green, 2 or 3 times pinnately divided; *leaflets* deeply divided into obovate-obtuse lobes; *upper leaves* with peculiarly irregularly cleft stipules. *Racemes* dense at first, much elongating in fruit, 5- to 11-flowered; *lower bracts* shortly stalked, much divided, becoming progressively smaller and less divided up the raceme; *pedicels* erect, 5–15 mm long, elongating to 10–20 mm long in fruit. *Flowers* purplish blue to clear blue, sometimes rather pale and only darker toward the tip; *sepals* whitish, deeply divided into long teeth; *outer petals* with broad and obtuse limbs, usually with a short crest that does not reach the apex; *spur* short, 5–7 mm long; *inner petals* 9–10 mm long. *Capsules* oblong, pendent, explosively dehiscent. Self-compatible.

This little weedy charm is immediately set apart from all other species in the genus by its irregularly cleft stipules. *Corydalis linstowiana* is a native of Central Sichuan, where it grows at the margins of forest at altitudes of 1350 to 3400 m (4400 to 11,150 ft). In the garden it flowers from spring to autumn and will seed around, often appearing far from the original location. It has been in cultivation for a couple of decades, and is sometimes sold as *Corydalis* 'Du Fu Temple'. The typical form of this species is biennial with a tap-root similar to a small pale carrot, but there are also annual strains, at least in the wild.

6

Additional Cultivated Genera

THIS CHAPTER COVERS all genera with zygomorphic (bilaterally symmetric) flowers, excepting *Corydalis*, which is the subject of chapter five. Included here are the two widely cultivated European species of *Pseudofumaria*, which were at one time classified in *Corydalis*. Also previously included in that genus and discussed here is the North American rock harlequin, *Capnoides sempervirens*, that is occasionally grown for its interesting bi-colored flowers. Two remarkable cliff-dwelling genera are also covered: *Rupicapnos* and *Sarcocapnos*. Both are found in Spain and North Africa and are cushion plants grown by rock garden enthusiasts. In addition we discuss *Fumaria*. This large genus includes few ornamental species but contains a widely encountered weed of gardens and agriculture, the common fumitory *F. officinalis*. In contrast to the plants appearing in the previous two chapters, none of the species included here have been hybridized in gardens, and almost no cultivars have been named.

Capnoides   PLATE 105
Rock harlequin

> Annual or biennial herb, erect, branched. *Stems* to 80 cm tall; basal and lower stem leaves with long petioles, upper stem leaves sessile. *Leaves* 2 or 3 times pinnately divided, with obtuse ultimate lobes. *Inflorescences* few-flowered, branched cymes. *Flowers* zygomorphic, 12–15 mm long; *petals* pink or white, with yellow tips, one of the outer petals with a short rounded basal spur; *nectary* short, peglike; *style* persistent, green. *Fruit* linear, a many-seeded capsule. $2n = 16$. Self-compatible.

Rock harlequin (Plate 105) is a dainty plant best suited to a naturalistic garden, where it should be planted next to a walkway or on a prominent rock outcrop. This way its subtle beauty can be appreciated up close. Although the flowers of this North American species are rather small and not easily seen from a distance, they are nevertheless interesting since they are attractively bi-colored pink and yellow, or occasionally white and yellow. Along with the plant's propensity to grow upon sparsely vegetated granite domes, or balds, the bi-colored flowers have earned it the common name rock harlequin. This plant also, however, grows in rocky woodlands and in burned or otherwise disturbed areas, and is often found in very shallow, dry soils. Unlike many members of the family it has long-lived seeds. It is native throughout much of northern North America from Alaska to Newfoundland south to British Columbia, the north-central Midwest, and along the Appalachian Mountains to northern Georgia.

Capnoides sempervirens (Linnaeus) Borkhausen has been in cultivation at least since 1683. At that date it was grown in an Edinburgh garden run by James Sutherland, who later became director of the Royal Botanic Garden, Edinburgh, and in Uppsala Botanic Garden by Olof Rudbeck the Elder under the name "*Fumaria maj. perennis Americana.*" *Capnoides sempervirens* is usually biennial and in the first year forms a rosette of gray-green leaves and then flowers in late spring of the following year. The plant's flowering season is long, often lasting from mid May to early September.

Despite having the alternative common name of pale corydalis and having once been classified in the genus *Corydalis*, molecular data shows that *Capnoides sempervirens* is not particularly closely related to *Corydalis*. This should not be too surpris-

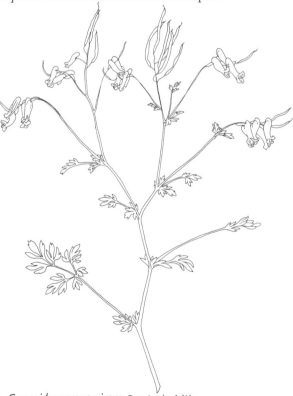

ing since its inflorescence structure, as well as its individual flowers, are more similar to those of *Dicentra* than they are to *Corydalis*. Of particular note, for those with an inclination toward botanical detail, is that the uppermost (terminal) flower in the inflorescence is fruiting when the lateral flowers are still fresh. In other genera with zygomorphic flowers (including *Corydalis*), the uppermost flower of the raceme is not truly terminal on the inflorescence axis and is usually the last to develop.

The generic name *Capnoides* means "like capnos" and refers to an early Greek name for the fumitories. The specific name *sempervirens* translates as evergreen, a reference to the species's graygreen leaf rosettes that persist through the first winter.

Capnoides sempervirens is commer-

Capnoides sempervirens. Drawing by Adèle Rossetti Morosini.

cially available from a few specialist sources (sometimes as *Corydalis glauca* or *C. rosea*) and is readily cultivated in a sunny or semi-shady site in slightly acidic, well-drained soil. Propagation is via seed, which germinates most readily when sown fresh, but can survive for many years in a natural seed bank. Once established, plants will self-seed and may with care be transplanted. In some gardens the species may self-sow with such abandon that it can become a nuisance. Nevertheless, unwanted plants are easily weeded out. The species is hardy to –20°C (–4°F). Flower color is variable. Flowers can be either pink with yellow tips, or less frequently, white with yellow tips. In gardens, the latter are often given the cultivar name 'Alba' and will come true from seed.

Fumaria   PLATE 106
Fumitories

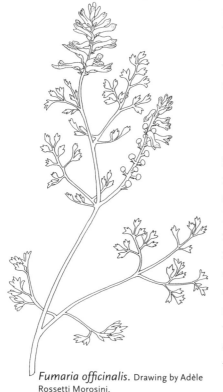

Annual herbs with suberect to reclining, branched, leafy stems. *Leaves* 2–4 times pinnately divided. *Inflorescences* terminal, leaf-opposed, in elongated racemes; *pedicels* short. *Flowers* zygomorphic, 5–15 mm long; *sepals* small to fairly large, entire or usually dentate; *petals* white or pink to purple; *upper outer petals* with a short rounded basal spur, usually darker toward the apex; *inner petals* usually tipped with dark purple; *nectary* present; *style* deciduous, white, semi-translucent. *Fruit* a globular, 1-seeded nut with two small depressions at apex. All species are self-compatible and many are regularly selfing.

Fumaria consists of 50 species and, after *Corydalis*, is the second largest genus in the family. Most of its members are European or North African and are concentrated in the Mediterranean region. However, *F. indica* (Haussknecht) Pugsley occurs in the Himalaya, while *F. abyssinica* Hammar is found on the high mountains of East Africa. Some of the European species, like common fumitory (*F. officinalis* Linnaeus), tall ramping-fumitory (*F. bastardii* Boreau), and small-flowered fumitory (*F. parviflora* Lamarck), have become naturalized outside of Europe as weeds. Many fumitories in fact are weedy and inhabit fields and other disturbed

Fumaria officinalis. Drawing by Adèle Rossetti Morosini.

ground. Two rare weedy British species, the western fumitory (*F. occidentalis* Pugsley) and purple ramping-fumitory (*F. purpurea* Pugsley), are worth mentioning because they are among very few plants with distributions restricted to the British Isles. They have presumably arisen late in history by a process called alloploidy (see under *Corydalis gotlandica*). Not all fumitories are weedy, however. Some are choicer plants that grow in crevices on limestone cliffs, like *F. macrosepala* Lidén in southern Spain, or in oak woods, like *F. mairei* Pugsley in North Algeria.

Many fumitories will, late in the season or if grown in shade, produce depauperate more-or-less cleistogamous flowers in which the floral characters are distorted. Even today the identification of *Fumaria* species is considered by many botanists to be a great challenge, and ripe dry fruits are usually needed for certain determination.

Few fumitory species are intentionally cultivated, but the common fumitory, *Fumaria officinalis* (Plate 106), is occasionally grown as a medicinal plant. Many are the virtues ascribed to this species. Herbalists have long used it to treat skin infections and various liver, kidney, and stomach complaints. Even today it is used in the treatment of eczema. The name *officinalis*, which Carl Linnaeus gave it in 1753, is Latin for "used in medicine." From John Gerard's herbal of 1633 we learn that it is "good for all of them that have either scabs or any other filthe growing on the skinne, and for them also that have the french disease" and further that it "doth take away unprofitable haires that pricke the eyes, growing upon the eye lids, the haires that pricke being first plucked away, for it will not suffer others to grow in their places," information that dates back to Dioscorides in the first century AD, and in part to Theophrastus 300 years earlier.

More often, *Fumaria officinalis* will make its own appearance in the garden as a weed. Though originally restricted to Europe, common fumitory has followed humankind since the Neolithic period (Stone Age) and is now ranked as the twelfth most common agricultural weed of the world's temperate regions. The species is particularly problematic in cereal and vegetable crops, especially as it is both self-fertile and can grow and flower even when temperatures are near freezing. In the garden it is not difficult to control by weeding, though this may have to be repeated over several years, since seeds can remain dormant in the soil for long periods of time. In fact, seeds of common fumitory have even germinated after lying buried for hundreds of years.

Like other members of its genus, *Fumaria officinalis* has an annual life cycle, a rather unkempt straggling habit, and deeply divided foliage against which the small flowers are hard to distinguish when observed from a distance. The deeply divided leaves have been likened to wisps of smoke arising from the ground. The peculiar smell experienced when the stems and leaves are damaged has also been likened to smoke.

Fumaria is a direct translation into Latin of the Greek *kapnos*, smoke, a name used for *Fumaria* and *Corydalis* in ancient Greece. It subsequently became fumus terrae (Latin), fumeterre (French), Erdrauch (German), jordrök (Swedish), and fumitory (English).

For those who are still eager to cultivate these species, most fumitories may be readily grown as long as they are given a light, well-drained soil. Even if they do become weedy, fumitories are easy to weed out. They have a very long-lived seed bank, making it necessary to remove plants over several years should they become firmly established. *Fumaria officinalis* is hardy to –30°C (–22°F), and is occasionally offered for sale.

Pseudofumaria   PLATE 107–108
Rock fumeworts

> Perennial herbs with branched stems to 40 cm tall. *Leaves* 2 times pinnately divided; *leaflets* deeply cut into obovate-obtuse lobes. *Inflorescences* terminal, 6- to 16-flowered, in loose racemes. *Flowers* zygomorphic, straight, 14–17 mm long, yellow or white to cream with the inner petals tipped yellow; *outer petals* rather broadly winged at apex, one outer petal with a short rounded basal spur; *inner petals* with an indentation only on the upper side; *nectary* present; *style* deciduous, whitish, semi-translucent. *Fruit* an oblong, 3- to 13-seeded capsule, with small elaiosomes.

The genus *Pseudofumaria* comprises two species, both of which are widely grown and will in suitable climates self-seed around the garden. Occasionally they can become a bit too invasive. Normally though they are well behaved and in any case are easily weeded out from areas where they are not welcome. They have attractive, deeply divided leaves, showy flowers, and a very long flowering season. The two species are quite similar in their habit but are instantly separable in flower. *Pseudofumaria lutea* (Linnaeus) Borkhausen (Plate 107) has yellow flowers, while *P. alba* (Miller) Lidén (Plate 108) has white to cream outer petals and inner petals of the same color with contrasting yellow tips. In addition, *P. alba* frequently has a glaucous covering on both its upper and lower leaf surfaces, while *P. lutea* is only ever glaucous on its lower leaf surface. Both species were at one time classified in the genus *Corydalis* but differ from that genus in their flower structure and hence have now been reclassified. *Pseudofumaria* is distinguished from *Corydalis* by having a whitish deciduous style, a feature it shares with the related genera *Sarcocapnos*, *Rupicapnos*, and *Fumaria*. Unique for *Pseudofumaria* are the unilaterally indented inner petals, an adaptation that facilitates a peculiar pollination mechanism (see chapter two).

The yellow-flowered *Pseudofumaria lutea* is the most commonly cultivated of the two species and is slightly more vigorous and less particular in its habitat requirements. In areas with moderate summer temperatures it has a very long bloom time and will flower from mid spring to early winter. In regions with warmer climates the plant also performs well but will pause flower production during the hottest summer months. It is native to the southern foothills of the Central and Western European Alps. As a garden escapee though, *P. lutea* has a much larger distribution across much of Europe. The species naturally grows upon cliffs and rock outcrops but will adapt equally well to life on walls and other artificial structures.

The second species, *Pseudofumaria alba*, is less commonly cultivated but nevertheless is available from several commercial sources. Again this plant is listed in most nursery catalogs as a corydalis and is often sold as *Corydalis ochroleuca*. The species sometimes has a shorter flowering season than *P. lutea*, but if regularly deadheaded and grown in a favorable climate, it will flower for much of the spring and summer. This species is native to northwestern Balkans and northern Italy but

also is widely naturalized throughout Europe as a garden escapee. Like *P. lutea* this species was once restricted to cliffs and rock outcrops but is now often found upon walls. For centuries large colonies have been naturalized on the city wall of the old town of Pola in Istria.

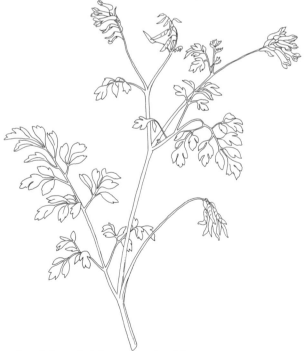

Both *Pseudofumaria* species have long been cultivated in Europe. English herbalist John Gerard grew *P. lutea*, the first of the two species to be introduced, as long ago as 1596.

Both species are readily cultivated but can sometimes be tricky to establish. In some gardens they resent disturbance, while in other, seemingly similar, locations they can be dug up, divided, and moved around. Once plants become established, propagation is usually from self-

Pseudofumaria lutea. Drawing by Adèle Rossetti Morosini.

sown seeds. Seedlings can be left to develop wherever new plants are desired and removed from other less favorable situations. In this way plants will often become established upon walls (Plate 107), between paving, and in other interesting sites where it would normally be difficult to get plants to grow or one would not think of planting them. In Philip Miller's *Gardener's Dictionary* of 1759 we read that it is "very proper for the Joints of Grottos," a reminder of a time when romantic Italian-inspired gardens were fashionable.

Both species of *Pseudofumaria* prefer well-drained, neutral to slightly alkaline soil and will grow equally well in a well-lit or shady site in most areas. Cutting back plants in summer will prolong bloom time and will also reduce the amount of self-seeding. Both species are hardy to –25°C (–13°F). In areas with mild winters these plants are evergreen, while in colder climates they will die down once the first hard frosts arrive.

Rupicapnos PLATE 109
Cliff-smokes

Annual to usually rather short-lived perennial, cushion-forming herbs. *Leaves* stalked, very glaucous and fleshy, 2 or 3 times pinnatisect or ternatisect with linear to oblong or lanceolate leaf lobes. *Inflorescences* terminal, 5- to 40-flowered, corymbose racemes on short peduncles; *pedicels* long. *Flowers* zygomorphic, white to pink or purple; *upper petal* with a short rounded basal spur; *inner petals* either narrowly crested and tipped blackish purple or with very broad undulate white wings; *nectary* almost as long as the spur; *style* deciduous, translucent. *Fruit* a hard-walled 1-seeded nut; fruit stalk sharply reflexed, lengthening, and eventually burying the fruit at the base of the plant.

Rupicapnos africana. Drawing by Adèle Rossetti Morosini.

This genus of seven species is remarkable in occupying a habitat that few other genera of plants have managed to colonize (but see *Sarcocapnos* below for a stunning example of parallel evolution). *Rupicapnos* species grow on steep, often overhanging limestone cliff-walls in northwestern Africa and in one case also in southern Spain at altitudes ranging from 500 to 1800 m (1640 to 5900 ft). Their natural habitat is so challenging that it is largely devoid of other plant life. The cliff walls upon which the plants grow experience large daily fluctuations in temperature; in the day the sun is very intense and the cliffs heat up, then at night air temperatures can drop almost to freezing. Furthermore, water is scarce and unpredictable in its supply, and soil is largely absent. On the positive side, these plants occupy a very stable niche with little competition and no large grazing animals.

To live in such an extreme environment *Rupicapnos* and *Sarcocapnos* have independently evolved a similar suite of adaptive features. Their stems are densely branched and have short internodes so that the plants form low cushions pressed tight against the cliffs. The stems and leaves are both fleshy and can store water. A covering of wax helps them hold onto this valuable resource. The juicy stems and leaves of these plants are unusually brittle since they almost completely lack strengthening tissue. Not wasting energy on wood allows them to invest their resources in growth, flowering, and seed production.

To establish the next generation of plants upon the vertical cliffs, these plants have evolved fruit stalks that elongate away from the light and thereby bury the nuts at the base of the parent plant or in a nearby crevice. The nuts may then be further dispersed by ants, which move them along the cliff walls. The ants are attracted to a nutritious, fat-rich swelling at the base of the fresh nut, a feature found also in *Sarcocapnos* and some species of *Fumaria*.

Rupicapnos africana (Lamarck) Pomel (Plate 109) is the most widespread of the species and is the only one that occurs in southern Spain as well as in North Africa. It has a scattered distribution throughout much of its range and exists as a series of discrete geographical races. Because these separated clusters of populations no longer exchange genetic material, they have frequently accumulated minor differences through the process of random genetic drift. The often very small populations, which in many cases were presumably derived from a single seed, further enhance this process. In the last revision of the genus this variation is described by the use of subspecies; in *R. africana*, for example, eight subspecies are recognized. Their identification is made difficult by the fact that these plants can be greatly modified by the environment and will look different if they are grown in a sunny or a shaded situation. More than one misguided author has described multiple species from a single cliff-face based on such environmentally induced variation.

Of the seven species of *Rupicapnos* only subsp. *africana* is apparently cultivated outside of botanic gardens. It has been grown since at least 1933, when it was first introduced to Britain. *Rupicapnos africana* is an attractive free-flowering species, which is best grown in a sunny situation either in a pot in an alpine house or, in areas with mild winters, outdoors on a vertical rock or tufa wall. It requires a gritty, alkaline soil with excellent drainage but is not particularly challenging to grow. Plants should be handled carefully, since in the first year they are shallowly rooted and throughout their lives they have very brittle stems that are liable to break if mishandled. Propagation is via seed, which is usually sown in the spring. All *Rupicapnos* species will set plenty of seeds through selfing. Germination can be sporadic since the seeds will often develop dormancy, which can be difficult to break. Plants will flower in the first year and in cold areas will behave as annuals, while in areas with a mild climate, individual plants may persist for up to 10 years. It is not easy to tell, however, if a plant is the original one, since self-sown seedlings will often grow up in the middle of the tuft and in time can replace it. *Rupicapnos africana* is available via specialist seed lists and from a few commercial alpine nurseries. It is marginally frost-hardy to –5°C (23°F).

Two subspecies of *Rupicapnos africana* are commonly found in specialist collections. Subspecies *africana* from Algeria has relatively narrow obovate fruit and narrowly lanceolate leaf-lobes, while subsp. *decipiens* (Pugsley) Maire from Spain has broader fruit and broader and fewer leaf-lobes. More rarely grown are subsp. *cerefolia* (Pomel) Maire and subsp. *gaetula* (Maire) Maire. The former is similar to subsp. *africana*, but immediately distinguished by its linear leaf-lobes. Subspecies *gaetula* is characterized by its small rounded fruit to 2.5 mm.

Sarcocapnos   PLATES 7, 110–112
Flesh-smokes

> Annual to perennial, cushion-forming, more or less fleshy herbs. *Leaves* very glaucous, simple to up to 3 times ternately divided; *leaflets* ovate to heart-shaped. *Inflorescences* terminal, 5- to 35-flowered, in corymbose racemes; *pedicels* long. *Flowers* zygomorphic, white or pale pink; *outer petals* broadly and abruptly dilated at apex, upper petal with a short rounded basal spur; *inner petals* tipped with yellow dorsal crests; *nectary* present; *style* deciduous, translucent. *Fruit* elliptic, 1- to 2-seeded; fruit stalk lengthening, sharply curved toward the base of the plant.

Sarcocapnos shares the peculiar adaptations to life on vertical or overhanging cliffs discussed previously for the genus *Rupicapnos*. In common with *Rupicapnos* species, the four species of *Sarcocapnos* are glaucous cushion-forming perennials or annuals that have very brittle, fleshy stems. The two genera are readily distinguished by both leaf and petal shapes. The leaflets of all *Sarcocapnos* species are rounded, while those of *Rupicapnos* never are. *Sarcocapnos integrifolia* Boissier deviates from the other species in having simple leaves. Furthermore, the outer petals of *Sarcocapnos* are more abruptly and broadly winged at the tips than in *Rupicapnos*. All *Sarcocapnos* species are rare in the wild, and individual populations may sometimes contain very few plants.

Sarcocapnos enneaphylla (Linnaeus) A. P. de Candolle (Plates 110, 111) is the species usually encountered in cultivation and has by far the largest distribution. It is found wild from the French Pyrenees down through the summer-dry, eastern half of Spain and, across the Alborán Sea, in a small enclave on the Moroccan coast. Given this relatively large distribution, it should not be surprising that *S. enneaphylla* was the first member of its genus to enter cultivation, around 1900. The other species were introduced roughly thirty years later. *Sarcocapnos enneaphylla* is an annual to short-lived perennial that grows on natural limestone cliffs, on steep road cuttings, and occasionally on walls from near sea level to 1300 m (4265 ft) in altitude. It is a very variable species and differs widely in its degree of succulence and density of hair covering. A form with particularly large rose-colored flowers has been distinguished as var. *saetabensis* (Mateo & Figuerola) O. de Bolòs & Vigo.

The fleshier-leaved, larger, and longer-lived *Sarcocapnos crassifolia* (Desfontaines) A. P. de Candolle is also occasionally cultivated. It is found on both limestone and schist cliffs at elevations from 800 to 3000 m (2625 to 9840 ft). It is distributed in southeastern Spain and northwestern Africa with many isolated populations, and has been divided into a number of lower level taxa. This species has a particularly strong and sweet fragrance. The South Spanish *S. speciosa* Boissier is very similar, but has longer spurs.

Sarcocapnos pulcherrima Morales & A. T. Romero-García (Plate 112) was described as recently as 1991. It is very similar to *S. speciosa* but has larger, rose-colored flowers and a less dense growth habit. Beautiful displays of this species may be seen at Presa del Pantano de los Bermejales southeast of Alhama de Granada in southern Spain, where large cushions dot the cliff sides (Plate 7). This species is likewise only rarely cultivated.

Sarcocapnos baetica Nyman is restricted in its distribution to southern Spain and is occasionally cultivated. It grows on vertical limestone cliffs at an altitude of 1200 to 2000 m (3940 to 6560 ft). The similar *S. integrifolia* deviates in fleshier, completely entire leaves.

Sarcocapnos pulcherrima. Drawing by Adèle Rossetti Morosini.

Sarcocapnos are best grown in a pot or on a tufa wall in the alpine house or, in areas with mild winters, on a vertical rock or tufa wall outdoors. All the species require excellent drainage and a gritty, calcareous soil. Propagation is usually via seed, which germinates most readily when sown fresh but which can, if necessary, be stored for a few years. With luck, the occasional cutting may also be rooted. *Sarcocapnos enneaphylla* and *S. baetica* are self-compatible and will produce seeds spontaneously; *S. crassifolia* and *S. pulcherrima* will not. However, at least *S. crassifolia* can be forced to produce a few selfed seeds if the stigmatic surface is mechanically disturbed. All four species are hardy to –5°C (23°F) and are available from specialist seed lists and a few commercial alpine nurseries. As with *R. africana*, the stems of *Sarcocapnos* are very brittle, necessitating careful handling of the plants.

Key to the Species of *Sarcocapnos*

1a. Plant short-lived; leaves with 7–18 leaflets; stigma asymmetric with a large flat crest . . . . *S. enneaphylla*

1b. Plant always perennial; leaves with 1–8 leaflets; stigma symmetric without a crest 2

2a. Flowers 5–6 mm long 3

2b. Flowers more than 8 mm long 4

3a. Leaves simple, fleshy . . . . *S. integrifolia*

3b. Leaves with 2–5 leaflets . . . . *S. baetica*

4a. Flowers pink, about 18–21 mm long; racemes often branched . . . . . *S. pulcherrima*

4b. Flowers white, 8–17 mm long; racemes rarely branched . . . . *S. crassifolia*

Appendix A
Useful Addresses

Specialist Societies

The Alpine Garden Society
Avon Bank, Pershore
Worcestershire, WR10 3JP
United Kingdom
Phone: 01386 554 790
Fax: 01386 554 801
E-mail: ags@alpinegardensociety.net
Web site: www.alpinegardensociety.net

Nederlandse Rotsplanten Vereniging
(The Dutch Garden Society)
Rob Koolbergen, Membership Secretary
Stelvio 15
1186 EE Amstelveen, The Netherlands
E-mail: NRWKoolbergen@hetnet.nl
Web site: www.rotsplantenvereniging.nl

North American Rock Garden Society
Jacques Mommens, Executive Secretary
P.O. Box 67
Millwood, NY 10546 USA
E-mail: nargs@advic.com
Web site: www.nargs.org

The Rock Garden Club Prague
[a.k.a. Klub skalnickaru Praha]
Marikova 5
162 00 Praha 2, Czech Republic
Web site: www.skalnicky.cz

Scottish Rock Garden Club
A. D. McKelvie, Membership Secretary
43 Rubislaw Park Crescent
Aberdeen AB15 8BT
United Kingdom
Web site: www.srgc.org.uk

Plant Sources

The nurseries that offer the widest selection of Fumariaceae are listed below. Information on where specific plants may be purchased in the United Kingdom and North America may respectively be found in the *RHS Plant Finder* and in *Andersen's Horticultural Library's Source List of Plants and Seeds*.

Arrowhead Alpines
P.O. Box 857
Fowlerville, MI 48836 USA
Web site: www.arrowheadalpines.com

Ballyrogan Nurseries
The Grange
Newtownards
Co. Down, Northern Ireland UK BT23 4SD
Phone: 028 9181 0451 (evenings)
E-mail: gary.dunlop@btinternet.com
(open by appointment only)

Beeches Nursery
Village Centre
Ashdon, near Saffron Walden
Essex, UK CB10 2HB
Phone: 01799 584362
Fax: 01799 584421
Web site: www.beechesnursery.co.uk

Buckland Plants
Whinnieliggate
Kirkcudbright, UK DG6 4XP
Phone & Fax: 01557 331323
Web site: www.bucklandplants.co.uk

Cambridge Bulbs
Norman Stevens
40 Whittlesford Road
Newton, Cambridge UK CB2 5PH
Phone: 01223 87176

Choice Plants
83 Halton Road
Spilsby, Lincolnshire, UK PE23 5LD
Phone: 01790 753361
Fax: 01790 752524
E-mail: jgunson@spilsby94.fsnet.co.uk
Web site: www.choiceplants.net

Christie's Nursery
Downfield, Westmuir
Kirriemuir, Angus, UK DD8 5LP
Phone & Fax: 01575 572977
E-mail: ianchristie@btconnect.com
Web site: www.christiealpines.co.uk

Crûg Farm Plants
Griffith's Crossing
near Caernarfon, Gwynedd, UK
   LL55 1TU
Phone: 01248 670232
E-mail: bleddyn&sue@crug-farm.co.uk
Web site: www.crug-farm.co.uk

Edrom Nurseries
Coldingham
Eyemouth, Berwickshire, UK TD14 5TZ
Phone: 018907 71386
Fax: 018907 71387
E-mail: info@edromnurseries.co.uk
Web site: www.edromnurseries.co.uk

Farmyard Nurseries
Llandysul, Dyfed, UK SA44 4RI
Phone: 01559 363389; 01627 220259
Fax: 01559 362200
E-mail: richard@farmyardnurseries.co.uk
Web site: www.farmyardnurseries.co.uk

Forest Farm
990 Tetherow Road
Williams, OR 97544 USA
Phone: 541 846 7269
Fax: 541 846 6963
E-mail: plants@forestfarm.com
Web site: www.forestfarm.com

Hythe Alpines
Methwold Hythe
Thetford, Norfolk, UK IP26 4QH
Phone & Fax: 01366 728543

Lazy S'S Farm
2360 Spotswood Trail
Barboursville, VA 22923 USA
Web site: www.lazyssfarm.com

Long Acre Plants
South Marsh
Charlton Musgrove
Somerset, UK BA9 8EX
E-mail: info@longacreplants.co.uk
Web site: www.longacreplants.co.uk

Odyssey Bulbs
P.O. Box 308
Berrien Springs, MI 49103 USA
Phone & Fax: 269 471 4642
E-mail: mail@odysseybulbs.com
Web site: www.odysseybulbs.com

Jānis Rukšāns
Bulb Nursery
Rozula
Cesis District, LV-4150 Latvia
Phone: 371 41 00 326
Phone & Fax: 371 41 33 223
E-mail: janis.bulb@hawk.lv

Pottertons Nursery
Moortown Road
Nettleton, Caistor
Lincolnshire, UK LN7 6HX
Phone: 01472 851714
Fax: 01472 852580
E-mail: rob@pottertons.co.uk
Web site: www.pottertons.co.uk

RarePlants (Paul Christian)
P.O. Box 468
Wrexham, UK LL13 9XR
Phone: 01978 366399
Fax: 01978 266466
Web site: www.rareplants.co.uk

Special Plants
Hill Farm Barn
Greenways Lane, Cold Ashton
Chippenham, Wiltshire, UK SN14 8LA
Phone: 01225 891686
E-mail: derry@specialplants.net
Web site: www.specialplants.net

Terra Nova Nurseries
P.O. Box 23938
Tigard, OR 97281 USA
Phone: 800 215 9450
Fax: 503 263 3152
Web site: www.terranovanurseries.com

Westonbirt Plants
9 Westonbirt Close
Worcestershire, UK WR5 3RX
Phone: 01905 350429

Chen Yi Nursery (Kaichen Nursery).
Included here because of the vast number
of their new *Corydalis* introductions, which
are now becoming widespread in cultivation, though usually under incorrect
names. It should be noted that nearly all
the plants offered have been directly collected in the wild, sometimes wiping out
whole populations, often from protected
areas. We do not endorse this practice.
Unfortunately, some unscrupulous nurseries in the West are now bulk purchasing
from this source, and, further compound-
ing the problem, since they are not themselves propagating these plants.

Sources of Other Supplies

The Seed Room
Kirstenbosch National Botanical Garden
Private Bag X7
Claremont 7735, South Africa
E-mail: seedroom@nbict.nbi.ac.za.
(source of liquid smoke)

Appendix B
Plants Recommended for Beginners

Corydalis 'Blue Heron'
Corydalis buschii
Corydalis cava
Corydalis cheilanthifolia
Corydalis 'Craigton Blue'
Corydalis flexuosa
Corydalis linstowiana
Corydalis malkensis
Corydalis nobilis

Corydalis omeiana
Corydalis scouleri
Corydalis solida 'George Baker'
Dicentra eximia
Dicentra formosa
Dicentra hybrids
Lamprocapnos spectabilis
Pseudofumaria lutea

Appendix C

Royal Horticultural Society Awarded Plants

Four awards have been given by the Royal Horticultural Society to members of the bleeding heart family. They are listed here in order of importance, starting with the most prestigious award. The information has been adapted from the RHS website, www.rhs.orkg.uk.

AGM (Award of Garden Merit). Given to plants of outstanding excellence for garden decoration or use (whether for the open garden or under glass). The award is only given following a period of assessment.

FCC (First Class Certificate). Given to plants of outstanding excellence for exhibition.

AM (Award of Merit). Given to plants of great merit for exhibition.

PC (Certificate of Preliminary Commendation). Given to a new plant of promise for exhibition.

In the list that follows, the date after each award indicates the year that award was received.

Corydalis afghanica subsp. *elegans*, PC 2003

Corydalis aitchisonii (as *C. nevskii*), PC 1988

Corydalis ×*allenii*, PC 1998

Corydalis ambigua, PC 1970; AM 1979

Corydalis angustifolia, PC 1995

Corydalis bracteata, PC 1969

Corydalis cashmeriana, AM 1938; FCC 1955

Corydalis caucasica, PC 1973

Corydalis cava, PC 2001

Corydalis cheilanthifolia, AM 1969

Corydalis chionophila subsp. *firouzii* (as *C. firouzii*), PC 1989

Corydalis darwasica, PC 1987

Corydalis diphylla, PC 1978

Corydalis flexuosa, PC 1990; AM 1991; AGM 2002

Corydalis fumariifolia, PC 1970 & 1973 (as *C. ambigua*), AM 1979

Corydalis haussknechtii, PC 2000

Corydalis henrikii, PC 2005

Corydalis integra, PC 1992; AM 1995

Corydalis 'Kingfisher', AM 2005

Corydalis macrocentra, PC 2000

Corydalis malkensis, PC 1973; AGM 1993; AM 1995

Corydalis maracandica, AM 1997; PC 1989

Corydalis nariniana (as *C. persica*), PC 1986

Corydalis nudicaulis, PC 2002

Corydalis oppositifolia (as *C. rutifolia* subsp. *kurdica*), PC 1978

Corydalis 'Persian Waif', PC 2001

Corydalis popovii, PC 1979; AM 1983; FCC 2003

Corydalis saxicola, FCC 1902

Corydalis schanginii, PC 1998

Corydalis schanginii subsp. *ainii*, PC 1995; AGM 2000

Corydalis sewerzowii, AM 2005

Corydalis solida 'Beth Evans', AM 1988

Corydalis solida 'Dieter Schacht', AGM 2000

Corydalis solida 'George Baker', AGM 1993; FCC 1988

Corydalis solida 'Highland Mist', PC 1995

Corydalis solida 'Jen Martin', PC 2000

Corydalis solida 'Mount Vermion', PC 1994

Corydalis solida 'Nettleton Pink', PC 1994

Corydalis solida 'Zwanenburg', PC 1999

Corydalis solida subsp. *incisa*, PC 1992; AGM 2000

Corydalis solida subsp. *incisa* f. *alba*, AM 1994

Corydalis thyrsiflora, PC 1994

Corydalis tomentella, AM 1937

Corydalis triternata, AGM 2000; PC 2002

Corydalis verticillaris, PC 1933; AM 1934

Corydalis vittae, AM 2001

Corydalis wilsonii, AM 1905

Dicentra 'Bacchanal', AGM 2002

Dicentra cucullaria, AM 1973

Dicentra cucullaria 'Pittsburg', PC 1989

Dicentra eximia 'Snowdrift', AM 1974

Dicentra 'King of Hearts', PC 2003; AM 2005

Dicentra 'Langtrees', AGM 1993

Dicentra peregrina (as *D. peregrina* var. *pusilla*), PC 1937; AM 1966

Dicentra 'Stuart Boothman', AGM 1993

Dicentra 'Tsuneshigo Rokujo', PC 1973

Lamprocapnos spectabilis (as *D. spectabilis*), AGM 1993

Lamprocapnos spectabilis 'Alba' (as *D. spectabilis* 'Alba'), AGM 1993

Rupicapnos africana, PC 1957

Sarcocapnos crassifolia, AM 1972

Sarcocapnos enneaphylla, AM 1936

Appendix D
Measurement Conversion Tables

To convert length	Multiply by
Millimeters to inches	0.04
Centimeters to inches	0.39
Meters to feet	3.28
Kilometers to miles	0.62

Millimeters	Inches
1 mm	$1/32$ in
2 mm	$1/16$ in
3 mm	$1/8$ in
5 mm	$3/16$ in
6 mm	$1/4$ in
8 mm	$5/16$ in
10 mm	$3/8$ in
12 mm	$1/2$ in
15 mm	$5/8$ in
20 mm	$3/4$ in
25 mm	1 in
30 mm	$1\text{-}1/8$ in
35 mm	$1\text{-}3/8$ in
40 mm	$1\text{-}1/2$ in
45 mm	$1\text{-}3/4$ in
50 mm	2 in

Centimeters	Inches (Feet)
1 cm	$3/8$ in
2 cm	$3/4$ in
3 cm	$1\text{-}1/8$ in
4 cm	$1\text{-}1/2$ in
5 cm	2 in
6 cm	$2\text{-}3/8$ in
7 cm	$2\text{-}3/4$ in
8 cm	$3\text{-}1/8$ in
9 cm	$3\text{-}1/2$ in
10 cm	4 in
15 cm	6 in ($1/2$ ft)
20 cm	8 in
25 cm	10 in
30 cm	12 in (1 ft)
35 cm	14 in
40 cm	16 in
50 cm	20 in
55 cm	22 in
60 cm	24 in (2 ft)
70 cm	28 in
80 cm	32 in
90 cm	36 in (3 ft)
100 cm	40 in

Meters	Feet
0.5 m	$1\text{-}1/2$ ft
1 m	$3\text{-}1/3$ ft
2 m	$6\text{-}1/2$ ft
3 m	10 ft
4 m	13 ft
5 m	16 ft
6 m	20 ft
7 m	23 ft
8 m	26 ft
9 m	30 ft
10 m	33 ft

Kilometers	Miles
1 km	0.6 mi
3 km	1.8 mi
5 km	3.0 mi

Glossary

Acuminate Narrowing gradually to a point, with concave sides.

Acute Tapering to a point at an angle less than 90°, with straight sides.

Alkaloid An organic nitrogen-containing bitter-tasting basic substance with pharmacological effects. Examples are: strychnine and morphine. The Fumariaceae are very rich in alkaloids.

Alloploidy The process of chromosome doubling of a primary hybrid resulting in a new (sexually) reproducing species.

Alternate (leaves) Arranged singly at each node, not opposite or whorled.

Annual A plant that completes its life cycle, from seed to seed, in one year and then dies (compare biennial and perennial).

Anther The terminal pollen-containing part of the stamen.

Apex The tip; the position farthest away from the point of attachment.

Apical Located at the apex.

Arcuate Arched like a bow.

Axillary Arising from the angle between a leaf and stem.

Biennial A plant that completes its life cycle, from seed to seed, in two years and then dies (compare annual and perennial). The distinction between biennial and winter annual (germinating in autumn, and surviving through winter as a leaf rosette) is gradual.

Bilaterally symmetric Same as zygomorphic.

Bisymmetric Having two planes of symmetry, like a canoe.

Bract An often reduced leaf subtending a pedicel or an inflorescence branch.

Bracteole A small, often paired, leaf situated on the pedicel.

Bulbil Small bulblike very condensed dispersal unit, sitting in leaf axils or in the inflorescence.

Bulblet Very small subterranean bulb forming part of a cluster, usually functioning as dispersal units.

Cauline On, or pertaining to the stem.

Chasmophyte Living on steep cliffs.

Cleistogamous Flowers that self-fertilize, without opening.

Cordate Heart-shaped, with the sinus at the point of attachment.

Corolla Collective term for the petals.

Corymb A flat topped inflorescence, in which the pedicels of the lower flowers are longer than those of the upper flowers.

Cotyledon The first leaves produced by a germinating seedling, in flowering plants either paired or single.

Crenulate With very small rounded teeth along the margin.

Cultivar A cultivated, named clone (perennials) or constant seed strain (annuals).

Cyme An inflorescence in which the main axis is terminated by a flower that often opens before the lateral ones.

Cymose With flowers in a cyme.

Deciduous Of organs that are shed from living tissue, like leaves falling in autumn.

Dehiscent Opening when ripe to release the contents, as of fruits and anthers.

Diploid Having two sets of chromosomes; the normal condition in most organisms.

Disjunct Occurring in widely separate geographic areas.

Dorsiventral Flattened from top to bottom, so that there are flat upper and lower surfaces.

Elaiosome Usually fat-rich seed appendage, attracting ants and aiding dispersal.

Elliptic A rounded shape that is broadest at the middle and narrower at the two equal ends.

Emarginate Having a shallow apical notch.

Entire Without teeth or lobes.

Erect Upright.

Erecto-patent With an orientation intermediate between erect and spreading.

Fascicle Arranged in tight bundle or cluster.

Filament The stalk of an anther.

Fusiform Shaped like a spindle; tapering toward both ends.

Geniculate With abrupt kneelike bends.

Geophyte Bulbous, tuberous or rhizomatous perennial with short growing season.

Gibbous Swollen on one side.

Glaucescent Slightly glaucous.

Glaucous Surface covered with a bluish-gray waxy bloom.

Habit The overall form and mode of growth of a plant.

Habitat The normal environmental conditions for an organism.

Hybrid Progeny resulting from two different species or subspecies. In plant breeding also used for progeny from two different cultivars of the same species.

Inflorescence An ultimate branch with flowers and associated bracts.

Laciniate Cut into narrow, irregular segments.

Lamina The broad expanded portion of a leaf.

Lanceolate Lance-shaped; at least three times longer than wide and widest below the middle.

Leaflet A segment of a compound leaf.

Mucro A short abrupt point at the end of an organ.

Naturalized Introduced or escaped, and self-perpetuating outside of cultivation.

Nectar A sugary liquid secreted in flowers, often contained in spurs or other specialized structures.

Nectary A structure (gland) that secretes nectar.

Nut A one-seeded non-dehiscent hard fruit.

Ob- Opposite to the typical orientation (for example: oblanceolate; obovate).

Obtuse Blunt or rounded at the apex.

Opposite Arranged in pairs (compare alternate).

Ovary The lowermost part of the pistil containing the ovules.

Ovate With the outline of an egg, attached at the broad end.

Ovule A complex structure containing the egg; the precursor of a seed.

Papillae Minute rounded, nipple-like bumps.

Pedicel Stalk of an individual flower.

Peduncle Stalk of an inflorescence.

Perennial A plant that flowers in successive years (compare annual and biennial).

Petal A segment of the corolla, usually attractively colored or white.

Petiole Leaf stalk.

Pinnate (of a compound leaf) With leaflets arranged in two opposite rows.

Pinnatisect Pinnately cleft to the middle.

Placentation The arrangement of ovules in the ovary.

Pyrophilous "Fire-loving"; of plants that benefit from intermittent fires.

Racemose Of an inflorescence in which the main axis continues its growth and it is not terminated by a flower; the uppermost flowers typically open last (see *Corydalis popovii* for a rare exception).

Rhizome A persistent subterranean stem bearing roots and leafy shoots.

Rosulate With all the leaves arranged in a basal rosette.

Saccate With a sac; bag-shaped.

Scale-leaf A small membranous leaf at the base of the plant.

Scapose With flowers borne on a leafless peduncle arising from a basal rosette.

Section (as a taxonomic term) A subdivision of a genus.

Seed A fertilized ovule.

Self-compatibility Ability to form fertile offspring following selfing (compare self incompatibility).

Self-incompatibility Inability to produce offspring following selfing, due for example to inhibition of growth of pollen tubes (compare self-compatibility).

Selfing When pollen is transferred from the anthers to the stigma of the same flower or to a stigma of another flower on the same plant.

Sepal A segment of the calyx; in most plants green and persistent and enclosing the petals in bud, but in Fumariaceae early or late deciduous, often petaloid, and not covering the petals in bud.

Sessile Without a stalk.

Spur A saclike or tubelike basal extension of a petal, usually enclosing a nectary.

Stamen The male reproductive organ of a flowering plant. Made up of filament and anther.

Stigma The apical usually sticky portion of the style that receives the pollen.

Stipule Usually small paired leafy or membranous appendages at the base of the petiole.

Style Stalk of the ovary that bears the stigma.

Subspecies A subdivision of a species with a few conspicuous morphological differences and a marked difference in distribution from other subspecies of the same species.

Talus A sloping mass of rock debris at the base of a cliff.

Taxon (plural: taxa) Any formally named grouping of biological organisms, for example family, genus, section, species, etc.

Tendril A twisting, threadlike structure by which a twining plant grasps an object or another plant for support.

Terete Cylindrical in cross section.

Terminal Positioned at the apex or end of a structure or stem.

Ternate Set in threes; of a compound leaf: with three leaflets.

Ternatisect More or less deeply cleft into three parts.

Tetraploid With four sets of chromosomes; that is, with twice as many as the normal diploid condition.

Torulose Cylindrical with alternate swellings and constrictions.

Tuber A swollen rhizome of a geophytic plant.

Tufa Calcareous deposits precipitated where spring water emerges from the ground and releases acid gases; soft porous calcareous rock in which, for example, chasmophytic plants can be grown.

Umbel A flat-topped inflorescence in which individual pedicels arise from almost the same point.

Vicariant Closely related taxa (such as species or subspecies) separated by the same geographical barrier.

Zygomorphic With one plane of symmetry, like a human face.

Select Bibliography

Baskin, J. M., and C. C. Baskin. 1994. Nondeep simple morphophysiological dormancy in seeds of the mesic woodland annual *Corydalis flavula* (Fumariaceae). *Bulletin of the Torrey Botanical Club* 121: 40–46.

Beattie, A. J. 1985. *The evolutionary ecology of ant-plant interactions*. Cambridge: Cambridge University Press.

Biodiversity of the Hengduan Mountains Region, China. 2006. http://maen.huh. harvard/:8080/china (accessed 1 August 2006)

Botanic Gardens Conservation International. 2006. http://www.bgci.org.uk/ (accessed 1 August 2006)

Dietrich, Friedrich Gottlieb. 1804. *Vollständiges Lexicon der Gärtnerei und Botanik*, vol. 4. 1st ed. Weimar. (*Fumaria spectabilis*, page 245)

Duke, J. A., and E. S. Ayensu. 1984. *Medicinal Plants of China*. Algonac, Michigan: Reference Publications.

Fedde, F. F. 1936. Papaveraceae. In A. Engler and H. Harms, eds. *Die natürlichen Pflanzenfamilien*. 2nd ed., 17b: 5–145. Leipzig: Engelmann.

Flora of China Editorial Committee. 2006. Flora of China online. http://flora.huh. harvard.edu/china/ (accessed 1 August 2006)

Fukuhara, T., and M. Lidén. 1995. Seed coat anatomy and phylogeny in Fumariaceae. *Botanical Journal of the Linnaean Society* 119: 323–365.

Grey-Wilson, C. 2000. *Poppies: a guide to the poppy family in the wild and in cultivation*. Revised ed. Portland: Timber Press.

Hegi, G. 1958. *Illustrierte Flora von Mitteleuropa*. 2nd ed. (F. Markgraf), IV (1).

International Plant Names Index. 2004. http://www.ipni.org/index.html (accessed 1 August 2006)

Lidén, M. 1986. Synopsis of Fumarioideae with a monograph of the tribe Fumarieae. *Opera Botanica* 88: 1–136.

Lidén, M. 1989. The genus *Corydalis* in Nepal. *Bulletin of the British Museum (Natural History) Botany* 18: 479–539.

Lidén, M. 1993. Fumariaceae. In K. Kubitzki, ed. *Families and genera of vascular plants*. Berlin: Springer-Verlag. 2: 310–317.

Lidén, M., T. Fukuhara, J. Rylander, and B. Oxelman. 1997. Phylogeny and classification of Fumariaceae, with emphasis on *Dicentra sensu lato* based on the plastid gene rps16 intron. *Plant Systematics and Evolution* 206: 411–420.

Lidén, M., and R. Staaf. 1995. Embryo growth in tuberous *Corydalis* species. *Bulletin of the Torrey Botanical Club* 122: 312–313.

Lidén, M., and H. Zetterlund. 1988. Notes on the genus *Corydalis*. *Quarterly Bulletin of the Alpine Garden Society* 56(2): 115–130.

Lidén, M., and H. Zetterlund. 1997. *Corydalis, a gardener's guide and a monograph of the tuberous species*. Pershore, England: Alpine Garden Society Publications.

Lord, T. 2002. *The Encyclopedia of Planting Combinations*. Richmond Hill, Ontario, Canada: Firefly Books.

Macior, L. W. 1970. The pollination ecology of *Dicentra cucullaria*. *American Journal of Botany* 57(1): 6–11.

Maloof, E. J. 2001. The effects of a bumblebee nectar robber on plant reproductive success and pollinator behavior. *American Journal of Botany* 88: 1960–1965.

Mathew, B. 2001. Earning their spurs (*Corydalis*). *The Garden* 126 (3): 184–187.

Morales, C., and A. T. Romero-García. 1991. A new species of the genus *Sarcocapnos* (Fumariaceae) from eastern Andalusia (Spain). *Plant Systematics and Evolution* 177: 1–10.

Olesen, J. M., and J. T. Knudsen. 1994. Scent profiles of flower colour morphs of *Corydalis cava* (Fumariaceae) in relation to foraging behaviour of bumblebee queens (*Bombus terrestris*). *Biochemical Systematics and Ecology* 22(3): 231–237.

Ownbey, G. B. 1947. Monograph of the North American species of *Corydalis*. *Annals of the Missouri Botanical Garden* 34(3): 187–260.

Popov, M. 1937. Papaveraceae. In V. A. Komarov, ed. *Flora of the USSR* 7. Moscow.

Salinas, M. J., A. T. Romero, G. Blanca, R. de la Herrán, M. Garrido-Ramos, C. Ruíz-Rejón, C. Morales, M. Ruíz-Rejón, and V. Suárez. 2003. Contribution to the taxonomy and phylogeny of *Sarcocapnos* DC. (Fumariaceae). *Plant Systematics and Evolution* 237: 153–164.

Stern, K. R. 1961. Revision of *Dicentra* (Fumariaceae). *Brittonia* 13: 1–57.

Stern, K. R. 1968. Cytogeographical studies in *Dicentra*. I. *Dicentra formosa* and *D. nevadensis*. *American Journal of Botany* 55(5): 626–628.

Stern, K. R. 1997. *Dicentra* and *Corydalis*. In Flora of North America Editorial Committee, eds. *Flora of North America*. Oxford: Oxford University Press. 3: 341–347.

Stern, K. R. 2004. *Dicentra* and *Corydalis*. Flora of North America online. http://www.efloras.org/florataxon.aspx?flora_id=1&taxon_id=10351 (accessed 1 August 2006)

Stern, K. R., and M. Ownbey. 1971. Hybridization and cytotaxonomy of *Dicentra*. *American Journal of Botany* 58(9): 861–866.

Su Zhi-Yun, and M. Lidén. 1997. *Corydalis* in China. I: Some new species. *Edinburgh Journal of Botany* 54: 55–84.

Svensk Kulturväxtdatabas (SKUD). 2004. http://skud.ngb.se (accessed 1 August 2006).

Sweet, Robert. 1838. *The British Flower Garden*. London.

Wen, J. 1999. Evolution of eastern Asian and eastern North American disjunct distributions in flowering plants. *Annual Review of Ecology and Systematics* 30: 421–455.

Wu Zheng-Yi, Su Zhi-Yun, and Zhuang Xuan. 1999. Fumariaceae. In Wu Zheng-Yi, ed. *Flora Republicae Popularis Sinicae* 32 (in Chinese).

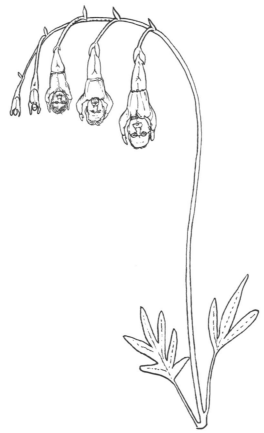

Manypeeplia upsidedownia with authors.
Drawing by Paul Harwood; modified from E. Lear,
1871, *Nonsense Songs, Stories, Botany and Alphabets*,
Charing Cross, London: R. J. Rush.

Index of Plant Names